Managing With Computers

Terry Rowan is a management consultant, who
has specialised in computers for over 21 years –
most of which was spent with the Urwick Group
as a Director of Urwick Dynamics. He was
seconded to Australia in 1983–84 as Director in
charge of computer consultancy services. He is
now a Senior Manager with Price Waterhouse,
following the merger between the Urwick Group
and Price Waterhouse. He is the author of several
articles on the use of computers, particularly in
manufacturing control; apart from extensive UK
experience, Terry Rowan has worked in 17 overseas countries including the USA and USSR.

T. G. ROWAN
B.A., A.C.I.S., D.M.S., M.I.M.C., M.B.C.S.

Managing With Computers

New and revised edition

Pan Books London and Sydney

First published in Great Britain 1982 by Pan Books Ltd,
in association with William Heinemann
This revised edition published 1986 by Pan Books Ltd,
Cavaye Place, London SW10 9PG
9 8 7 6 5 4 3 2 1
© T. G. Rowan 1986
ISBN 0 330 29143 2
Photoset by Parker Typesetting Service, Leicester
Printed and bound in Great Britain by
Cox & Wyman Ltd, Reading

Contents

Acknowledgements

This book is very much a personal commentary on success and failure in the use of computers in a variety of organizations in both the public and private sectors. However, I have drawn on the experience and knowledge of my colleagues, past and present, much of which is embedded in the course notes and case studies used at the Urwick Management Centre, Slough. I am indebted to my colleagues for their help and encouragement and to UMC for permission to use some of their material to amplify aspects of the book. However, the responsibility for any errors of fact, interpretation or judgement is solely mine.

Finally, I should like to acknowledge the forbearance of my wife, Anne, in putting up with the inconveniences caused by the preparation of the book and for typing the manuscript. Her help in modulating the vagaries of style and grammar was invaluable and any residual dissonance is all mine.

1 Introduction

Introduction

At the end of 1984 it was estimated that there were over 50,000 computers in use in the United Kingdom, in public and private organizations, ranging in capital costs from a few hundreds of pounds to several millions. These machines are being serviced by almost a half a million people in categories of job which did not exist a generation ago. Worldwide, the figures are half a million installations with a dependent job population of perhaps 25 million. In the United States alone it is forecast that the total market for computer equipment and related services, currently about $100 billion, will be $200 billion by 1990 and will still be rising.

The growth in a technology, which barely existed in the early 1960s, has been dramatic and continuous, fired by a necessary and parallel development in marketing techniques which has been quite outstanding. The situation is often confusingly dynamic for the businessman, with few weeks going by without announcements of new products, major technological advances, improved cost performance ratios and myriad allied services, many bearing inscrutable names, mnenomics, or just plain numbers that convey little or nothing to the uninitiated.

The early 1980s has also seen a massive extension of computer technology into the domestic market, with many thousands of families acquiring home computers of varying degrees of sophistication and similarity to their larger electronic brethren. Predictably, the majority of these acquisitions end up being used merely as games machines, and recent signs indicate the virtual collapse of the mass computer market.

The range of activities to which computers have been applied is vast and there are few aspects of our working and leisure lives which are not influenced in some measure by computer technology. As likely as not, John Citizen:

- will work for an organization which uses some form of computer power;
- will be paid, taxed, insured, billed, rated and mortgaged by data processing equipment;
- will eat, wear, drive or use products that have been designed, planned, made and distributed by computer;
- will, at least once, play an electronic game, perform a domestic administrative chore or pursue a hobby using a home computer;
- will communicate on, by or through media that are feasible only because of the products of the electronic age.

However, while most people may be affected by computers, they are rarely involved directly in their use and have little or no influence on the selection of targets, nor on the efficiency and effectiveness with which computers are applied. These activities are critically dependent on the interplay between computer specialists and the management of an organization who, together, might represent only a tiny proportion of the employees. Under any circumstances we might feel entitled to ask how well they fulfil these responsibilities but, in an uncertain economic environment, where technological changes occur frequently, rapidly and often dramatically, there may well be an implicit right in insisting upon superior performance.

Judging by the reactions to the advent of microtechnology, which have been mildly hysterical or euphoric depending on persuasion and age, the livelihood of John Citizen may soon be threatened by a host of half perceived and as yet ill-defined changes in his working conditions, typified by such concepts as the fully automated office and the factory operated by robots. In such circumstances, even the role of the manager in its conventional form will be questioned and traditional methods of organizing and controlling a workforce will become obsolete.

The reality of these threats (or opportunities), their long-term consequences and the best ways for society to respond to them are debatable and for the moment unclear to all except politicians and pundits. However, what is certain is that the pace of technological development is unlikely to slacken, that the costs of equipment will continue to decline and that a growing number of organisations will make greater use of computers. Unfortunately, it is almost also certain that:

- most new users will make the same mistakes as were made in the 1960s, 1970s and early 1980s;
- many existing users will fail to profit by past errors and will perhaps even compound them;
- a significant proportion of users will not obtain the expected benefits of computer applications; and
- too many computer projects will take longer, cost more and achieve less than was originally anticipated.

In the past 25 years I have seen some splendid computer applications, come across companies whose growth and profitability have been founded on the benefits of data processing, and known many organizations that could not exist in their present form or even at all without the support of computers. It is a genuine source of regret that, during this period, I have also seen or heard of many more organizations with a disappointing and occasionally disastrous history of computer usage.

This book is about both kinds of organization – the successes and the failures. From the failures we can learn lessons without incurring the costs and from the successes we can extract guidelines to improve the effectiveness of our own computer projects.

Common mistakes

As we look at different facets of the application of computers in organizations, it will be possible with the aid of case histories to identify the errors which are most commonly made. In my experience they fall into four broad categories.

Computers are different

There is a fundamental misconception, embraced by many prospective and existing users, that computers are somehow different from other items of capital investment and that computer departments are uniquely dissimilar from other parts of the organization. There are many reasons why an ordinary level-headed manager might accept or acquiesce to these propositions, which are patently absurd and positively dangerous.

1 He may be too busy running the company or pursuing the main purpose of the organization and he may consider, with justification, that computers are not a priority concern.

2 He may be seduced by the blandishments and promises of computer salesmen, the technical briefings of his specialist staff or the aspirations of prospective users in the organization.
3 He may be persuaded to relax his standards by a variety of pressures that in themselves may not be quantifiable:
   ● what the competition is doing;
   ● what the media tells him everybody who is anybody, and wants to remain somebody, is doing.
4 He may not understand or may be fearful of the whole concept of computer technology.
5 He may be caught up in the prevailing 'technological hysteria' which has swept many companies into expensive investments in computers.

For whichever reason, the acceptance of the idea that computers are different leads to some unfortunate results.

Firstly, there is usually a relaxation of standards normally applied when assessing capital projects, and decisions are often made without proper regard to payback periods. Contrast this attitude with the difficulties faced by a manufacturing director wishing to introduce new plant, costing in many cases far less than the total investment in a computer project.

Secondly, having lost the initiative in evaluating the first expenditure, management is poorly placed to re-apply standards for return on investment when operating experience shows that the equipment needs to be enhanced or replaced. By that time the organization is committed to computing and may be in no position to withdraw, even if it is considered. Furthermore, when enhancements/replacements are being evaluated, the supporting evidence is almost always technically oriented and general management may be ill-equipped to challenge it.

A third more insidious effect is that, having begun by treating computer projects as a different form of corporate investment, management also discards a proven method of controlling them. Individual applications may be loosely evaluated and any subsequent excess costs or delays in achieving benefits become part of the accepted pattern of development. The computer department will either have no budgetary framework to work within or financial controls will be purely nominal. The computer manager, without precise objectives and agreed criteria for measuring performance, will be effectively unmanageable.

The belief that computers are different will necessarily colour the choice of manager employed to control their use, so it is hardly surprising that most computer managers are selected from the most senior technical men, present or obtainable. You may be lucky, but the chances are that you will place this loosely justified and potentially uncontrollable project in the hands of an able technician with no management experience, no track record, no training and no grounding in project management.

Abdication by top management
On the other hand you may recognize, as an increasing number of top managers do, that computer projects should be properly justified and the computer department should be operated and controlled like any other function. You may insist that all capital expenditures and increases to the computer budget are subject to costs/benefits evaluation and that performance against these criteria is consistently monitored.

Unfortunately, many senior managers who follow these good practices also believe that their job ends when they sign the cheque or accede to a new authorization. From that point, their participation is nominal or, worse, they initiate a process of delegation which often ends with a low level manager having responsibility for computing without any real means of controlling it. It may become difficult and time-consuming to obtain policy decisions, to agree priorities, to allocate resources and to direct corporate efforts. The effect this has on a computer project can be quite devastating; computer staff become disillusioned, users are frustrated, costs tend to increase and benefits recede. Many researchers have found, and my experiences as a consultant confirm this, that the root cause of many computer failures is the abdication of responsibility by top management and the lack of a consistent computer policy.

Underestimation
A common problem in the application of computers is the underestimation of the amount of work involved. This is not merely a question of the experience of the estimators; it may be a compound of several factors.

1 The over-willingness of management to believe the case presented by computer salesmen or their in-house technical

staff. A classic example is the oft-quoted claim that a computer will reduce inventory by up to 20%. What management is rarely told is that the precise mechanisms for achieving control have not been established and that computerized inventory control frequently leads to a significant *increase* in stock before any reductions occur.

2 The failure to appreciate the enormous complexity of some applications, particularly those which interface with many other procedures in an organization, e.g. production planning and control.

3 The setting of impossible or over-ambitious target dates that may be totally unrelated to any intrinsic feature of the proposed application or the work content. Many dates are set by senior management on the basis that:
- x months seems a reasonable amount of time;
- they coincide with the start of a financial year or the intro-duction of a new product;
- they are convenient from the general point of view of the business as a whole.

4 A superficial assessment of the preparedness of users to accept and absorb a fundamental change in their working environment. We are all creatures of habit; none of us likes change. Fear, ignorance, reluctance, lack of training are all rocks of resistance on which many computer projects have foundered.

5 The failure to make adequate provision for the review and renovation of working methods, manual procedures and clerical disciplines before the introduction of a new computer system.

There is a disquieting implication that many of these omissions have a delusive quality, where wishful thinking becomes a substitute for adequate planning.

Lack of user participation

There is clear and conclusive evidence that computer applications which are developed with the full participation of the prospective user tend to be more successful and to achieve the objective benefits. In spite of this experience, many projects are initiated and pursued without the involvement of the user, without a thorough exposure of requirements and often on premises that are largely based on an academic assessment of the application area by com-puter staff.

There are many factors that might contribute to an inadequate level of user participation in the development and implementation of computer systems.

1   The most common cause is the failure of communications between computer staff and users, which may by induced by:
   ● a jargon and experience barrier that no amount of training or appreciation courses may overcome;
   ● a professional arrogance on both sides;
   ● wholly inadequate training of computer staff;
   ● the reluctance of users to nominate and second senior experienced staff to computer projects.
2   The influence of the prevailing computing environment.
   ● Do existing applications, file structures or hardware/ software features severely limit the options available to the next prospective user?
   ● Does the computer department have a consistently poor image of project achievement and indifferent user relationships?
   ● Is there a high turnover of computer staff which inhibits the development of a consistent relationship?
3   The lack of a suitable mechanism, or corporate tradition, for bringing together multidisciplined teams, task forces or working parties. This may be exacerbated by the geographical dispersal of prospective users.
4   The inability of the average user to articulate his requirements adequately for computer development purposes. How often have you experienced that momentary amnesia when asked the nature of your job or how it might be improved? For many people, their job is a collection of physical/mental activities which are rarely viewed as a logical whole.

As we shall see, the growing disillusionment of users with centrally coordinated computer projects and the increasing availability of cheap computer power have fostered user independence and have begun the eclipse of conventional approaches to data processing.

The responsibility of management

Whichever way you look at them, the consistent element in these common errors is the failure of management to recognize, accept or exercise the responsibilities that would normally be expected of them and that they would wish to carry out for any other part of their organization. On the other hand, a general manager should be able to rely on the functional competence of his senior executives and feel confident about delegating the major part of his responsibilities for their areas. In those respects, many computer managers fail to provide adequate managerial support and are often motivated by the pursuit of technical objectives that are irrelevant to the aims of the organization. The success of computer projects depends almost entirely on achieving the right balance of managerial and technical skills and this is rarely a state that is reached spontaneously. It requires effort on the part of both the manager and the technician.

The purpose of this book

The purpose of this book is to help management understand the nature of computer activities and recognize the importance of the contribution which they can make to the exploitation of a novel resource for the benefit of the organization as a whole. It is written to encourage managers to manage and to enable them to dismiss, knowledgeably, any spurious claims about the special nature of computing or computer staff.

Although the content is addressed principally to executives with general management responsibilities, it is hoped that many senior functional managers will find useful guidance here, particularly those users wishing to exert more influence over the application of computers in their domain. For these purposes, I have included descriptions of approaches and techniques for project management that may not yet be wholly acceptable to computer departments. Nevertheless, I urge computer managers to consider the contents of this book; they may not agree completely with my assessments and advice but they can hardly dispute some of the more distressing facts that are reported.

Finally, a word to the growing number of users who are attracted to microcomputers or small business systems, costing a few hundred or at most a few thousands of pounds. Your total investment in computer development may never exceed the cost of one senior clerk and, consequently, you may not see the relevance to your circumstances of the experience and advice recorded here. Indeed, if you were to follow the guidelines indicated for more elaborate computer projects, you would undoubtedly spend more time and money than your probable investment in computing warranted. Nevertheless, your investment and the expected benefits from computing are presumably related to the on-going success of your business and they deserve no less management attention for being small.

The dilemma for the user of small machines is to determine the level of research cost justified in reaching a decision about equipment and software and the amount that should be devoted to the subsequent application of computer techniques in the business. A crude measure would be to allocate say 10% of the probable capital cost as an allowance for an appraisal of the investment and to budget for an annual expenditure in staff time which is at least equal to the capital cost. Thus, for an expected outlay on equipment and software of, say, £5,000, you should allocate £500 to evaluate the equipment options and budget the equivalent of one person per year to introduce and maintain computer applications. Obviously, if you require expert advice, £500 will not purchase very much consultancy but it might be sufficient for one man-week of support from a software house or a longer period from one of the many reputable freelance operators.

Alternatively, if you have the confidence, you could evaluate the options yourself, provided that you have a clear idea of what you are seeking and take a realistic view of the nature of future requirements and their impact on the choice of computing facilities. For example, the favoured micro may be perfectly adequate for a modest stock-control application but may be insufficiently powerful or capacious to cope with a large sales ledger, which might be the next application. If the micro cannot be expanded you may need a second machine, whereas some prior thought might have pointed to a different computer. Micros are too often acquired in haste, with a lot of enthusiastic amateurism and little planning, and end up as executive toys. Quite recently, discussing the expansion of an existing central computer with a client, the managing director deplored the past proliferation of cheap microcomputers in the company, each costing £800, which had distracted potential users from the central service. In his words, the machines had set back data processing for a decade as managers had tried to short-cut the learning process and had ended up with a hotchpotch of small unrelated jobs that offered no discernible benefits.

Although many parts of this book describe approaches that are more pertinent to computer projects which are likely to cost over, say, £20,000, the principles that they reflect are just as valid for investments at lower figures. The user of small machines still needs a degree of certainty about his requirements, should have a sufficient understanding of the basics of computing to deal confidently with suppliers, and should have the knowledge to motivate and oversee the exploitation of the device in his business. As a minimum, the prospective user of a microcomputer or a small business system should:

● identify the main applications that are likely to crop up in the next two years;
● establish a broad estimate of the number of records to be stored for each application and the peak input/output transaction rates;
● identify two or three mainstream equipment suppliers;
● ask the suppliers to demonstrate how their equipment and software would carry out these jobs; and
● then keep close control over the phasing and introduction of computer applications.

It should take no more than about ten days to accomplish the first four stages and the amount of time you devote to the on-going supervision of data processing developments is likely to be less than the equivalent of one person full-time, although several people may be involved.

There is no doubt that microcomputers are the current dominating force in the development of data processing systems and, with computing features that match the power and capacity of many mainframe predecessors, they offer a vast potential to an ever-widening user market. At the ever-present risk of being overtaken by events, we offer guidelines, in Chapter 4, on the selection and use of microcomputers at all levels of business activity.

Format
The book is in four main parts.

The first part, which includes this general introduction, is concerned with providing background material on the nature of computers and the people who service them. The essential features of the hardware and software are described in non-technical terms and with relevance to the kind of decision you may be called upon to make. The application of computers has created a whole range of new jobs, most of which are filled by young and, in many respects, organizationally inexperienced people. We examine the real need for this resource and the problems of controlling it.

The second part examines the alternative sources of computing power and establishes guidelines for selecting the one most suitable for your organization. We emphasise the importance of justifying computer projects and the ways in which potential applications should be evaluated. The development cycle for all but the simplest applications can be long and arduous, calling for a combination of skills and experience that is not always available and is often misdirected. We look at the critical stages in systems development, at the importance of good project management and the increasing influence of the user in dictating how requirements should be met. In particular, we examine how new techniques in systems design, the invention of new languages for non-technicians and the explosive growth in software facilities have brought dramatic changes in the speed with which organizations can begin to make use of computer facilities.

In the third part we look at the ways in which computers have been applied to the principal functions of the business or organization. This review examines individual applications and the various attempts to develop fully integrated systems covering wide areas of the business which extend beyond established departmental boundaries. We examine the growing recognition of information as a resource and the attempts to manipulate it for the purposes of the enterprise, through planning and control systems and management information services. We consider how the power of the computer can be harnessed to drive virtually all administrative and control functions and whether or not the fully automated office is a practicable objective.

If an enterprise decides to introduce computers on anything other than a minor scale, it will have to consider the problems of organizing and managing a totally new resource. In the fourth part we consider how you can establish a structure that is best suited to your organization, and we describe the most appropriate management practices that should follow. We also examine how this new function affects other parts of the organization and its impact on people. In particular, we explore the emergent threat to industrial relations posed by the progressive commitment to computer systems and the increasing reliance on specialist staff.

The use of case material

Most of this book is the product of personal observation of good and bad practices in a wide variety of organizations, in both public and private sectors, in the United Kingdom and in several foreign countries. I have made extensive use of case material which is wholly based on real-life clients or the known experiences of other organizations. Naturally, I have preserved their anonymity – to protect the guilty – but it is possible that the reader may find uncomfortable parallels with his own situation. If he does it will underline the popularity of the mistakes being made rather than the uniqueness of his own position. I would like this book to be a sort of Highway Code for computer users. It may not stop accidents happening and it cannot prevent recklessness, unsocial behaviour and vehicular unreliability. However, if users recognize the signs, and can be persuaded to follow directions, it may reduce both the incidence of mishaps and their consequences.

2 Hardware and software

Introduction

Modern computing involves many complex activities and any attempt to describe them briefly runs the risk of over-simplification, with all the dangers attendant upon a little know-ledge. On the other hand, there is not a great deal of point in the average manager filling his head with technical details and attempting to match the accumulated knowledge and experience of the computer specialist. Nevertheless, an analysis of the pitfalls involved in applying computers to business problems and guidance on evasive action must be founded on some understanding of the nature of computers and an awareness of the ironmongery you may be called upon to pay for out of profits.

You may already have a sufficient appreciation of computer hardware and software and wish to skip this chapter entirely. For those readers with more time on their hands, I have tried to describe the key features of computers without excessive use of jargon, although this is rather difficult in a technical field. If you encounter a word or phrase with which you are not familiar and it is not defined in the text, you should find a working definition of it in the glossary of technical terms given in Appendix 1.

What is a computer?

I have yet to see a definition of the word 'computer' that is both succinct and uniquely descriptive of the beast we have in mind. This is partly a function of the continuous evolution of the tech-nology and also the fact that what constitutes a 'computer' may differ significantly from one organization or environment to another.

For our purposes we will define a computer in the following way.

A collection of electronic devices which is capable, under the control of a program of instructions, of carrying out arithmetic, manipulative and processing operations on business data.

The bits that you can kick and fall over are known as hardware and the programs of instructions that make the hardware work are known as software.

Representation of data

From the general manager's point of view, the way in which data are represented and manipulated within a computer and its peripherals is largely irrelevant. It is sufficient to know that numbers and characters can be uniquely identified by electronic impulses or by the state of some device or component. Nevertheless, you are likely to be bombarded with technical terms or jargon by salesmen or your advisors and it may be some comfort to know the difference between a bit, a byte and a word.

Most of you will be familiar with the techniques used by Morse code and semaphore to represent numbers and letters and to convey whole messages. The representation of data within computers is based fundamentally on a similar simple structure known as binary arithmetic.

The decimal numbering system is designed to the base 10. The number 747 actually means the sum of:

$(7 \times 10^2) + (4 \times 10^1) + (7 \times 10^0)$

or:

$(7 \times 100) + (4 \times 10) + (7 \times 1)$

In binary arithmetic, the numbering system is designed to the base 2; each digit can only take the value of 0 or 1. By this system the decimal number 5 becomes:

101

which means the sum of:

$(1 \times 2^2) + (0 \times 2^1) + (1 \times 2^0)$

or:

$(1 \times 4) + (0 \times 2) + (1 \times 1)$

Although I have been impressed by the skill of school children in manipulating binary numbers, in practice the use of this form of arithmetic is unwieldy and prone to error; for example, the decimal number 747 is represented in binary by:

1011101011

However, in computing terms, binary provides an ideal structure for recording data because the two binary digits (bits) 0 and 1 can be represented by the state of an electronic device, e.g. is the device on or off, magnetized or unmagnetized?

Thus, by recognizing the 'states' of groups of devices in a predetermined fashion, similar to the combinations of dots and dashes in Morse code, it is possible to record, manipulate and move data within a computer system.

In technical terms there has been an incredible development in the physical nature of the devices used to represent data, from the early days, when one electronic valve equalled one bit, to the present situation, where several million characters can be represented on a suitable magnetizable surface.

While these features may fascinate the technician and be advanced by the salesman as unique selling points, they are not particularly relevant to your choice of computer, provided they are proven and reliable. You will be much more concerned with power and capacity and in this respect you will be advised that the machine has x thousand bytes or words of storage. All this means is that the internal structure of the computer is based on a specified unit of storage which, in the case of a byte, is 8 bits, whereas a word will contain 16 or 24 bits, depending on the manufacturer. With 8 bits it is possible to represent any decimal digit, any letter of the alphabet and a range of special characters, e.g. a £ sign.

The functional components of a computer

In spite of the rapid advance in the design of computers in the past 30 years, they will consist conceptually of five functional components:

1 input
2 output
3 storage
4 arithmetic and logic
5 control

Their interrelationship is illustrated schematically in Figure 2.1.

At one time, these functions were synonymous with the actual hardware 'boxes', but this is no longer necessarily the case with modern computers, in which one box may house several functions or, alternatively, one function may be distributed over a number of units.

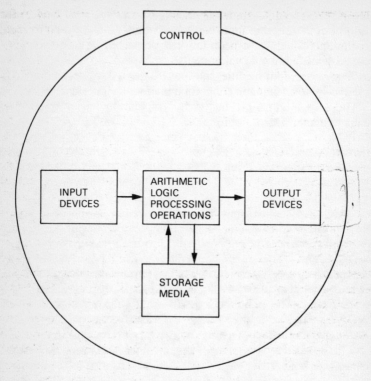

Figure 2.1   Components of a computer

Input

Input is the means whereby data and instructions are entered into a computer for subsequent processing. Input facilities are available in a wide variety of forms and the choice of media can be highly significant for your applications. Among the more commonly used facilities are:

- punched cards and punched paper tape, in which the positioning of punched holes represents data in coded form;
- magnetic tapes or disks on which data are recorded in machine readable form;
- equipment capable of reading characters, optically or magnetically;
- keyboard input from a variety of terminal units.

More specialized computer applications may use such devices as light pens to generate input or utilize equipment designed to read documents which have been marked up according to a predetermined code. Future developments are likely to include handwritten and voice input facilities, although these features are at present a long way from being in common use.

There are a number of factors to bear in mind when considering your particular input requirements.

1 Firstly, data capture and preparation are essentially non-productive parts of the computing process and you should endeavour to minimize the time taken to get input into your computer. If it is practicable and economic, opt for some form of direct data entry.
2 Ideally, aim to place responsibility for the availability and accuracy of input data with the originators, as opposed to a specialized data preparation unit, even if this means investing in a few more items of equipment.
3 Try to integrate data capture with normal office procedures and have the equipment operated by the staff of the function concerned.

Output
Output is the means by which the computer communicates the results of past or current data processing to the user.

The most common forms of output device are the line and character printers which produce reports, tabulations or official documents at speeds typically in the range 100–2,000 lines per minute. High speed laser printers are becoming available which can print the form design as well as the content of official documents, but we would not expect to see them in common use until prices come down considerably.

By far the most significant development in output devices has been the trend towards visual display terminals, with or without hard copy printing facilities, and this trend is expected to dominate computing activity in the future. Using these devices, which normally consist of a keyboard and a screen similar to a television set, users can enquire about computer records, call up reports and receive messages.

I am not aware of any computer installation that operates without a printer, but whether or not output terminals are used depends very much on the type of application. In considering your own needs, you should be guided by a few basic ground rules.

1 Do all you can to restrict the volume of printing. Computers are notorious producers of wastepaper, largely because systems designers have failed to evaluate the real needs of the end user or the manager's wish to reproduce the existing paperwork systems.
2 If the application is suitable, encourage the use of visual displays to cut down on hard copy output.
3 If printed output is considered essential, make sure it is used, and carry out periodic audits to identify any changes in requirements. In one audit, carried out after about three years of computer operation, one company discovered that over 80% of computer tabulations were discarded without being used.

Storage
There are two basic types of storage associated with computers which, for convenience, we will call working storage and backing storage.

Working storage The working store or main memory of a computer fulfils three principal functions.

1 It contains the computer program(s) which carry out the processing and control activities needed to complete a job.
2 It is the area into which input data is received and information for output is compiled.
3 It is the area in which all calculations, data manipulation and processing takes place.

The working store can be visualized as a matrix of pigeon holes in which each compartment can be separately identified and designated to contain a piece of data or a computer instruction or be available as a temporary storage or work area.

If a salesman is offering you 'a System X with a 32Kb memory', he is indicating that the size of the working store (memory) consists of 32,000 bytes (of 8 bits each), which in itself is not particularly illuminating.

The amount of working storage you require for your installation will be influenced by, for example:

- the size of the input/output/file records you wish to manipulate;
- the size of your programs and the complexity of the calculations you wish to carry out;
- the amount of space that has to be allowed for the specialized programs that control the computer (see Software below);
- the number of terminals connected to the computer if it is an on-line system.

The size of the working store or main memory of the computer is one important measure of the capacity of the equipment; another is the size and efficiency of the backing store.

You will encounter two acronyms describing forms of computer memory, namely ROM and RAM. ROM stands for read only memory; it contains instructions to the computer and generally cannot be modified by the user. RAM, on the other hand, is random access memory; it is normally used to store data and applications software and is under the control of the user.

Backing store If the computer was equipped solely with main memory, it would be little more than a highly sophisticated programmable calculator and would have severe limitations for commercial work in which large volumes of data have to be processed, filed and retrieved. Even for quite small businesses, the storage required for customer files or for stock records may run into millions of characters and it would be quite impractical to consider holding this amount of data in the working store.

The large scale storage capacity needed for most commercial data processing jobs can be provided by a variety of media, but is typically provided by either, or both, magnetic tape, in reel or cassette form, or magnetic disks of different sizes. Depending on the power of the computer, it is usually possible to connect more than one magnetic tape or disk storage unit to the machine and thereby to provide tens or hundreds of millions of characters of backing store. If you consider that such capacity would be excessively indulgent and possibly wasteful in your business, be advised that Parkinson's law operates in a pure form in computing; jobs expand to fill the capacity and features available.

Tapes and disks have different storage characteristics, which influence the ways in which they are used. On magnetic tapes, data are recorded serially and it may be necessary to read the whole tape in order to locate a specific item, e.g. a stock record. In contrast, the surfaces of magnetic disks are divided into tracks which are individually addressable such that, by a system of indexing, it is possible to go direct to the record required and read it into the working store. Furthermore, by reading disk tracks sequentially, the disk can be treated as if it were a magnetic tape.

Because of these characteristics, magnetic tape tends to be used where records are normally processed in sequence, such as the preparation of a weekly or monthly payroll, or where relatively cheap, large volume archiving is required, e.g. to store last year's sales invoices. Magnetic disk storage is preferred where random or selective access to data is required, for example to update 50 stock records out of an inventory file of say 1,500 items. Disk storage is also essential for any application which is based on the interactive use of terminal devices, either to enquire of or to update specific records. With most modern computers, magnetic disks in one form or another are now the standard media for providing backing store.

The type and size of the backing store and the flexibility with which it can be increased are important factors in assessing your needs, but you should also consider efficiency. Basically, this boils down to the speed at which records can be transferred to and from the storage device – these movements of data will dictate the overall performance of the system.

Arithmetic and logic
At the heart of every computer are the electronic devices that carry out the arithmetic and logic functions which are basically:

- addition
- subtraction
- multiplication
- division
- comparison

Of these functions, the most powerful is the facility to compare values within the computer and to select a course of action (or set of program instructions) as a consequence of the comparison. From the earliest days, this feature has been likened in popular terms to the ability to 'think', but the computer is essentially a moron, designed to follow rigidly prescribed rules and is incapable of original thought. Having said that, however, I stand to be contra-dicted by the growing amount of research in the field of artificial intelligence (AI), involving the use of computers to solve problems that appear to require human imagination or intelligence, acquired through a learning process. However, this development will hardly effect the vast majority of users of computers in business for many years to come.

Although the functions performed by the arithmetic and logic units of the computer are fundamentally simple, the real power of the machine stems from the very high speeds at which it performs those functions. Modern computers will carry out many thousands of calcu-lations per second and will do so effortlessly and consistently. Large mainframe computers are usually rated in terms of their ability to process millions of instructions per second (MIPs); smaller machines are rated in thousands of instructions per second (KIPs), although microcomputers with very powerful MIP ratings are now commonly available.

In practice, of course, the process of executing a commercial routine is a mix of arithmetic and logic instructions and data movements within and between components of the system, and these internal speeds may not be the critical factor in selecting hardware, i.e. the application may be dominated by the speed of access to backing store rather than the internal working speeds.

Control

If arithmetic and logic are at the heart of the computer, the control unit is very much the brain. The function of the control unit is to select the program instructions to be executed (from working storage), to interpret them and to control their execution by activating input, storage, arithmetic, logic and output devices.

Programming

When they are powered up, the machines we have described are only capable, by and large, of delivering a powerful and possibly fatal electric shock. To perform a useful purpose they have to be activated and controlled by 'software', consisting of lists of instructions (pro-grams) written by human beings (programmers). Before describing the different types of software required to operate a computer, it would be as well to introduce the concept of programming.

Each computer has a defined repertoire of instructions, pre-determined by the manufacturer, which the control unit can recognize, interpret and execute. Each instruction may be a basic simple step, for example 'read', 'write', 'add'. When the systems analyst has completely defined the proposed system, the programmer must break the system specification down into a series of simple logical steps, each of which can be translated into the specified instructions allowed by the computer. The complete set of instructions necessary to execute a given job is called a program. When the program has been written it is transferred permanently to the computer storage medium. Each time a particular job is run, its program is read into the computer and is usually held in the working store throughout the computer run, during which time the computer reads and executes the instructions in the specified sequence. At an early stage in the program, one of these instructions will cause the computer to read in the first input transaction (e.g. the first customer order). After executing the procedure for this transaction and recording or storing the results it will then be instructed to repeat the process with the next transaction, and so on, until the last transaction has been dealt with and the job is finished. Human intervention, except in most unusual circumstances, is both undesirable and impractical. The program must therefore be so comprehensively designed that it will not only deal with, for example, all the different types of orders (which may require many different procedures), but also produce all checks, intermediate results and exceptions.

With the earliest computers, each instruction coincided with a simple machine function and was represented numerically, which meant that programming in 'machine language' had to be meticulously accurate and comprehensive, otherwise nothing happened, simply because programmers were prone to 'grammatical errors'. An advance on machine language was the introduction of assembler programming which was closer to a real life expression of the instructions, in so far as the code for addition was 'ADD' instead of some digital concoction. The need for simpler programming led to the development of high level languages in which the ways in which programs were defined and expressed were very much closer to natural language than assembler techniques. Indeed one of the objectives of high level languages was to encourage the programming of computers by non-specialists, although this has not happened to any great extent in business computing. The most commonly used high level language is Cobol (Common Business Oriented Language) but you will also frequently come across applications programmed in RPG (Report Program Generator) language, and Fortran (FORmula TRANslation) which is principally for scientific use. Other languages in common use include PL1 and various forms of Basic.

Generically, these languages are known as procedural languages because you have to tell the computer what to do via a set of predefined procedures, incorporated in programs. For reasons that will become clearer in later chapters, the use of procedural languages prescribes a lengthy and detailed systems development cycle and creates on-going maintenance problems. A great deal of progress has been made recently in the development of non-procedural languages – known as 'Fourth Generation Languages' (4GL) – designed to facilitate the production of computer application programs. Broadly, there are two types of 4GL: those intended for use by computer professionals; and those that can be applied by the end user. Clearly, these 'user-friendly' languages could have a major impact on the exploitation of computers by the average user, especially when they become commonly available on microcomputers.

Both the power and the disadvantages of fourth generation languages were well illustrated in an assignment I undertook a few years ago, when 4GLs were in their infancy and confined to mainframe computers.

A real-time system, developed by 4GL, was showing very poor operating performance and we were engaged to review the system. It emerged that the system, which was quite complex, had been developed in four man-years by a combined user/DP team, as compared to an estimated 40 man-years if the application had been developed by conventional means. The user was delighted with the system.

Unfortunately, as the system was extended to each new segment of the business, computer operating performance deteriorated and additional disk units were required. Quite apart from the costs involved, there were clearly going to be physical and practical limits to the extension of the system.

Eventually a hardware solution was found, to give respite while parts of the system were re-designed or tuned to give higher performance. This was not easy as there was virtually no systems documentation available.

There are some simple guidelines to be drawn from this example.

1   A good 4GL will provide a fast method of developing prototype systems.
2   These systems may be inefficient in day-to-day operation and performance should be monitored to identify shortcomings and, where necessary, these should be eliminated by re-design or re-programming using conventional methods.
3   Whatever suppliers may say, most 4GL still require a degree of technical input and are not so 'user friendly' that users can be left entirely to their own devices.
4   Do ensure that systems are properly documented.

Generally speaking, a computer program must specify a problem in complete detail and, what is more, it must cater for all possible exception conditions. Whereas Nellie, your average clerk, has the power of reason and discretion, and a store of background information on which to call if unusual conditions arise, the computer does not have this frame of reference unless the programmer, acting as your agent, is able to create it in the machine in the form of tables, instructions and parameters. Given the complexities involved, it is hardly surprising that a recent survey revealed that 90% of errors in computer systems were caused by program faults.

Software

Although modern computers may include the 'hard-wiring' of some functions, generally speaking the hardware components that make up a computer configuration will not work without software, which activates the devices through the control unit.

As you may be aware, there are broadly three types of software:

• system software;
• utilities; and
• application software.

System software
System software is usually, but not invariably, supplied by the computer manufacturer and will consist, inter alia, of the following items.

1 One or more programming 'languages' for the use of your programmers, together with a compiler or translator.
2 An operating system which, depending on its versatility and comprehensiveness, may include the following features:
   - an overall device and program control module which enables the control unit to function;
   - input, output and file handling and routing modules that present data in a form that can be manipulated or processed.
3 Programs for the control of the interface between the computer configuration and external devices such as communications facilities, terminals, etc.

If the computer manufacturer does not supply this type of software, the user will have to write it for himself, as one had to in the early days of computing. Nowadays, this process is tedious, complex, time consuming, error prone and extremely costly. Fortunately, as these functions are generally common to all users, the suppliers have sensibly saved us the trouble.

When selecting a computer, you should pay close attention to the availability and robustness of the system software provided by the manufacturer. This is an area where you may have to rely on technical guidance, but there are some basic questions you can ask.

- Are the programming languages/compilers that are being offered in common use, i.e. are they known by most computer staff?
- Does the operating system have all the requisite features and has it been proven in general use?
- How much extra equipment/storage capacity do we need to provide room for the operating system?
- Is the system software unique to this model of the machine or is it usable, and therefore will my programs operate, on other models from the same manufacturer?

No prospective user who has ambitions for his business to grow should ignore the implications of that growth for his data processing facilities. Is the black box and its software capable of expansion?

Utilities

Utilities are programs that carry out functions which are common to much of the computer processing carried out by most users. These functions include:

- routines for the sorting-merging of data;
- facilities for dumping or copying data from one medium to another, e.g. disk to tape, tape to printed output;
- security routines;
- facilities for the generation of printed reports on an ad hoc basis.

Because these programs are not fundamental to the activation of the hardware, there may be some functions that are not provided as standard software by the manufacturer. Prospective buyers of computer systems should be wary of acquiring equipment solely on the basis of hardware costs, as they may find that they have to write some essential utilities for themselves or purchase them elsewhere. These accretions can add appreciably to the cost.

Application software

You have acquired your computer, you have satisfied yourself that the supplier can provide adequate system software and utilities and now you wish to apply the machine to those business problems for which it was originally intended.

To do so, you will have to provide written computer programs that address those problem areas. These programs are known as application software and may be offered up to the computer as either:

- application packages; or
- bespoke systems.

We will examine the pros and cons of packages in a later chapter and so, for the purposes of this description, it is sufficient to recognize that there are certain basic business procedures, such as payroll, financial book-keeping and stock control, which are common to most organizations and which are capable of 'general solutions' in data processing terms.

Thus, many computer suppliers and hundreds of software houses will be happy to sell you, say, a generalized sales ledger or a stock control system; all you have to do is to 'plug' it in and provide the parametric data unique to your business environment. At least, that is the theory...

The alternative is to write your own programs, which involves the application of the techniques described in the programming section earlier in this chapter. For many computer users, the development of bespoke systems becomes a maze of frustration, excess costs and management bewilderment.

Hardware costs are becoming less and less significant as the determining factor in the selection of a computer system. As equipment costs decline, in some cases quite dramatically, more emphasis is placed, quite rightly, on the importance of the software facilities provided by the manufacturer or by the multiplicity of software vendors who hasten to supply a successful machine with the necessary systems software and utilities. This is particularly true for the first-time small business system user, where the availability of suitable software facilities is the key selection criterion.

Types of computing

Finally, a word on the types of computer processing that you will hear referred to by equipment salesmen and by computer specialists:

* batch processing;
* real-time processing; and
* on-line processing.

Ideally, it will be the characteristics of your applications which will determine which mode of processing will be the most suitable for your needs. It should never be the blandishments of salesmen, nor the technical aspirations of your staff.

Batch processing

As the term implies, this type of computing involves the processing of data in batches. It was the original method of data processing and remains the most common one in use. Batch processing has the following features.

* Transaction data is collected and coded on a regular predetermined basis.
* Transaction data is prepared for computer input and processed according to a predetermined and regular schedule.
* It involves a significant amount of manual/computer inter-

action during the processing cycle, e.g. input preparation and entry, file handling, output control and distribution.
- In between batch processes, computer files are not updated and are not therefore an accurate reflection of the real position.

The most typical example of a batch system is the processing of a weekly or monthly payroll.

Real-time processing

The term originates from the field of process engineering, where it describes a system in which input signals are converted to output actions in a virtually continuous mode in order to allow continuous control of a process or an environment. In data processing terms, a real-time system is one in which an input transaction immediately updates a record to bring it into line with the 'real' world, and the result of the change influences the system's response to the next transaction.

Perhaps the most well-known example of real-time processing is an airline seat reservation system, which requires:

- immediate up-to-date knowledge of available seats;
- immediate recording of a reservation;
- a barrier on allocating the reserved seat to the next transaction.

The fact that you may have suffered double booking is a reflection of the airline's commercial policy rather than a failure of the real-time system.

Real-time processing implies several users who are, more or less, permanently connected to the computer in an 'on-line' mode.

On-line processing

This type of computing is frequently confused with real-time, but the terms are not interchangeable. A real-time system must be on-line but an on-line system need not operate in real-time.

For example, Nellie in stock records could have a terminal through which she could:

1 update a stock record immediately, i.e. in real-time;
2 enter a batch of transactions for subsequent processing i.e. on-line data entry for a batch system;

3 enquire as to the status of a stock record without having the facility to update it, i.e. on-line enquiry.

Generally speaking, real-time systems are complex and expensive to develop and run, and potential users should have a very clear idea of the likely benefits before committing themselves to this type of computing.

3 People

Introduction

The financial director of an organization for which I worked several years ago was prone to unannounced walkabouts, much to the dismay of his departmental managers. On one occasion, passing through the computer department for which he was responsible, he noticed a long-haired, bearded, casually dressed young man apparently just staring into space and quite oblivious to his surroundings. After observing this phenomenon for some minutes, the financial director asked the systems manager who the young man was and what he was supposed to be doing.

'He is a programmer,' came the reply, 'and he is thinking.'

'Really?' said the director, for whom cerebral exercise was an indulgence. 'Well, I should get rid of him and let him do his thinking on someone else's time.'

Although the incident occured some time ago, it illustrates an attitude which persists today in spite of the much wider use of computers and the recognition of computing as a growing and important occupation. On the other hand, the behaviour and work patterns of many computer staff have done little to improve their image, which I believe to be generally poor.

The financial director was struck by two relatively trivial features of the computer man, his unconventional appearance and his method of working, that distinguished him from other company staff. He might, with more justification, have picked on other characteristics which have tended to set computer staff apart from fellow employees.

Typically, computer staff are:

- younger, academically better qualified but less experienced than their counterparts in other functions;
- articulate, more egalitarian and less susceptible to the traditional disciplines of the workplace;

- inclined to an inflated view of their new 'profession' and the contribution it makes to the organization and to society at large;
- more highly paid than other staff, to a level that often distorts existing pay structures and may sometimes be divisive;
- traditionally more loyal to the computer than the organization which they currently serve.

Some members of the computer fraternity would also claim that they work harder and longer, often during unsociable hours. However, most cases of prolonged overtime I have examined have had more to do with poor estimating, inadequate planning or a lack of productivity than with missionary zeal. It has been said that computer staff are truly creative and while this may be a justifiable description of the original work of some specialists, particularly in the software field, it is hardly correct to portray the vast majority of developments by computer staff as anything other than a re-work of existing systems.

Nor should management be misled by the tendency of computer staff to project their skills as a vehicle for the introduction of new theories of organization, management and information handling. By and large, these staff do not have the depth of understanding of human relations and organization theory to substantiate this approach, nor am I convinced that the average data processing application demands it. What is more, most managers would sacrifice their place in the forefront of management theory in favour of systems that work in practice and contribute to the efficiency or effectiveness of the business. In terms of the episode with the financial director, they would prefer more 'doing' and less thinking, but this view is no more tenable than the idea of an army of 25-year-old systems analysts marching to the rescue of British industry.

There is also that sneaky feeling that with the development and exploitation of cheap computing power and the growing range of software aids for the non-technician, we may not need computer staff in the same numbers or doing the same jobs as we have in the past. Management and user confidence has increased enormously in the 1980s, and the specialist finds it difficult to retreat behind jargon and mystique, particularly if the manager has acquired a machine or learned a language that may be unfamiliar to him. We are entering the 'throw away' age in computers, where a manager can acquire quite powerful equipment for a few thousand pounds, can write or buy a program for a few hundred and can throw it away and start again if it fails to satisfy or outlives its purpose.

By the same token, theoretically, there is no reason why we as individuals could not be DIY solicitors, doctors or motor mechanics if we read the right books, watch certain television programmes or attend evening classes. Sensibly, however, we do not attempt open-heart surgery or complex litigations. Similarly, before you rush out to buy a personal computer, it would be as well to recognize that there is, at a much lower level, a background of knowledge, experience and skill which the computer expert can call upon and the average manager should not attempt to reproduce.

The purpose of this chapter is to examine the nature of the jobs that have been created by the introduction of computers into organizations, to elucidate their real purpose, to dispose of some of the myths that surround computer staff and to offer guidelines to management on the control of an important resource.

The nature of the jobs

In the previous chapter we examined briefly the chief characteristics of hardware/software and looked at what was involved in converting a simple clerical procedure to a computer application by writing a program. It was a grossly over-simplified example of the process of development of a computer system, but you will have recognized the two basic stages involved.

Firstly, we had to define the problem in terms of WHAT was required and then, using our computer and its facilities, we designed a solution that determined HOW those requirements would be met. These are essentially the stages of systems analysis (WHAT) and programming (HOW). In spite of excessive elaboration of tasks over the years and the proliferation of job titles and specializations, these remain as distinct functions, whether or not they are carried out by separate individuals. Organizations which ignore this distinction run a serious risk of designing systems to suit their facilities rather than to suit users' needs, and perpetuating the confusion of ends and means which has bedevilled many computer projects.

I have always thought the analogy between computing and

engineering to be most fruitful when distinguishing the nature of the different jobs involved in bringing a product (a system) into being.

1 The product is conceived by a design engineer (the systems analyst) in response to a specification based on market needs. The engineer will be assisted by inputs from marketing, production and finance and the end product will be a synthesis of these requirements.

2 The conversion of the design into a production item is the responsibility of the production engineer (the programmer) who will determine and plan the manufacturing process to make the best use of the firm's facilities, will decide which jigs and tools are needed and will specify material and labour content.

The production engineer may refer the design back to the design engineer because it proves difficult to manufacture and the design may have to be altered, and, similarly, the programmer may suggest changes to a system to make it easier to produce (program) or to operate on a production basis. In spite of this important interplay between functions, design and production remain essentially separate and involve different skills.

In both engineering and computing, there is a third group of people which contributes substantially to the process of delivering a product that satisfies the end users' requirements. These are the operators, the production staff who set and operate the machines and apply resources on a day-to-day basis to maintain a production schedule. These tasks also involve separate skills but, like engineering manufacture, are increasingly open to the introduction of automation in one form or another.

These three types of computer jobs – systems analysis, programming and operations – perform as the intermediaries between the source of computing power and the user and his problem, as illustrated in Figure 3.1. A wry illustration of these relationships is shown in Figure 3.2. I am reliably advised that this diagram has been used over decades in many descriptions of professional activity and thus its origins and attributions remain unclear.

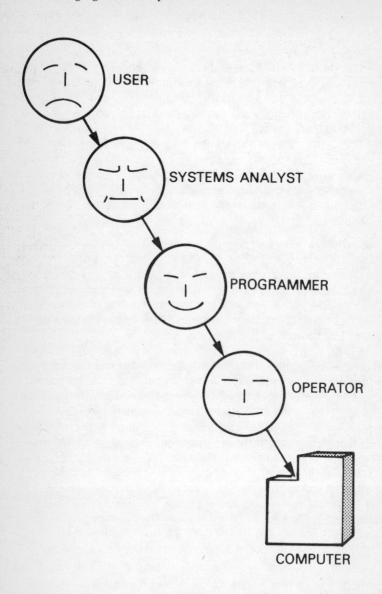

Figure 3.1 The intermediaries

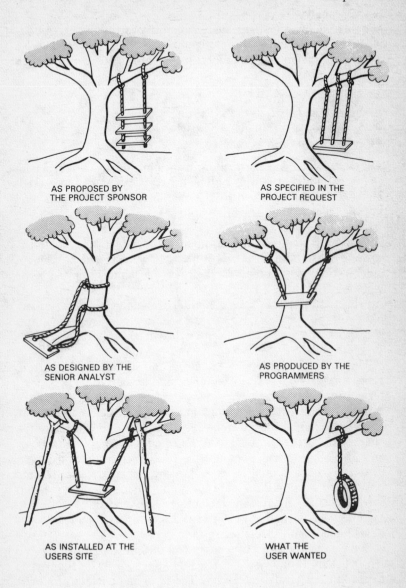

AS PROPOSED BY
THE PROJECT SPONSOR

AS SPECIFIED IN THE
PROJECT REQUEST

AS DESIGNED BY THE
SENIOR ANALYST

AS PRODUCED BY THE
PROGRAMMERS

AS INSTALLED AT THE
USERS SITE

WHAT THE
USER WANTED

Figure 3.2 Development process

Systems analysis

We have defined systems analysis as the process of determining what the user needs and of designing a computer system to meet those requirements. This process will involve a number of related activities:

- a feasibility study
- the detailed analysis of the existing system
- evaluation of alternative approaches
- preparation of an overall specification

These activities will be dealt with in more detail in subsequent chapters, but the following outline is necessary for an understanding of the work involved in systems analysis and the skills and knowledge that should be brought to bear.

A feasibility study At the feasibility study stage, the analyst is seeking to establish if the problem posed by management is amenable to solution by computer. In order to reach this conclusion, he will have to acquire a sufficient understanding of the nature of the existing system to see how computer techniques can be applied. However, he does not have to design the computer solution at this stage; indeed to do so would probably handicap any subsequent developments.

The analyst will interview managers and staff about the current procedure(s), he will study the operation of the system in general terms, concentrating on the flows of information into and out of system, and he will collect data that describe the parameters of the procedural model (because that is what it is). He will relate the characteristics of the model to his knowledge of computer facilities and of similar systems, because the probability is that this application has been computerized before by somebody else. Having established a prima facie case for a computer system, he should provide management with the information necessary to enable them to decide whether or not to allocate further resources to the development of the proposed system.

Some organizations put a great deal of time and effort into the feasibility study of a systems area, and I am not convinced that this expenditure is always necessary. The form and content of a feasibility study, to achieve maximum impact on management, is discussed in more detail in Chapter 5.

Detailed analysis If the results of a feasibility study are favourable, the next step is to carry out a detailed analysis of the existing system. Some theorists will argue that it is unnecessary and possibly an encumbrance to analyse the current situation and that, given the parameters of the problem, it is perfectly possible and acceptable to design a computer system without reference to the operation of existing procedures. After all, is not this the way in which successful general application packages are designed? However, this claim is made invariably by designers of systems and never, to my knowledge, by users. It would be foolhardy of the systems analyst to specify a new computer system without, first of all, becoming thoroughly familiar with the purpose, structure and operation of the existing system.

There are several reasons for an approach which at first sight may appear irrelevant, if you intend transforming the procedures dramatically.

1 As a matter of professional pride and discipline, the analyst should know as much as possible about the area under review, in order to convince management and prospective users that he knows what he is talking about.
2 At the detailed analysis stage you will identify problem areas, shortcomings, procedural quirks and exceptions that were not dreamed of at the feasibility stage. Your system must cater for or obviate every one of them.
3 The analyst is acting as an agent of change – a hackneyed phrase, but true – and none of us likes change. There will be resistance, reluctance and obfuscation of the issues. The analyst's prime responsibility and opportunity is to use the detailed investigation to get to know the prospective users, to allay fears, to win their confidence and to sell himself and the concept of computing. It is a kind of seduction and is best carried out face to face.
4 Getting to know the system and the people who operate it will provide invaluable material for planning conversion and implementation. Believe me, if Nellie says a system will not work, then it will not work, whatever its merits.

So my advice to the analyst and his manager is to pay proper attention to the operation of the existing system and ensure that they understand its purpose, the inputs, outputs and information flows, the processing rules, the management controls, the exceptions, the volumes of data to be dealt with, the relationship with other functions and the objectives of the proposed change. All these findings should be fully recorded in a fashion that both the user and the expert, but principally the user, can understand and agree upon.

Evaluation of alternatives Whether or not the feasibility study postulated a particular approach to computing, the job of the analyst carrying out the detailed investigations will include the consideration of alternative methods of achieving the end result. He will have in mind either an existing computer installation or a general idea of the facilities the organization may acquire. His deliberations will be conditioned to some extent by these facilities, but his conclusions may also influence them. For instance, although you may have a highly centralized computer function, the demands of this new application may call for some decentralized computing power, say in the form of remote direct data entry.

In any event, the analyst will be assessing the requirements of the proposed system in terms of its demands on computing resources and will be considering such issues as the following.

- Should the application be batch or on-line?
- Should computing power be centralized or localized?
- How should input be offered up to the computer?
- How should output be presented to the user?
- Could the same objectives be achieved with only partial use of data processing facilities?

The last question is perfectly valid at the stage of a detailed investigation, notwithstanding the direction given by the prior feasibility study, and is an additional reason why the existing procedures should be thoroughly examined.

The overall specification Having established the prospective user's requirements and looked at ways in which they could be satisfied, the analyst will prepare an overall specification which is variously known as:

- the proposal
- the user requirements
- the functional specification

- the business requirements specification

Personally, I prefer the last description.

Whatever its name, I would expect to find that it was a document that dealt comprehensively with the overall design of the system, with the functions required by users, with the inputs and outputs, with the data to be held or manipulated and with the interfaces with other procedures. There should also, at this stage, be a clear idea about the method of converting to a new system, the amount of training required by the staff estimated to operate it and the proposed timetable. Unlike the feasibility study, which will have given the 'ball park' assessments of the computer resources needed to develop and implement the system, the business requirements specification should provide and substantiate more detailed estimates of the specialist staff, computer time and other resources required.

The business requirements specification is designed to meet two main objectives: to secure user agreement and acceptance of the proposed system; and to provide management with the justification for authorizing subsequent work and expenditure on the proposed project. Management is the final arbiter and could at this stage decide to modify their aspirations on the grounds of costs; alternatively they could cancel the project because of inadequate justification. If the development process has been properly planned and monitored, it is most likely that management will take a decision to go ahead on *some* basis. However, they should not shrink from a decision to cancel if their commonsense or gut-feel suggests that this would be the right course of action. After all, at this stage they have spent only a fraction of the amount that they could be committed to if the proposed system is a non-starter.

The systems specification So you have decided to go ahead, and the analyst's next set of tasks is to convert the business requirements specification into a form that more accurately reflects the ways in which the proposed application will make use of computer resources. Within the systems specification:

- input/output will be defined in data processing terms;
- file contents will be described;
- processing rules will be specified in detail, down to the last most unlikely exception;

- and, without losing sight of user requirements, the analyst will begin to consider how best to use the facilities at his disposal.

At this stage, hopefully and sensibly, the analyst will involve the experts in programming in the formation of a computing and programming strategy for the proposed system.

Programming

You may feel that it has taken a long time to translate Nellie's problem into a form on which we can base a computer program. Unpalatable and costly though it may be, the process of systems analysis can be lengthy and often laborious, but my experience suggests that the number of problems encountered at the programming stage is inversely proportional to the amount of time devoted to systems work.

This must be so: the programmer's task is to convert procedural steps into instructions that will activate the computer, and if any of those steps are omitted or imprecise, the ability of the program to function must be impaired. It is insufficient to advise the programmer that Nellie updates a stock record with a new transaction; in order to program the activity, we also need to know, for example, that:

- a stock movement must consist of wholly numeric data and its absolute value may not exceed a certain quantity;
- if the posting of a transaction causes a negative balance, we take certain actions;
- if we cannot post a transaction we need to refer it in some way;

and so on. The history of systems developement so far suggests that specifications are rarely precise enough to eliminate misunderstandings, and I have yet to hear of a program of any significance which worked correctly on the first pass.

We have defined programming as the set of techniques or tools with which we apply computing resources to the solution of our problem. Utilizing these techniques involves a number of activities:

- the design of program specifications
- flowcharting
- coding
- testing

Like so many activities in computer developement, these tend to merge or be confused, almost always to the detriment of the final product.

Program specifications The way in which the proposed application is specified by the analyst may not be the best approach to constructing the system in terms of a programming strategy that makes optimum use of the computer's capabilities. This does not mean necessarily that the analyst is unfamiliar with the machine, although this is sometimes the case, but rather that the programmer is a specialist who should know it very well. He will have at his command the skills, knowledge and past experience that come from constant exposure to the problems of program construction and data manipulation. This frame of reference will guide him in deciding such matters as the most efficient file or record layouts, the scope for combining certain functions to avoid excessive access to storage and the effective use of software aids.

Ideally, the systems analyst will have involved a senior programmer at an early stage in the design of the system in order to avoid any complete nonsense in its structure. In any event, the first task in the sequence of programming activities is the interpretation of the systems specification into a number of program specifications. This should be carried out by the chief programmer, if there is one, or the senior programmer allocated to the project. It will involve the following steps.

1 The detailed study of the systems specification and liaison with the analyst concerned.
2 Design of the file and record layouts to support the system.
3 Deciding on the number and type of programs required to meet the specification and preparing an overall schema for the system.
4 Preparing a specification for each program, including:
   • input/output/file contents;
   • a flowchart of the modules that make up the program;
   • processing rules for manipulating the data.
5 Estimating the work required to code and test each program.

These steps should be completed for the whole system *before* any code is initiated. Some programmers will argue against this cautious level-by-level approach, merely because they are anxious to get to grips with actual program writing. However, in my experience, if you start coding before you have a complete understanding of the system at a strategic level and have resolved all structural problems, you will almost certainly find that some programs or modules are incompatible and will subsequently have to be modified or rewritten. By analogy, if you were building a house, you would hardly start constructing the kitchen or the outhouses before you had an overall design, including the routing of mains services, etc.

The level-by-level approach is a proven technique and is known variously as 'top down' programming, structured programming or modular programming. Whether or not he had been formally trained in these methods, a good programmer will usually follow a similar route. Apart from the advantages of logical and compatible construction, the method has the considerable benefit of enforcing a disciplined approach to documentation.

An important step in this process is the one concerned with estimating the work required to code and test each program. It is only at this stage that the validity of programming estimates made during the feasibility study and systems specification phases can be confirmed. Regrettably, many initial assessments are revealed as optimistic and the aggregation of such program estimates usually results in an increased total cost of implementing the system. It is a fact that estimates are rarely reduced as the specification of the system is progressively refined and knowledge of the size and complexity of the system becomes more detailed. We will examine the process of estimating more closely in a later chapter.

Flowcharting The program specification will include an overall flowchart that illustrates the main functions to be performed. The programmer to whom the program is allocated will use this schema to aid his initial understanding, but he should then prepare a much more detailed flowchart that virtually mirrors the individual computer instructions necessary to carry out the processing. Until the job has been charted in detail, and has been approved by his senior, he should not attempt any actual coding. This approach is consistent with the level-by-level progression into detail that ensures a full understanding of requirements before proceeding to the next stage.

Coding Finally, the moment the programmer has been waiting for – coding of the program from the flowchart can begin. The programmer will select from the repertoire of computer instructions and utilities the commands that are required to carry out the functions of the program. Ideally, he will be working to some predetermined installation standards that prescribe, for example, the maximum size of program or module and how to use certain instructions. He may be barred from using some commands or techniques because experience has shown that they are time-consuming or difficult to amend if something goes wrong. In spite of the care taken, it is highly likely that something *will* go wrong because of mistakes in using commands, through faulty logic in the flowchart or as a result of misunderstanding in breaking down the specification in the first place.

Testing These faults or 'bugs' may be detected at any stage; some may lie for months or years and spring upon the unsuspecting user long after the program has been operating successfully, for example if a part of the program dealing with an unusual set of conditions is suddenly called into execution for the first time. When you consider the many thousands of paths that make up a program, which attempts to cater for all possibilities, it is not surprising that some prove faulty or that some freak data hits the system. Although these faults occur in spite of testing, many arise because of inadequate attention to the tedious process of proving a program.

Quite the most irksome task for programmers is some form of 'dry run' through the logic of the program, without the aid of the computer. This might merely involve simple desk-checking with the assistance of a fellow programmer, or it might call for a major presentation of the program to a gathering of colleagues. In any event, the programming supervisor should vet the program against the original specification before authorizing compilation and testing by the computer.

Once the program has been coded and checked, it has to be compiled. This means offering it up to the computer for translation, via a compiler, into a working program. At this stage some faults will be identified which will be in the nature of 'grammatical errors' in the use of the programming language. These should be eradicated and the program should compile successfully on the second pass. If you find that programs require several compilations before they are ready to run you should begin to question the competence of your programming staff, especially the supervisors.

Having achieved a 'clean' compilation, the next step is to test the operation and logic of the program, module by module, and finally in its entirety, by submitting it to test data. Some simple rules need to be observed.

1 Do take the trouble to plan the test sequence and the structure of the test data, including the results you expect.
2 Always start with error-free data so that you know if the program will work at all. Having established that, you can progressively introduce 'dirty' transactions.
3 Do not persist with subsequent tests if you cannot pass data through the opening parts of the program. In other words, finish cleaning each room before you pass on to the next one.

These tests should trap most bugs, but they may not find them all. Here again, you should keep track of the number of test shots taken by the programmer, as this is an indication of the quality of programming and the efficiency of your test procedures.

In one installation I visited, it became clear that the delayed implementation of an important system was largely due to the fact that one program had not passed the testing phase. We discovered that the program had been submitted for 65 tests but, as soon as one bug was fixed, another was detected. Closer examination of the program revealed that no prior checking had been carried out and the program was riddled with errors that had not been reached yet but were plain to see. The programmer was using the computer to check a rather slipshod program when most of the faults could have been eliminated beforehand. It is worth noting that the installation had no method of recording and controlling the number of test shots and the actual figure came as a surprise to management.'

When the program eventually passes the test imposed by the programmers themselves, it will be subjected to an equally thorough and tense systems test set by the users. The program, by now part of a whole system, will be exposed to a comprehensive range of operational data which should reflect the conditions under which the system will run.

Programming aids With some computers, generally the larger ones, but including some minicomputers, the programmer is able to use a terminal connected on-line to the machine to develop his programs. Using a video screen, he can write, amend, compile, test and document his program and offer it up for a systems test. These aids tend to increase overall programmer productivity by up to 20%, but they are expensive to use. Whether or not these methods are employed, the programming disciplines we have described are equally relevant and may be more critical because of the costs involved.

The increasing use of the fourth generation languages mentioned in the previous chapter has had a marked effect on the traditional systems development cycle described above. These languages can be used to construct 'prototypes' of proposed computer applications very rapidly, via a user/technician/machine *trialogue*, and thus expedite the refinement of user requirement at an early stage in systems development. To date, they have had their greatest impact in the hands of the computer expert whose productivity has increased between two- and ten-fold in the production of program code.

Operations
The position of computer operations has changed significantly over the years. In the early days, the job of operating a computer was largely physical and involved loading and unloading cards, tapes, disks and paper and pressing buttons. Developments in system control software and increased complexity of the operating environment enhanced the technical content of the operations task and called for a higher degree of skill.

To-day, there are further developments which, far from extending the skills of the operator, are tending to erode the work content and could lead eventually to the demise of the operator as a separate job category. These developments include:

- improved automation in the running of computer applications, especially on large machines, where operations tend towards machine-minding, with fewer staff;
- the increase in decentralized on-line operations, such that computer jobs can be initiated and controlled remotely by users;
- improved reliability of hardware and software, allowing for a great deal of unattended running, for example, to produce

major volumes of output or carry out housekeeping routines;
- the spread of mini- and microcomputers which can be built into normal office procedures and run by existing staff;
- the growth in personal computing, where the user controls his own operations.

The significance of these changes for the general manager, especially in an organization with a sizeable operations staff, is that they may provoke industrial relations problems because of possible job losses. These problems are discussed in a later chapter.

The qualities required

A manager, seeking to fill any important functional post in his organization, will evaluate any potential candidates under three broad headings:

- basic skills and knowledge
- experience
- personal characteristics

A satisfactory score on these three aspects is fundamental to any type of job, be it engineering, accounting or marketing, and the same rules apply to the recruitment of data processing staff.

Basic skills and knowledge

We have examined briefly the nature of the jobs carried out by computer staff and it will be apparent that a considerable range of skills and knowledge are brought into play during a computer project. These include:

- a knowledge of computers and their potential uses;
- the investigation and recording of often complex procedures and documentation;
- interviewing techniques;
- the ability to collect, manipulate and evaluate statistical data;
- oral and written communication;
- flowcharting and design skills;
- the ability to analyse and synthesise case material; and
- knowledge of programming techniques.

You will recognize in this list some elements of other similar service functions – O & M, work study, statistical analysis, operations research. It would be fair to acknowledge that computer systems analysis not only owes part of its genetic inheritance to these earlier management sciences but also provides an important stage in their current development.

Experience

As with most disciplines, these skills can be taught in the classroom and knowledge can be acquired by diligence. However, it is self-evident that these skills are enhanced if the practitioner has a lot of experience of applying them and, in particular, if they are combined with a knowledge of the functional areas being studied. Thus, if you are planning to use computers in manufacturing control you will save time, money and a modicum of grief if you begin by recruiting computer staff who know something about the area. Similarly, an accounting application will benefit substantially from the allocation of computer staff who have an understanding of, or possibly a basic training in, accounting and book-keeping principles.

> I well remember meeting a young systems analyst who was a brilliant computer scientist with a depth of background in technical programming and little else. At the end of a lengthy discussion of a sales ledger and sales analysis application, to which he made a thoughtful if unremarkable contribution, he turned to a colleague to ask, 'tell me, what is an invoice?' He learned quickly and now runs a successful computer services company.

Clearly, accountants and production managers will have more confidence in computer staff who can demonstrate experience in their areas.

Personal characteristics

It is theoretically possible to design and program a computer system without going anywhere near the prospective user, particularly in areas which have been well researched elsewhere. Regrettably, this is the approach adopted by some computer staff, either as individuals or in following the standard data processing practice in the organization. This approach can work at the programming stage; indeed, it is often desirable to keep the programmers away from the user. However, it is totally wrong for systems work and can be disastrous for the process of project management and implementation, where contact with the user should override all other considerations.

In terms of the personal characteristics of a systems analyst, this participative and interactive approach to systems development calls for similar qualities to those attributed to successful salesmen: a degree of extroversion; the ability to show an interest in and get on well with people; patience; tact, an understanding of the organization's social structure; a willingness to compromise. All these qualities, which are mostly innate, are rarely taught, and tend to develop with exposure to live situations. Without these characteristics it will be harder to bring about the changes that are inevitably associated with computerization and on which, quite probably, the expected benefits depend. The job of the systems analyst, as we will be constantly reminded, is to act as an agent of change, and persuasion is a major part of that role.

By comparison, the job of programming calls for less worldly and mature characteristics: it is vital to be capable of logical thought; to be industrious, painstaking and methodical; and to be capable of participating in a team approach to the solution of the systems problem. However, by and large, the programmer will not be called upon to deal with managers and with user staff, nor to assess, argue and arbitrate on their needs, nor, finally having won Nellie's confidence, to coach her in the use of her terminal.

Job titles

We have talked about two main job categories, the systems analyst and the programmer. We nodded in the direction of the third important, but not fundamental, category of operations staff. Not many years ago, these classifications were sufficient to describe not only the functions performed but also the title of the job holder, subject to such distinctions as trainee, junior or senior grades. However, as you may be aware, in data processing there is now a proliferation of job titles which owe their origins to organizational development, technological changes and resultant personal aspirations. While you should be aware of these gradations, you should not lose sight of the principal distinction we have made between systems analysis and programming, of which they are mere perturbations.

Organizational development

Some data processing departments are now quite large, employing several hundred people and, in terms of the budgets they wield, they operate like small- to medium-sized companies. Organization structures, management practices and staffing policies have had to develop in line with this growth and have created quite interesting management problems (see Chapter 12.)

It would have been difficult to found some of these larger structures on a simple categorization that catered purely for systems analysts and programmers. Among other effects, it would have perpetuated a very shallow structure, with perhaps two or three levels between the boss and the office boy. In addition, the approach to computing has changed, such that organization structures have had to recognize the growth of functional/application areas and the orientation towards project teams. Specializations have emerged that reflect both development practices and technological advances. As a result, in the larger computer department, we may find such interesting titles as:

- business analyst
- business systems analyst
- senior systems analyst/systems analyst
- project manager/project leader
- team leader
- analyst/programmer
- senior programmer/programmer
- lead programmer
- principal analyst (or programmer)
- application programmer
- systems programmer/software programmer

as well as variations that recognize levels of experience and specialization. In one company I visited, there were 17 different titles to describe only 40 individuals.

Technological changes

Advances in computing and related fields, and the new skills these changes have identified, have also led to new types of jobs being created, for example:

- database administrator
- database programmer

- communications programmer
- network controller
- real-time programmer

and so on. On the emergence of a new title, it is quite interesting to attempt to draft a revised job specification; it invariably turns out that we are talking about an additional level of knowledge rather than a distinctly different function.

Personal aspirations

Many data processing job structures have been created in order to provide a means of advancement for computer staff and, more importantly, a salary structure that gives them the opportunity for progression. They also allow management some flexibility in the constant struggle to retain and motivate staff who can just as readily go elsewhere.

Job specifications

Whether or not formal job specifications exist for computer staff depends on the style of the organization they serve. Most large companies and public and private institutions have job descriptions of some form, if only as a basis for the pay structure. Where they exist, they are usually out of date in some respect and generally consist of the job title, a broad statement of the scope of the job and then a list of the main duties of the incumbent. There may be additional commentary on superior/subordinate relationships, on authority to spend money, hours of work, etc. In my opinion, most of the job descriptions which follow this common pattern are not much help to the job holder, nor to his manager who may wish to check if he is fulfilling his duties correctly. For instance, how does a manager verify that a systems analyst is 'ensuring that systems are designed to meet users information requirements', that he is 'planning and controlling the work of the programmers', or that a computer programmer 'produces tested and proven programs ready for operational use'?

These are extracts from typical job specifications in which duties are described in the form of the activities that should occupy the job holder. There is usually no quantitative comment which indicates how the activity should be carried out or how it should be measured in terms of results. These requirements are sometimes catered for in the establishment of installation standards, but how much more pertinent it would be to fix specific criteria of performance for each task in a job description, especially if you take the precaution of inviting the job holder to participate in setting them. For instance, you could agree with programmers that a clean program should be available for testing after a maximum of three compilations; that a program should be fully tested after x test shots or y minutes of computer time; that, overall, the programming process should be completed at the rate of z instructions per day.

This type of goal setting, management by results – call it what you will – is fairly common now in general and functional management and I see no valid reason why similar techniques cannot be applied to data processing activities. It has the additional advantage of providing a basis for staff appraisal and can be linked successfully to salary structures. To give further illustration of this approach, I have included in Appendix 2 some detailed examples of results-oriented job descriptions for computer staff in the larger installation.

The use of external resources

It will not have escaped your notice that we are well into the 1980s with a shortfall in the supply of computer staff. Estimates of the unfulfilled need in the UK vary from 20,000 to 30,000, of which about two-thirds are reckoned to be systems analysts and programmers. Even if this gap in numbers could be miraculously closed overnight, the real problems of effective computer usage would not be solved because of the below-average quality of the staff available. The reasons for the disparity between supply and demand are fairly clear.

1 The rapid growth in the introduction of computers, especially in the late 1970s.
2 The inability of public and private training schemes to keep pace with the increased demand for staff.
3 The stretching of existing resources over a larger number of small installations.
4 The drift of experienced staff into computer service companies or into management roles in user companies.
5 A reducing productivity level among staff of lesser experience,

which is reflected in a demand for more men rather than better methods.

The effect on average remuneration has been startling, even in an industry renowned for high salaries; staff costs are now the largest single component in any data processing budget, accounting for up to 60% of total costs. Some organizations, tired of the constant hassle of acquiring staff, worried about internal pay relativities and concerned about the quality of work, have turned to external computer service companies to provide resources. Other users, especially of small computers, have realized that their needs can be met by software packages or by a few bespoke systems and that they do not require a permanent data processing staff once those applications have been implemented. It is small wonder that the demand for external systems and programming resources is increasing at a rate of about 30% per year.

Recently I reviewed the £15.0 million budget of the computer division of a large organization, using the Urwick Overhead Activity Profiling Method. It emerged that several million pounds were expended annually on subcontract services which were almost certainly subject to a margin of about 30% on cost. However, the company was content to follow this route rather than take the resources on board as permanent staff because of the overhead they would incur (sic). In my view it was more a reluctance to develop a sensible personnel policy and manpower planning that could handle technicians in a basically clerical environment.

Obviously, external computer resources are expensive and they are not wholly immune to the problems and deficiencies that beset in-house staff. They may also overrun on development projects and misunderstand requirements, so in what circumstances should you consider using a software house rather than your own staff?

When to use
The use of external computer staff should be seriously considered when one or more of the following conditions prevail.

1   You are a new prospective user with a small computer and relatively few standard applications in mind. For example, if you merely wish to convert financial ledgers to a computer,

then you would be well advised to look for a suitable package among the several that will probably be available for your machine, and employ a software house to implement it for you.

2 Where there is a determinable project that can be readily identified and specified and can be subcontracted on a turnkey basis; for instance, the commissioning of a stand-alone minicomputer in a remote location where it is dedicated to one task such as acting as a sender/receiver of data.

3 If you have an overload in systems development that cannot be absorbed in the medium term and the prospective user is pressing for implementation. This is a common practice among large computer installations, and some household names have retained one or more software houses for several years.

4 When you are seeking a particular expertise that your own staff do not have or specialist software which can only be acquired elsewhere. For example, with the upsurge of interest in office automation, there is a demand for skills and software to link computers with office devices which is unlikely to be satisfied internally.

5 Where a series of bad experiences with internal computer performance – high costs, project overruns, poor productivity, lousy systems – lead you in despair to seek more reliable resources.

6 If, having considered the costs and man-management problems, you decide that you do not wish to build up an in-house computer department. The ultimate stage of this policy is to turn everything – development and operating – over to a service company that will provide either a bureau service or will manage your installation for you. This latter approach, known as facilities management, is similar to the common practice of subcontracting all catering services in an organization.

However sound your reasons may be for turning to external resources, you should not be deluded into thinking that all your problems are eliminated. You cannot subcontract your management obligations to ensure that you get value for money, that services are delivered on time and in good order and that objective benefits are achieved.

Nevertheless I believe, on balance, that the use of properly controlled external resources can be highly beneficial to the user.

- In spite of the high cost, it is likely to be less expensive in terms of productive hours.
- You will probably get better systems, which is good for you and the economy.
- It transfers the responsibilities for recruitment, training and the control of skilled staff to the experts.
- It removes eccentrics from your organization, leaving you to devote your energies to your real business.

Obviously, it does not have to be an all-or-nothing choice and it is certainly sensible to have some in-house expertise, if only to manage the use of external resources.

The future

Some people forecast that the imbalance between the supply and demand for computer staff will disappear and perhaps reverse in the late 1980s and early 1990s, and that their specialist skills will become redundant. This interpretation is based on a number of developments that are likely to accelerate.

1 The expected further decline in the cost both of hardware devices and of improved software facilities.
2 The growth in personal computing fostered by these technological/commercial changes.
3 The effect of de-skilling of the systems development process, especially in programming, which will enable the average man to design systems with the aid of sophisticated software.
4 An increase in the amount of basic training in computer skills given in schools, in further education and in the professions.
5 Wider availability and reliability of packages and a greater willingness on the part of users to sacrifice optimization for quick, cheap and reliable solutions.

Who knows what else may lurk beyond the current technological horizon? Voice-actuated computing that would enable systems to be developed by a man-machine dialogue? It is certain that we have not reached the end of the road in technical developments, judging by the vast amounts spent on research by the principal manufacturers.

However for the foreseeable future, as managers wishing to apply computer techniques, you will have to contend with the current environment in which systems analysts and programmers have to be motivated and controlled. This is a responsibility which is often shirked, managers frequently appearing reluctant or unable to apply to computer staff those standards of man-management which they commonly use with other functions. For their part, some computer staff have taken advantage of relaxed management styles and are quite happy to move on if the going gets rough. It is time for both sides to acknowledge their responsibilities and for management to manage and computer staff to deliver.

4   The sources of computing power

Introduction

In the early 1970s, if you wished to acquire a computer your choice, by and large, was restricted to a relatively small number of manufacturers, each supplying a range of related machines for which the starting price might be as 'low' as £100,000. Where smaller and cheaper equipment existed, it was not always possible to guarantee compatibility with larger computers and this could inhibit growth and lead subsequently to expensive conversion costs. As a result, there was a vast untapped market for computing facilities which was either unsatisfied or had to make use of computer service bureaux, advanced accounting machines and the like. Because of the heavy capital and resource costs involved, those organizations which did install computers naturally adopted a centralized approach and concentrated on achieving high utilization of equipment. As a result, within those organizations, there was often a queue of patient prospective users, waiting their turn for access to the limited central computing and development resources.

Technical developments and breakthroughs in production technology, particularly in the manufacture of silicon chips, allied with considerable marketing flair on the part of the manufacturers, have changed the position dramatically. Not only have the mainstream manufacturers developed smaller and cheaper equipment, but also the opportunities presented by a bigger market have attracted hundreds of new suppliers into the fray. As a result, a prospective user is spoilt for choice and may be bewildered by the array of equipment and services now on offer. As an indication of the change that has come about, a survey in 1981 revealed that there were 210 companies supplying microcomputers and allied services. In 1985, there were over 700 different makes of microcomputer and over 5,000 software products marketed by well over a thousand suppliers. The average prospect might have a hard time deciding which company to contact, even supposing that he is right to look at a microcomputer rather than a larger machine or some form of external service. Unfortunately, many managers are attracted by the cheapness and kudos of microcomputers and have given inadequate thought to their possible limitations and the alternatives that may be available. I would like to persuade managers, who state categorically 'I need a microcomputer; which one shall I have?' to think more flexibly and say, instead, 'I need a source of computing power; how best can it be provided?' It may take a little longer to arrive at a decision, but it could avoid an expensive mistake.

An investment company acquired a specific microcomputer largely on the grounds that it was recommended by an executive in another company who had had successful experience with the equipment. The configuration cost £20,000 which was at least double the price of many similar machines that could have provided the same facilities. After a year, it was realized that the growth of the company was outstripping the capacity of the computer and the management was faced with the choice of buying a duplicate configuration or scrapping their investment to date and starting again with a bigger machine. Rather embarrassing for a company specializing in the analysis of investment decisions.

If this company had allocated the proper amount of time to considering future as well as present needs and shopped around a little, with the aid of technical advice, they would not have wasted so much time and money. On the other hand, there is a substantial record of success stories.

A small company supplying components to the motor industry decided that its delivery performance could be improved by acquiring a microcomputer. Without much hesitation, the managing director went to a well-known retail outlet, purchased a well-known microcomputer, bought two modules of a production control package and implemented them successfully for about £10,000. Within a very few months their planning and control of manufacture and their delivery performance had improved substantially. Mind you, they did have the part-time assistance of a consultant!

Types of computing power

Most textbooks or reference works will attempt to define the difference between mainframes, minicomputers and microcomputers in technical terms and will usually fall foul of the next advance in technology which will contradict some part of their definition. These days it is equally dangerous to base definitions on realtive costs and cost/performance ratios, as these factors are constantly changing. For our purposes it is sufficient to acknowledge that if you need higher processing speeds, larger storage capacity, more facilities and greater flexibility then you are moving up the scale of computing and will tend to pay more for those features and for the supporting services such as systems analysis and programming. Our working definition of the various sources of computing power is therefore based on the facilities that are usually associated with each level of computing.

Microcomputers

The first thing to say about microcomputers is that they are exceedingly cheap in data processing terms. The central device, consisting usually of the logic, control circuitry, memory, a keyboard and a screen, can be acquired for a few hundred pounds. However, at this level, it is not much more than an elaborate electronic calculator and to transform it into a data processing machine calls for the addition of input/output devices and some form of backing storage. Even so, the total cost of providing a balanced configuration is unlikely to exceed four figures; if it does you may be looking at the wrong machine.

Although a relatively small outlay will acquire quite a powerful machine, you must recognize that there may be significant limits to what you can achieve with it. Its internal speeds may be relatively slow in computing terms and this may make certain standard requirements, such as sorting data, rather time-consuming, especially as the machine may not be able to do anything else. The amount of backing store, in the form of diskettes or larger capacity hard disks, that the microcomputer can support may also be limited, perhaps to less than 10 million characters, and this will restrict the number of records you can hold. Printing facilities tend to be slow and variable in quality, although there have been marked improvements in the performance of 'letter quality' printers.

These machines are now supplied with a range of systems software, comparable to the facilities available on larger machines, and the large number of software suppliers are responding well to customers' requirements and beginning to provide a wide range of software and application packages. Packages are remarkably cheap and easy to implement but they have to conform to the limitations of the machine and its operating system, often specifying an upper limit to the file sizes they can handle, e.g. a stock recording and control package that will maintain up to 1,000 stock items, or a sales analysis package that is limited to so many transactions. However, at this level of computing there is no reason why users cannot construct simple applications for themselves, and I have seen some excellent examples of systems written by managers to analyse the order book, to provide cash flow forecasts and to facilitate quality control. The ubiquitous and versatile spreadsheet has done much to encourage user exploitation of microcomputers.

The beauty of microcomputers in data processing terms is that, because of the low costs involved, you can afford to use the machine to refine your requirements and, if you have to abandon one approach and try another, the cost is relatively insignificant. Furthermore, you do not require a permanent in-house technical staff, although you may need to consult with an expert from time to time.

We are already in the next phase of technical development for microcomputers which will see faster input-output devices, greater disk storage capacity and facilities that will enable machines to talk to each other, share expensive peripherals and be linked to larger mainframe computers.

Minicomputers

Today's average minicomputer is often more powerful than the mainframes on which many senior data processing staff learned their trade several years ago; furthermore, they can be acquired for a fraction of the cost. The price range is very wide, say £10,000 to £100,000, overlapping that of microcomputer configurations at the bottom end and smaller mainframes at the higher level.

Compared with a micro, a typical minicomputer:

- will be several times faster;
- will have a more comprehensive repertoire of programming commands;

- will usually support more than one programming language;
- will be provided with a broader range of systems software and utilities;
- will have faster input/output devices and larger storage capacities;
- will be capable of supporting a network of terminal devices; and
- will be able to communicate with other computers.

Because of these technical features and the variety of options they present to the systems designer, we are now in the realm of the computer expert although not wholly within his grasp. There are some excellent software aids to enable programs to be developed fairly quickly by non-technicians and an increasing range of application packages are available that can be implemented without great difficulty, if users are prepared to moderate their aspirations to match the facilities. Furthermore, because minicomputers generally do not require a specially controlled environment, nor much in the way of operating attention, they can be integrated quite successfully with normal office routines.

One of the manufacturing divisions of a large company concluded that the increasing volume of paperwork and complexity of its planning and control procedures merited consideration of computer facilities. Management had no access to in-house expertise but did have a thorough understanding of the division's requirements. With part-time external assistance, production management carried out a feasibility study, evaluated equipment and software and finally selected a particular minicomputer and a production control package.

During the following 12 months, five modules of the package were successfully implemented by internal staff with only 30 days external assistance. The computer and the system, which has on-line facilities, have become part of day-to-day office activity and no specialist staff have been engaged.

Mainframes

The distinction between a large minicomputer and the small mainframe becomes blurred when they are both capable of supporting on-line systems from a central location. I suppose that one of the principal differences is that with the largest minicomputer there is eventually a limit to growth, whereas mainframes are usually part of a family of computers that theoretically provide unlimited capacity for expansion. Some manufacturers will claim that their minis and mainframes are wholly compatible, but users may find that there are software barriers that are difficult or expensive to surmount.

For our purposes, it is sufficient to know that mainframes are capable of providing bigger, better and faster facilities which are invariably centralized in an organization. These facilities will include:

- processing speeds rated in millions of instructions per second rather than thousands;
- backing storage amounting to thousands of millions of characters;
- multiple input/output devices;
- the capacity to support large terminal networks and communications facilities, world-wide if necessary;
- the ability to run several jobs at once or to be configured as more than one machine;
- a comprehensive range of systems software, utilities, design aids, programming languages and application packages; and
- a framework of controls, protocols and disciplines that make it extremely difficult for the average user to communicate directly with the computer.

At this level of computing we are very much in the hands of professional data processing staff and the computer function becomes a necessary and formal part of the organization structure.

Terminal facilities
Our thesis is that the user wants access to computing power and that the source of that power is largely irrelevant as long as he can depend upon it, in which case it will be apparent that if a computer can support remote locations reliably via some kind of terminal device, this may be all that some users will ever need. The nature of the terminal device will vary according to the type of application, the volume of data, the pattern of transmission and the need for local processing; it could be as simple as a teleprinter or a visual display unit, or it could be a minicomputer connected to a mainframe. The user may be using his terminal merely to enter

input data and to receive output or he may have complete control over the initiation of his jobs and also have ad hoc access to computing capacity, subject to established rules.

Under these conditions, the computer is exploited in a manner analogous to the use of public utilities, such as electricity or water. The consumer plugs in, switches on, draws on the resources that are centrally available and, after use, disconnects from the supply. The analogy with a public utility can be extended further to acknowledge the existence of companies who specialize in the provision of computing power to any prospective user.

External services

In the preceding paragraphs the computer options available to users were described in terms of their availability within the organization. As you may be aware, it is not necessary to have your own equipment in order to gain access to computing power, there being well over 200 UK companies providing commercial bureau services and many large users who are prepared to sell machine time. These companies offer a variety of services to prospective users, including the provision of on-line facilities via a terminal located on the client's premises. Alternatively, the customer may adopt a batch approach, for example on payroll, in which data are submitted on a regular, scheduled basis and output is delivered subsequently by the bureau.

Until the advent of cheap micro- and minicomputers, the use of a computer service bureau was often the most attractive entry method for organizations taking their first steps in data processing. Service bureaux are responding to the threat posed by micros to their markets by extending and diversifying their services and introducing more competitive charging structures. For the prospective user, who does not wish to take on the burden of an in-house installation and its staff, the service bureau remains a very attractive proposition; indeed, there are many large organizations with a significant data processing workload who prefer to leave it with a bureau, even though they might be able to justify their own machine.

Selecting your source

There are some general rules for deciding on the ultimate source of computing power, although it is surprising how often they are ignored.

Firstly, never restrict your choice to one supplier, even if you are an existing user and have a sitting tenant providing computer services. However good a current supplier may be, it is probable that his attention to your needs will improve if he feels that his customer base is threatened; healthy competition for your future business is more likely to yield a better deal than a bland assumption that it will stay where it is. On the other hand, you should resist the temptation to invite more than, say, four suppliers to tender for your business, otherwise the process of selection and liaison with suppliers becomes a major, and largely unproductive, administrative task.

Secondly, you should ensure that your requirements are agreed internally and prepared in writing before approaching any supplier and that every supplier is given identical information. When proposals are received they should be checked initially for conformation with that specification, otherwise you will find yourself comparing apples with pears and pears with oranges, and being none the wiser at the end of it. Accordingly, you should resist the marketing 'razzmatazz' that usually accompanies the tendering process, or at least keep it in perspective.

Thirdly, you should nominate one person to be the focal point for all dealings with prospective suppliers, even if you have to take him out of a line job for a limited period. By this means you can be sure that all tenderers are operating to the same guidelines, and you can also limit the irritating practice of some suppliers who attempt to pick off and influence other executives in the organization. Depending on the circumstances and the potential size of the tender, suppliers may wish to undertake their own fact-gathering survey before submitting proposals. There is absolutely nothing wrong with this approach, provided it can be accomplished within the timescale set by you and is free of charge – I see no virtue in potential customers paying possible suppliers to help sell their wares.

Selecting a computer supplier
If, as a result of a feasibility/justification study, you have decided that you should install your own equipment, you will have to select a suitable machine from a computer supplier. There are several stages to this process.

- Specifying your requirements in detail.
- Pre-selecting a shortlist of potential suppliers.
- Issuing the tender, and subsequent liaison with suppliers.
- Evaluating the proposals submitted by the suppliers.
- Negotiating a contract with the successful tenderer.

The amount of time and effort devoted to these tasks and the degree of attention to detail will be dictated, to a large extent, by the scale and complexity of the applications and the proposed solutions. For a small business with a limited requirement it may take only a week to prepare a specification, whereas for a large organization it may be necessary to spend several months defining requirements before approaching suppliers; the whole process might be completed in a few weeks for one organization or it could take a year or longer to satisfy more elaborate requirements. Whichever situation you may be in, you should bear in mind that inadequate consideration at a time when you are under no obligation could result in decisions which are difficult to reverse or amend when you have entered into a firm contractual arrangement.

Specifying requirements The specification of your requirements should follow naturally from the completion of the initial studies, which should provide basic information about:

- the jobs to be carried out by the computer;
- the current and estimated future size of those jobs in terms of volumes of input, the number and type of records to be held, the amount of printing, etc.; and
- the timescales within which these jobs have to be accomplished, e.g. daily, weekly, monthly, and so on.

If you are contemplating on-line systems you will have to give guidance on the likely volume of transaction traffic the computer will have to cope with and the level of service that users will expect.

In addition to physical and logical information about individual applications, the specification should also include material about your organization, its principal activities, the business objectives and the contribution that a computer is expected to make. This information is designed to put the proposed computer development in the right perspective for the supplier and facilitate his understanding of your needs. Guidance on the content of a formal specification of requirements is given in Appendix 3.

To facilitate your review of proposals and to establish the initiative from the outset, you should make it clear that you expect the tenders to conform to a particular layout and to answer specified questions. This will avoid the unhelpful practice of some suppliers who interlard your requirements with sales material, dissertations on software strategies, and such like, all of which can be provided separately. You should also state the criteria against which the tenders will be evaluated and indicate if any one of them is of critical importance. Typical criteria might be:

- 'All processing must be completed by xxxx hours each day'
- 'The on-line system should have a minimum availability of 98% and average terminal response time should not exceed 4 seconds'
- 'The whole print load must be completed within 2 hours'

but they will be dictated by the particular characteristics of your environment.

Pre-selection As I have indicated, there is no great benefit in putting out a tender to more than about four suppliers, even though, in the small business systems field, there may be hundreds of possible contenders. The feasibility study may have given guidance on this issue, if only to establish ball-park figures for costing purposes, or there may be other criteria which influence the composition of a shortlist. For instance, the computer may have to be compatible with equipment in a sister organization or the supplier may have to have a particular expertise. A common source of inspiration, particularly when purchasing small machines, is the experience of friends or business associates, but this can be misleading if their applications are totally different. Obviously, a lot will depend on whether or not you plan to build up in-house expertise or if you intend relying wholly on your supplier. Factors that should be considered in arriving at a shortlist of potential suppliers include the following.

1   The history, size and financial soundness of the company.
2   The size of the customer base, especially in your area.
3   The amount of engineering and systems support available.
4   The extent of the hardware/software product range.

5   Reputation and image, as evidenced by customer reactions.
6   Experience and expertise in your field.

Initial guidance on possible candidates can usually be obtained from your professional or trade association, from management bodies such as the BIM, from computing or trade journals and from organizations associated with the computer services industry, e.g. the National Computing Centre. One thing is certain – you will not be short of advice.

The invitation to tender Depending on the scale of the proposed computer system, the suppliers might respond to your invitation to tender within a week or so or they may need a couple of months to do justice to your requirements and their equipment. In any event, you should impose a degree of formality on the process and make provision for:

- the formal issue of your document;
- a formal briefing;
- subsequent visits from the supplier to clarify or amplify the specification;
- a final submission date; and
- a sales presentation in support of the tenders.

At this stage, I would not encourage invitations from suppliers to visit other installations. If you do this you will be obliged to give each supplier the same opportunity; furthermore, such visits are time-consuming and are rarely critical factors in making your choice. They are more important when you have settled on one supplier and wish to confirm claims or check up on doubtful issues and, even then, you should attempt to make your own arrangements.

Evaluating proposals At this stage the manager who has no technical support may feel exposed and uncertain when examining the manufacturers' proposals. With the exception of a review of the cheapest microcomputers or small business systems, it is inconceivable that he should attempt an evaluation of any size or complexity without some technical advice. If he does so, he may be tempted to give undue weight to commercial factors, such as cost, and to ignore quite critical technical characteristics that could lead to problems at a later stage. For example, in the days when main memory was an expensive element in a configuration it was not unknown for salesmen to under-quote in their proposal in order to preserve a competitive edge. Invariably, after the equipment was installed and had failed to perform satisfactorily, the customer was faced with the cost of paying for a minor enhancement to his system. Fortunately, with the continuing decline in hardware costs, it is less onerous now to 'buy your way out of trouble', although this practice should not be encouraged.

On receipt of the tenders, your first task in carrying out the detailed technical and commercial evaluation should be to assess each proposal individually in relation to the specification which the supplier was asked to meet. This assessment should include the resolution of such questions as:

- Does the supplier demonstrate a proper understanding of your overall requirements?
- Does the proposal meet the criteria set by the specification?
- Does the recommended equipment provide sufficient power and capacity to cope with the expected workload in the time allowed?
- Are the methods proposed for dealing with individual applications acceptable to the users?
- What provisions are made for growth in volumes and in the range of applications?
- Which software tools, aids and packages are recommended and on what basis are they supplied?
- How much support does the supplier offer and on what terms?
- Are arrangements and charges for engineering maintenance acceptable?
- What are the costs involved?

This review of individual proposals will almost certainly generate queries and the need for additional information. If the supplier has misunderstood your requirements he may have to carry out further work.

Having satisfied yourself that the suppliers have understood the specification and have responded in accordance with your instructions, your next job is to compare them with each other. There are several techniques for doing this, ranging from a straightforward points allocation for specific features to comprehensive simulations of the actual workload on a comparable machine. This latter approach is essential if you propose adopting a major on-line system.

Contract negotiation All suppliers will have some form of standard contract for the sale, hire or leasing of their equipment, but because they regard it as standard does not mean that you have to accept it. With few exceptions, suppliers are prepared to negotiate aspects of the contractual arrangement and the associated financial details. The rules are self-evident.

- Study the contract closely and take legal advice.
- Identify those aspects you are unhappy with or where you feel a commercial advantage can be gained.
- Sign nothing until you are satisfied with the final contract and any attachments.

Using external services

In all probability, if you have opted to use a computer service bureau instead of acquiring your own machine, you will have a particular application or small group of related systems in mind, e.g. payroll, financial ledgers, sales analyses. It is rare for an organization to decide from the outset to place the whole of its expected data processing workload with a service company, but this may be the decision finally reached.

The process of appointing a computer bureau is similar to that of selecting an equipment supplier, in that it imposes the same self-disciplines, which you ignore at your peril. It is just as important when choosing a bureau to have a full statement of your requirements, to preserve multiple options, to insist on a formal tendering process and to establish a framework of criteria against which to measure proposals. On the other hand, there are some interesting differences, in that service bureaux have a hand-holding responsibility which is not often demanded of manufacturers.

Specifying requirements You may decide to subcontract the detailed definition of requirements to bureau staff who will carry out a systems study before quoting for your work. Whether or not you are charged for this study will depend on the amount of effort involved, whether it is competitive, and whether the bureau will be asked to undertake the development and implementation of the system on their machine. There are advantages to this approach.

1   The study will give you an opportunity to get the measure of bureau staff and to establish a working relationship.
2   Having done the study and prepared their own specification rather than estimating from your own specification, the bureau will be better placed to form estimates for developing and operating the system.
3   If you do pay for the study, you are not obliged to place the remaining work with the bureau.

The principal disadvantage of an uncompetitive study is that you have to make a rational prior assessment of prospective bureaux and choose one on a relatively unstructured basis.

Pre-selection The choice of a bureau is also subject to different constraints. If you are looking for a batch service, you will obviously concentrate on bureaux operating in your immediate area in order to minimize the logistics involved in input-output handling, transport, etc. Even with an on-line system (remote job entry/remote batch entry/enquiry) where you will have a terminal device on your premises, you may wish to be close to your supplier, even though there may be no technical necessity to do so. However, as most bureaux are now offering on-line facilities it is unlikely that you would be forced to look very far from home.

Factors to be considered at the pre-selection stage, and which might lead you to opt for one bureau from the beginning, are similar to those applied to the shortlisting of manufacturers.

1   The history, size and financial soundness of the company.
2   The size of their client base in your area.
3   Their range of services and support, including packages.
4   Reputation and assessments of levels of service by existing customers.
5   Knowledge of your type of business and the proposed application and general expertise.

You should also assess the bureaux in the light of your longterm plans, especially if you have the objective of bringing your data processing work in-house when it has built up to a suitable level. If you plan to install a computer eventually, and wish to preserve your investment in systems and avoid major conversion costs, then choose bureaux with mainstream computers and software, not fringe machines, however good they may be.

Invitation to tender There are several ways in which you can make
use of a computer service bureau. Ideally you should make it clear
in your invitation to tender which option you favour or, if you are
in doubt, how you expect the bureaux to present the options.
These options include the following possibilities.

1 You have no computer staff and no intention of recruiting.
   You have a specific requirement but have not carried out any
   detailed studies. You require a proposal which distinguishes:
   - the charge for a systems study;
   - the costs of developing and implementing the application
     as:
     – a package
     – a tailored system
   - the costs of running the system at the bureau including:
     – data preparation/entry
     – any equipment requirements
     – processing charges
     – any other costs
     and how these may vary with volume/frequency, etc.
2 Alternatively, you may have a tight systems specification or an
   intention to use a package, in which case you are principally
   interested in:
   - development and implementation costs; and
   - annual running costs.
3 You may intend developing and implementing the system with
   your own resources and merely wish to buy time on the bureau
   computer.

If you have any particular requirements, such as ensuring compatibility on future hardware/software, these should also be
stated.

Evaluating proposals The process of evaluating bureau proposals
is similar to that adopted for equipment tenders. You should
ensure that the bureaux understand your requirements and have
responded with the information you have requested. However,
comparing the merits of competing proposals presents a different
set of problems.

1 First of all, few bureaux have the same charging structure or
   even a similar charging philosophy. Many bureaux will base

their estimate of running costs on the probable use of machine resources, such as central processor and disk utilization, but their estimate will be influenced by:

- their conception of the way the system will operate;
- their particular equipment configuration; and
- their software facilities.

Because these three factors may be different for each bureau, it is not always a simple matter to determine which is the most cost effective approach. For example, the number of times the system accesses disk files is a critical element in constructing running costs; if the software is inefficient it could lead to very high charges. Thus, even though the estimates for total annual operating costs at different bureaux may be similar, the make-up of those costs may have quite an important impact on actual charges when the system is implemented. The answer is to request a detailed breakdown of costs for each phase of processing and to compare the methods used and the assumptions made by the competing bureaux.

2 Because a part of your business procedures will be conducted off your own premises by persons not directly responsible to you, it is important to satisfy yourself and your colleagues that adequate provision is made for security, confidentiality and responsible performance. You would be perfectly justified in reviewing the administration of the bureau and asking to meet the managers and staff concerned with your project.

3 If you are delegating the detailed development of your application to a bureau, you would be most unwise to assume that you will have no responsibility for the project. On the contrary, a good bureau will insist on the active participation of the client throughout and will be anxious to identify decision points at which your involvement is crucial, e.g. 'signing off' the systems specification before programming is authorized. It is important to compare the bureaux in terms of the arrangements they propose for:

- maintaining liaison
- progress reviews
- project planning and control
- systems and programming methods
- documentation
- training and conversion
- maintenance

The methods they have used to construct their proposals and the way they are presented will provide an initial guide to the quality of their approach.

Contract negotiation Bureaux tend to have less complex contracts than equipment suppliers and they are usually more flexible in negotiation. One aspect to which you should pay particular attention, however, is the question of ownership of the systems which the bureau develops for your use. If the system is based principally on one of their packages, adapted for your needs, then the probability is that ownership remains with the bureau and you could not remove the application and run it elsewhere. On the other hand, if you have paid good money for the development of a system, unique to your requirements, you should ensure that your ownership is acknowledged in the contract. If you expect to make prolonged use of the bureau (a commitment that incidentally would influence favourably any question of proprietory rights) you should be clear about the arrangements for increasing or modifying the standard price structure, as your case for using a computer could be demolished by an alteration to the charging algorithm.

Selecting an application package
Whether you install your own computer or choose instead to make use of a service bureau, you may wish to acquire an application package rather than develop your own systems. There are several reasons why you may adopt this approach.

1   It is usually quicker and cheaper to implement compared with developing a system from scratch. The exceptions arise where organizations acquire a package, proceed to modify it to their needs and invariably end up with a costly and only partially successful application.

Some time ago I was analysing a client's data processing budget and came across an item of £10,000 allocated to package maintenance. On enquiry, I established that some years earlier the client had selected a general ledger package which had an excellent reputation in the market. The snag was that it was written for machines supplied by manufacturer A and was not available for their machine, which came from manufacturer B. Undeterred, the company set about rewriting the package with the help of the originators. It was not a success, because of different facilities, and absorbed excessive amounts of machine time. At the end of five years, the company had spent enough to acquire several general ledger packages outright.

I am astonished that even quite sophisticated computer users continue to make this foolish mistake for marginal benefits that are often illusory. Far better for the user to settle for 90% satisfaction of requirements than to devote time and money to achieving an additional 5% improvement.

2 If you are at all uncertain of your ultimate requirements, a package may provide an ideal vehicle for experimentation and refinement while giving operational support and experience for users. I have seen this approach adopted by a company that ran a factory loading system on a bureau for a number of years, even though it had an in-house computer processing other manufacturing applications. From this experience they were able to design and develop a system more suitable to their needs.

3 The vendor may have experience or expertise that is unique or rare, for example computer aided engineering or construction industry packages, and it would be uneconomic to duplicate it or attempt to re-invent the wheel.

Factors to be considered In recent years there has been a dramatic increase in the number and variety of packages available to users, promoted not only by the growth in the market for small business systems and computers generally but also by a growing realization that little is sacrificed by opting for a generalized solution and much is to be gained in efficiency by not assuming the burden of development costs. As a result, for any given application area, the prospective user may be faced with a choice of dozens of suitable packages, each claiming to meet his needs. The only answer is to adopt a disciplined approach which – yes, you have guessed – is based on a definition of your requirements, an analysis of the features offered with the package and an assessment of related commercial issues. Guidelines for the selection of a software package are given in Appendix 4, but particular attention should be paid to the following aspects.

1   All packages are generalized solutions and have to be adapted to suit individual users. This process of adaptation is known as 'customization' and may be accomplished by the use of parameter tables, by special interface programs or by some other means. As a prospective user you should establish how simple this process will be, what is involved, what it will cost and who pays.

2   Make sure that you establish all the costs involved, including the charges, if any, for:
   - the basic package
   - forms, manuals, operational aids
   - customization
   - maintenance
   - conversion
   - support
   - training
   - subsequent enhancements
   - renewals
   - machine time

   Can you buy or hire the package once and use it in several locations or is each use a separate contract and an additional charge?

3   Which machine configuration and software environment is required and who is responsible for maintaining the package's compatibility with subsequent releases of system software?

4   Seek a demonstration of the package, preferably in a working environment, and invite comments and suggestions from current users.

Employing consultants or a software house

This chapter has been concerned with possible sources of computing power and the multitude of ways in which this power can be channelled to the user. We have looked at the work involved in selecting equipment, in choosing a computer bureau, and at the tasks arising from a decision to introduce application packages. If you are new to computers and have no technical support, you may be daunted by the apparent difficulties and may consider employing consultants or a software house to assist you. Even if you are an established user with in-house data processing staff, you may not be in a position to allocate resources to carry out evaluations, or, having made an assessment, you may welcome a second opinion. In Chapter 3 we considered the advantages and drawbacks of using external staff and concluded that in prescribed circumstances they could be a valuable additional resource. If you arrive at the same conclusion, you have then to consider the question of how to select a suitable source of external staff.

Consultancy or software house? I shall be taking a grave risk of offending colleagues and competitors alike in attempting to distinguish between the services offered by a consultancy and a software house, especially when each can, and often does, operate successfully in the others' domain. Nowadays, some consultancies provide systems and programming services and may also market application packages; software houses undertake technical consultancy assignments, almost certainly offer packages and may also have rights to market computer equipment. Nevertheless, there are important differences between the two types of organization and in the work that is normally assigned to them.

1 A consultancy will tend to have a much higher proportion of staff with a management, business or functional background allied to technical skills. In contrast, the majority of software house staff will consist of project leaders, systems analysts, programmers and specialists.
2 Consultancy fee rates will usually be higher than those of a software house because they reflect the general level of experience among the staff. On the other hand, consultancy assignments tend to be shorter in duration than the contracts awarded to software houses.
3 Clients will opt to use consultants when they are seeking impartial advice, guidance, second opinions or support at a senior level. Clients will tend to use a software house to obtain specific technical knowledge or to develop a particular project.
4 Consultants are often used by clients:
  ● to carry out feasibility studies;
  ● to specify requirements;
  ● to evaluate hardware/software/services proposals;
  ● to develop a computing policy or an overall systems plan;
  ● to manage projects;
  ● to audit systems or whole installations;
  ● to select software houses.

5   Software houses are sometimes used to carry out any of the above tasks except, hopefully, the selection of a software house. The ability to provide managerial and functional experience will depend on the type of software house and the quality of the individual assigned. However, by and large, the special skills of a software house reside in their technical knowledge and their ability to design, develop and implement systems.

Making a choice There are hundreds of consultancies and software houses to choose from and if you have never used one before you may not know where to begin. In such circumstances you can seek initial advice from any one of the following bodies:

- the British Institute of Management
- the Institute of Directors
- the Management Consultants' Association
- the Institute of Management Consultants
- the National Computing Centre
- the British Computer Society
- the Computer Services Association
- your trade or professional association

Unless there are very good reasons to the contrary, you should always look at more than one firm and you should adopt a fairly formal approach to selection.

1   This means, firstly, drawing up clear and unequivocal terms of reference; nothing is more likely to lead to an unsuccessful assignment than a flabby or imprecise brief.
2   Unless the proposed assignment is small, you should expect the competing firms to carry out some form of preliminary survey, at their own expense and without obligation to you. The purposes of this survey should be to confirm their understanding of your requirements, to enable them to estimate the work involved in meeting the terms of reference and to provide the basis for their detailed proposal. It also gives you the chance to assess the qualities of the firms through their representatives.
3   Proposals should be evaluated in terms of how effectively they respond to your brief and how they relate to each other. You would also be well within your rights to ask to meet the con-

sultants who are proposed for your work, as they may not be as acceptable to you as the individuals who are selling the assignment.

4   You should ensure that adequate provision is made for managing the assignment, for liaison with you and your colleagues and for documenting the results of the project.

You should not ignore the possibility that the proposed consultancy may qualify for assistance under one of the grant aid schemes operated by the Department of Trade and Industry. These schemes have proved particularly successful in introducing small businesses to the use of microcomputers, via an initial study and selection of equipment for which the client pays a fairly nominal fee.

In considering the use of this type of external resource, you should not ignore the potential benefits to the organization arising from consultants or specialists working in conjunction with your own data processing staff rather than replacing them. The whole existence of these service firms depends on their exposure to a wide variety of situations, often international in character, and their accumulation of knowledge and experience normally unavailable to in-house staff.

5   Justifying the use of computers

My feeling is that once we have taken the decision to install a computer, we will then be able to concentrate on how it can best be used. (unsuccessful computer user)

Introduction

In previous chapters we have looked at the physical attributes of computing devices and software and at the nature of the skills required to exploit them. We have seen the variety of ways in which this power and these skills can be placed at the disposal of the prospective user. It will be apparent also that the world of computing is essentially dynamic and decisions about computer usage taken today might be eroded by some technological change or dramatic cost reduction introduced next week. Some managers become terribly agitated about this possibility and, fearful of being marooned by some technical or commercial innovation, are reluctant to commit themselves to a long-term computer strategy. This is a pity because, in my experience, the setting of clear objectives for computing and the adherence to a consistent, albeit flexible, computing policy are more likely to yield benefits to an organization than the pursuit of technical excellence. The foundation for successful data processing must be an honest assessment of the contribution that computing can make to the aims of the organization and on a realistic evaluation of the probable costs and potential benefits involved.

Why bother?

A prospective purchaser of a microcomputer or alternatively an existing computer user, faced with a major enhancement of his current installation, may both be tempted to question the need to justify their intentions. This is a valid point of view. In the one case, the microcomputer may be so cheap that it could be regarded as an out-of-pocket expense, costing less than an additional employee and having much more potential. Similarly, the existing user may feel that, because of limitations to growth or capacity, he has no option but to increase his computing facilities, indeed that it is an inevitable corollary of being in computers at all. While I sympathize with these attitudes, I believe them to be dangerously seductive rationalizations which, if applied generally to investment decisions, would have disastrous consequences. Whether you are spending £5,000 or £50,000, you are automatically depriving yourself of the benefits of an alternative application of those funds, even if that alternative is merely to leave the money on deposit, earning interest. It is really quite extraordinary how organizations that normally apply objective standards to other investment decisions seem to approach the justification for using computers in a highly subjective and often unstructured way. Whether you do it yourself or have other staff working on it, whether you take one day considering the pros and cons or allocate several weeks to a detailed examination of the economic case, there are many good reasons for carrying out a formal justification.

1 It forces a close examination of all aspects of the proposal and eliminates any poorly conceived ideas or objectives. For instance, any claim that the proposed project will reduce staff will have to be demonstrated, particularly since general experience suggests that redundancies rarely occur.

2 It provides the opportunity to ensure that all possible costs have been taken into account. For example, the clerical costs involved in preparing the initial basic data for a computer system may be overlooked or understated, especially if it is assumed that the extra work can be accomodated within normal operations.

3 It focuses attention on expected benefits, and particularly on the mechanisms by which those benefits will be achieved. One thing is certain: such benefits do *not* automatically accrue and have to be pursued positively. For example, although it is true that the use of computer techniques will assist with the reduction of inventory, it is not always recognized that one of the first effects of computerization may be to increase stocks, as the model endeavours to bring inventory into a correct balance. Unless positive, non-computer action is also taken to

eliminate surpluses, excess stocks may persist for some time and, more importantly, user confidence in the system may be impaired.

4   The process of justification and realistic assessment of costs/ benefits provide the mechanisms for ranking potential applications and highlighting the priorities that should be applied. These priorities may not accord with the aspirations of individual executives, who want their job done first, but it may make more sense for the organization as a whole.

5   A formal approach to justification will at least require a proper consideration of the alternative courses of action, which might include:
   ● Do nothing
   ● Improve manual procedures
   ● Use a computer service bureau
   instead of installing your own equipment.

6   Depending on the scale of expenditure involved, the prospective user may have to budget for a net outflow of funds over more than one financial year before a positive return is achieved. Any organization that ignores the initial evaluation of an investment that can affect subsequent years automatically loses the ability to control such investment. The distinctive feature of capital investment is that the organization is committed to a broad policy for some time ahead and, if decisions are taken on inadequate bases, or as a matter or urgency, intuition or ambition, it may be forced to live with a bad decision for many years.

A large manufacturing company had been a user of one computer supplier's equipment for over a decade. When the time came to replace the existing computer with larger, more versatile facilities, the in-house data processing department carried out a detailed technical and systems study of the options available to the company. They concluded that, in spite of the probable conversion cost and the delays to new developments, the company should change its supplier. The case was soundly based and well argued.

For totally subjective reasons, the board of directors insisted that the company should remain with their existing supplier. After three years of almost constant hardware and software problems, involving considerable extra expenditure and a lot of user/data processing aggravation, the board conceded that the decision was incorrect and the policy was reversed.

7 The disciplines involved in a formal justification will clarify the computing objectives of the organization and will provide the criteria for measuring the achievement of those objectives. By these means, the performance of a computer project can be monitored at both a management and a detailed level. For example, if an application is justified because it will reduce administration expenses to a given ratio, or maintain costs per transaction at a prescribed level, the design, development and subsequent operation of the system can be assessed against these criteria.

Whether you are an entrepreneur or a manager with a responsibility to some ultimate authority, you are clearly entitled to construct your own rationale for the decisions you may be called upon subsequently to defend. My plea, however, is that you do not delude yourself about the reasons for adopting a particular course of action and its ramifications, that you observe good business practices and that you ascertain the potential benefits of computer usage in a realistic fashion. It should be apparent that whereas it may be feasible to apply computers in your organization – and by and large if you can describe your problem a computer can deal with it – you may not be justified in doing so. In my opinion, founded on long experience and observation of both good and bad computer projects, all prospective users, large or small, should adopt an approach to justification that distinguishes:

- The delineation of the problem area
- The definition of key requirements
- The consideration of *all* possible alternatives
- The evaluation of expected costs/benefits
- The next steps

Even a one-man business contemplating buying a microcomputer from a local shop would benefit from jotting down his assessment of the key points under these headings, perhaps with the help of his accountant, before making a final decision. For a larger organization, or where a more complex investment decision is involved, the investigation and evaluation will be more elaborate.

The justification study

Feasibility or justification studies are not unique to the world of computing, being a long-established feature of the preliminary stages of major investment decisions involving, for example, civil or construction engineering projects; there are feasibility studies to site new airports and new factories and to consider the creation of new urban communities. What they all have in common is a structured attempt to define needs, to elucidate problem areas, to conceive overall solutions, to consider alternatives and to assess viability, before an extensive commitment of resources is undertaken. Feasibility studies remind me of a simplistic definition of economics as being 'the study of scarce resources with alternative uses'.

Not all prospective users of computers would accept that their proposed investment warrants an elaborate study. However it is not the length of the study, nor the amount of manpower applied that is important; it is whether or not the quality of the decision is improved by taking more care and whether future success is more likely because the possibility of failure has been examined. To illustrate the factors that should be considered at this initial stage I propose to describe a fairly formal approach to justification, from which you can extract the features that will be helpful in your particular environment.

The aim should be to produce an authoritative statement of need and a positive recommendation. The feasibility study team should report to a management group which is either set up especially for this purpose or to one which already has an executive role. The team should present its findings and justify its recommendations to this group, to whom it should look for a decision and subsequent authorizations.

Purpose and objectives

The aims of a feasibility study are to confirm that the application of computer techniques in an organization will actually contribute to its future well-being and to explore the implications of authorizing a full-scale systems development project. Whatever the original motivation may have been – ambition, envy, whim, competition, rising costs, staff problems – the initiation of a feasibility study presupposes that some sensible prior demarcation has occured that defines the target area(s) in a logical and manageable way. For example:

- 'Study the problems of computerizing stock recording and control procedures'
- 'We are having problems with our centralized cash collection procedures. Can the computer help?'

Ideally, the study should have clear terms of reference and specific objectives set by management. For instance, a feasibility study for a computer-based stock recording and control system might have one or more of the following objectives:

1 To reduce stock levels
2 To minimize 'stock-outs'
3 To reduce the clerical and paperwork burden
4 To improve levels of customer service
5 To control several stock locations
6 To minimize outstanding purchase commitments

As some of these aims may conflict, it is essential that the objectives of the study are clear and that the bases for trading off between desirable goals are clearly understood.

You will have noticed that I have given examples of specific problem areas, although it is not uncommon for organizations with no previous history of data processing to mount much more general feasibility studies. For example, one could set up a study to examine the whole organization and report on the scope for using computers in any function. The generality of this brief often makes it difficult to set specific objectives, and if one is not very careful it becomes an exercise in which a solution (the computer) is looking for a problem (any problem). So, wherever possible, avoid general studies and go after those areas in which you are experiencing operating difficulties, resource problems, excessive costs, or where control could be improved or management information is inadequate.

The objectives set for study should be as precise as your understanding of the problem will allow and as much guidance as possible should be given on the quantifiable parameters which the persons carrying out the study may have to apply. Thus, the aim to reduce stock levels should be amplified with data on existing and target levels, the sources and costs of money, preferred timescales, and so on. If you wish to utilise computers in order to reduce your reliance on human resources, you must give an indication of how you expect this to be accomplished – by redundancy, by natural wastage, by eliminating overtime, by redeployment or by some combination of these methods? Quite apart from giving direction to the study, objectives that are set in this fashion provide the means of comparison between alternative approaches to the resolution of problems. It goes without saying that the objectives given to a feasibility study should reflect and contribute to the overall framework of corporate objectives that guide the activities of the organization. In this respect, those organizations that have long-term corporate plans are infinitely better placed to judge the contribution that computers can make than enterprises forced to consider data processing solutions to immediate or short-term problems.

Duration and manning
Obviously the duration of a feasibility study will be influenced by the nature of the problem areas under review and the extent to which they are geographically or organizationally dispersed. Returning to our stock control example, a study of inventory systems operating in several locations and the subsequent concoction of a common system will take longer to complete than a survey of the requirements of a single site. This may be so not only for the obvious physical reasons, but also because of the need to take account of differing managerial and operating environments when arriving at an acceptable solution. Nevertheless, I do feel that some organizations spend far too long on feasibility studies and I would tend to be highly suspicious of most surveys that exceed six man-months of effort.

Let's face it, the purpose of a feasibility study is not to develop a computer system. It is to acquire a sufficient understanding of requirements and possible solutions to enable the person carrying out the study to report convincingly to management whether or not it is feasible to use a computer and what would be involved in doing so. For most applications, this is relatively straightforward because:

- the proposed application will almost certainly have been tackled before by some organization;
- any computer man worth his salt should know the capabilities of computers in most application areas;
- he should also be able to assess the validity of a computer approach on the basis of the volumes of data involved and the complexity of the procedures; and

- he should be able to formulate in broad terms the nature of the computer solution and give first estimates of the potential costs and benefits.

At the risk of encouraging superficiality, I suggest that these conclusions can be reached at an earlier stage than in fact is the case in most feasibility studies, and furthermore can be attained without the excessive input of manpower which often results in a highly structured solution before a detailed analysis has taken place. Not only may this approach prejudice the design of the application, but it may also overlook quite important features that would have been uncovered in thorough systems investigation following the feasibility study.

> A financial institution wished to transfer a complex dealing system to its computer, and the proposal involved the use of an existing package covering about 40% of the functions to be converted. The feasibility study took eight man-months to complete and concentrated principally on the integration of this package with other routines; as a result it tended to go into great detail on the design of the system.
> The company used this specification as the basis for programming and found repeatedly that there were important features of the existing system which were not catered for in the misleadingly precise feasibility study. Dozens of programs had to be rewritten or modified and the system was over 12 months late in being implemented.

Thus, a feasibility study should not attempt to design the perfect solution; its principal purpose should be to provide sufficient information to management to enable them to decide whether or not they wish to spend more time and resources on developing a solution.

The composition of a feasibility study team will have a significant influence on the results. If the study is carried out by computer specialists, it should come as no surprise if the ultimate recommendation favours the use of data processing techniques, although I am assured that some systems analysts have vetoed computer solutions. Conversely, if no specialists are involved and you rely solely on staff who have no technical background, there will be an amount of aimless and unproductive activity and, whether or not the correct solution emerges, they are likely to underestimate the difficulties and costs involved. The ideal solution is obviously a blend of technical knowledge and data processing experience with the business, managerial and functional knowledge of the users. Bearing in mind that the feasibility study may be the first step in a major investment programme for your organization, it is imperative that management ensures the participation of prospective users and that the best brains are involved. In the context of our stock control example, one should make every effort to allocate an experienced senior member of the inventory management function to a feasibility study that may conceivably change the whole basis of control in the organization. Not only does this move ensure that the right level of functional knowledge is applied to the problem but it also encourages the credibility of the proposed solution among user staff and management. If the computer specialist also has knowledge of the inventory function and of similar applications, the likelihood of sound recommendations is doubly enhanced. As far as is practicable, the persons allocated to the study should be relieved of other responsibilities and should devote full-time attention to the tasks involved.

Structure of the study

The structure of a feasibility study should be geared to the nature of the output you expect from it. I suggest that the better surveys usually aim to produce a report that covers:

- the nature and purpose of existing systems;
- the shortcomings and problem areas;
- the scope for improvement;
- the alternatives available;
- the preferred solution;
- the preliminary estimates of costs/benefits; and
- the recommended approach.

Whether this report is contained in one or two pages or in 50 is in a sense immaterial, although it is clearly governed by the size and complexity of the project. However, what is important is that it contains unequivocal guidance on the decision management should make.

Investigation of existing systems No matter what other experts would have you believe, the study should begin with a thorough examination of the existing system. There are two principal reasons for this approach.

1 To guarantee the credibility of the solutions that may eventually emerge from the study. It is quite dispiriting to hear of cases where the prospective user, who after all may be a sceptical or hostile viewer of data processing, succeeds in attacking or demolishing a recommendation on the grounds that some important aspects have been overlooked or that certain requirements are not met by the proposed system.
2 A review of current operations may reveal opportunities to improve existing systems which can be pursued, whether or not a computer is introduced. Furthermore, it will highlight those activities or practices that would have to be altered substantially in order to cater for data processing techniques.

This part of the study should concentrate on examining and recording the key features of current procedures, the methods and documents in use, the form and content of the data and information flowing through the system and the volumes and frequencies of the data to be handled. However, this approach to fact-finding should not be a passive exercise and the team should be constantly but constructively challenging the information it is offered.

- 'Why is this task done?'
- 'Why is that report produced?'
- 'Is it necessary; could you operate without it or at a reduced frequency?'
- 'What do you do with this information?'
- 'What decisions are you required to make and within what timeframe?'

Shortcomings Usually, people who are exposed to this type of study are anxious to give their assessment of shortcomings and problem areas. Human nature being what it is, their views are rarely self-critical and may point away from their area of immediate responsibility; they will almost certainly not have the overview being built up by the study team. It is probable that the team will also identify inadequacies or faults that were unknown or ignored in current conditions and which individual users could not have dealt with. Typical of the findings in these circumstances might be evidence of:

- late receipt/despatch of data;
- lengthy paperwork processing cycles;
- redundant operations;
- duplicate records;
- inflexibility of procedures;
- lack of capacity in staff or the procedures;
- difficulties of communication with other functions;
- lack of management information;
- excess costs.

No one should be surprised by these findings. Organizations and the environments in which they operate are subject to change but systems rarely have the same dynamism or flexibility and tend to degenerate through time.

The scope for improvement In examining the opportunities for achieving improvements in the area under review, the study team should not feel inhibited by existing practices. They should be prepared to ask fundamental questions.

- 'Do we need this function/activity/system?'
- 'Can it be amalgamated or taken over by some other function/ activity/system?'
- 'Can its performance be improved by manual changes, a different management or an injection of resources?'
- 'Is the application of computer techniques the only answer to achieving better results?'

Most feasibility surveys will identify improvements that can be achieved in the short term, usually by a modicum of method study or a reorganization of work flow, but unfortunately these may not be pursued either because of lack of resources or because of concentration on the longer-term computer solution. This is a great pity where large projects are concerned, as it may be several months or years before a new system can be implemented and ultimate benefits materialize.

Evaluation of alternatives In their report, the feasibility study team must record their efforts at evaluating alternative strategies in relation to the objectives set for the study. It is in order to consider, as a first option, retaining the status quo or some modification of it before looking at different approaches; after all, if it is not possible to demonstrate the need for change it will be difficult to justify ways of bringing it about. For each possible approach, the team should describe its chief characteristics, the tasks involved and the likely costs/benefits that would accrue. The process of evaluation is described in more detail later in this chapter.

The preferred solution As a result of evaluating alternatives, the team should recommend the approach which they believe matches most closely the requirements of the organization and which they think will meet the objectives and criteria of performance in the optimum manner. This need not be the cheapest solution but hopefully it will be the one which in the long term will provide the greatest benefit to the organization. The preferred solution should be described or mapped out in sufficient enough detail to identify the overall design of the proposed system, the mode of processing, the source of computing power, the time and resources required to develop and implement the system and the way it should be introduced. Thus, for example, this part of the feasibility study report should tell the managing director that the preferred solution to his stock control problems is an on-line application with the VDU terminals linked to a central minicomputer, which should be based on a blend of packaged and bespoke systems that will take 18 months to implement.

Costs/benefits analysis The costs of implementing the proposed approach and the anticipated benefits should be thoroughly explored. This is a difficult and contentious area and warrants separate treatment, given on pages 106–13.

Evaluating alternative strategies

Theoretically, a feasibility study team could look at a whole range of possible alternatives to the present system, such as:

- Improved manual procedures
- Advanced accounting equipment
- A computer bureau service
- An intelligent terminal
- A time-sharing utility
- An in-house micro, mini or mainframe computer

In practice, it is probable that some of the criteria set by management for the study will automatically eliminate certain of these alternatives. For example:

- a ceiling on the total annual cost of the preferred solution may prohibit the use of an in-house mainframe computer;
- insistence on an in-house installation may cut out consideration of a bureau service;
- a desire to use a 'British' computer will significantly reduce the options available to the organization.

Additionally, the characteristics of the proposed applications will tend to favour particular solutions, or at least indicate the most likely paths. Large volumes of records or transactions, for instance, might point towards the use of a minicomputer rather than a micro, but fall short of the case for larger mainframe facilities.

There are three fundamental questions when considering the options at the feasibility stage, and the answers to them will establish the pattern for the organization's computing policy for some time ahead. The study team should form positive judgements on the following issues when it becomes evident that a computer is the most likely solution.

1   Should the application(s) be on-line or batch-oriented or a mixture of both?
2   Should we have an in-house computer facility or should we use external services?
3   Should we use packaged systems or should we aim for a custom-built application?

The sequence of questions is not critical and could vary from case to case. For some organizations there will be a firm intention to have their own computer and no arguments for use of a bureau will undermine it. In other situations the urgency to inroduce a particular application will be paramount, thus favouring the use of a package, even though some user requirements or aspirations have to be sacrificed. In order to simplify our examination of the issues involved, let us consider the situation where a company has set up a feasibility study to look into the scope for applying computers to inventory control, and the study team is evaluating the alternatives of:

- using a bureau;
- acquiring an in-house computer;
- considering package solutions.

We assume that they have done their homework on existing systems, they know problem areas and user requirements and they have formed estimates of the volumes of data involved, both currently and in the foreseeable future.

Using a computer bureau

The case for using a computer service bureau is strongest where one or more of the following characteristics apply.

1 Where the proposed system can be precisely delineated in terms of functions to be performed, with clear cut-off points for availability of input and presentation of output. A payroll, for example, is a classic bureau application.
2 Where volumes of data and records are relatively small and would not warrant the use of a dedicated machine.
3 If there are occasional 'one-off' problems to solve or infrequent processing requirements. For example, an annual revision of standard costs for labour, materials and overheads or a unique market research exercise.
4 The need to relieve peak workloads, whether or not the sub-contracting organization has a computer of its own.
5 Where the prospective user, perhaps uncertain of the problems and benefits of data processing, requires a gentle introduction to computing.
6 Where an organization wishes to have access to computer facilities that would be prohibitively expensive to acquire for themselves, e.g. occasional use of computer aided design facilities.

In these circumstances a computer service bureau has many advantages over the acquisition of in-house equipment.

Advantages of a computer bureau
1 The price charged by a computer bureau is an amalgam of all the costs involved in setting up and running a major data processing installation, including a profit element, and represents access to more powerful equipment, greater expertise, software and resources than the average user could possibly

afford for himself. So, in computing terms, the cost effectiveness of a bureau application can be very high.

2   Bureau costs will not only tend to be lower than a comparable in-house service, because of the spread over a number of customers, but they will usually be clearly defined and, being volume related, readily determinable for some time ahead.

3   The alternative to using a bureau, to whom you can subcontract the full technical responsibility for developing, implementing and running your application, is to recruit, pay, retain, direct and control your own data processing staff. Many organizations find running their business a sufficient challenge, without inviting additional problems that they may be ill-equipped technically and managerially to cope with; they are therefore content to leave such problems to the experts.

4   If there is any degree of uncertainty about the value of computing to an organization, using a bureau provides an ideal opportunity to sample the difficulties and the delights without incurring lasting obligations. It also enables staff to come to terms with the unique disciplines required in order to interface with computer applications, and to learn how to exploit data processing facilities.

5   Using a bureau gives access to expertise and experience that would be too expensive for the average user to acquire. Moreover, some expertise may be needed for only a limited period, until an application is designed and implemented, and it may not make sense to have a full-time staff member on board. This expertise may be encapsulated in software packages available from a bureau, thus enabling a prospective user to get off the ground faster than starting from scratch.

In the context of our inventory control application, we might favour a bureau service because the costs are relatively easy to establish. In broad terms, we can estimate the cost of storing n records and the charge for processing n input transactions and producing reports. The bureau may have a standard package which matches most if not all our requirements and we know that if the package is improved, or other facilities become available, we will be in a position to take advantage of them.

Disadvantages of a computer bureau

1 Whatever the technical and commercial merits of using a bureau, there are evident psychological barriers that some prospective users fail to overcome. In the first place, a user may feel uneasy or hesitant about passing control of an internal function to an outsider. He may be concerned that bureau staff will not have the same objectives nor the level of commitment shown by his own staff. In particular, he may be worried about the security and confidentiality of his affairs if documents and records are in transit or held externally. Good bureaux go out of their way to reassure prospective users on these doubts, but they are often sufficiently strong to tip the balance in favour of an in-house solution.

2 If, in spite of these worries, an organization still opts to use a bureau, it must recognize that there are new management problems to be dealt with because a new communication and control interface has been created. Somebody has to liaise with the bureau during system development, conversion and operations, as well as marshal internal resources. If these tasks are not properly identified and fulfilled, the potential for disruption to internal activities is greater than any mishap perpetrated by the bureau.

3 Although bureau costs may be initially attractive and determinable, they may rise in time, through inflation or through increased processing loads, to a level where continued use of the bureau would be uneconomic compared with an in-house installation. A cost conscious user will monitor charges to ensure that value for money is maintained, although he may find in practice that it is quite difficult, if not impossible, to unhook from a bureau.

4 A successful bureau will have many customers, possibly several hundred and, by the nature of most applications, they may all seek priority service at the same time, e.g. the end of the month. Hopefully the bureau will have geared its resources, particularly its computing capacity, to these peak demands, but things do go wrong and the individual user may feel frustrated by not having complete control over the situation.

5 First time users, by and large, start with one application; if it is successful they may then convert other systems to bureau operation. Unless they progressively introduce modules of a

pre-structured package, such as general ledger, the probability is that each function will be treated separately and they will end up with a number of stand-alone systems. Even with a framework of related packages, like general ledger, it is not uncommon to find that one part, say purchase ledger, is not acceptable to users and a novel system has to be developed. Thus using a bureau may not be conducive to the development of an integrated approach; if this is the ultimate objective, it may be better achieved by in-house means.

Such disadvantages may be sufficient to dissuade the feasibility study team from recommending a bureau for the proposed inventory control system. They may decide that, although satisfactory software packages are available, they do not wholly meet requirements and, in any event, the problems of passing data to and from the bureau and maintaining management control are likely to cause too many internal stresses.

Installing a computer
If the feasibility study team opts for the acquisition of an in-house computer, it is almost certain that, whatever its size, it will be capable of handling other work besides the inventory control system. The team's terms of reference may therefore have to be broadened to allow them to look at other potential applications, if only in general outline. However, the inventory application will yield the data necessary for sizing the machine in terms of the amount of storage required, the processing features and the volume and frequency of output. If few records are involved, say 400 – 500, it may be possible to make do with an inexpensive microcomputer, whereas if many thousands of records have to be stored, utilizing tens of millions of characters, the team will have to look at something bigger – either a minicomputer or possibly a mainframe.

Advantages of a microcomputer In the previous chapter we noted the tremendous advances in capacity, power and facility that have been made in microcomputer technology in recent years, to the point where even potential mainframe users may opt to use microcomputers.

1 The overwhelming advantage of the microcomputer is its low cost which, nowadays, is no longer a reflection of severely

limited facilities. For the right application, it provides an ideal dedicated resource; configurated as a network of linked machines, microcomputers offer a major challenge to both minicomputers and mainframe configurations.

2   A microcomputer requires no specialist staff and can be installed and applied with the minimum of training by user staff.

3   No special environmental controls are needed and machines can be installed in any office or factory location.

4   A vast range of systems software, utilities and application packages are now available, specially written for microcomputers and catering for every conceivable need.

5   For many potential users the speed and relative ease of implementation is a major attraction, enabling benefits to be achieved at an early stage of computerization.

6   Microcomputers offer opportunities for extending technology into office administration, performing tasks that would otherwise be ignored by computer experts.

Disadvantages of a microcomputer

1   A major disadvantage of the microcomputer is the seductive quality of the cost performance factor, which can fuel a strategy which may lead eventually to higher total expenditure on computing than might be necessary using a mainframe. For example, the development of networked microcomputers might prove more expensive than using a minicomputer or a mainframe supporting dumb terminals.

2   Notwithstanding the major technological improvement in the facilities available from microcomputers, there are still limitations on file sizes, multi-users capabilities and the quality of peripheral devices that may restrict some applications.

3   To date, there is a limit to the degree of sophistication in software in important areas such as database, security procedures and protection of data. Users should be aware that microcomputers are highly vulnerable to loss of data, either by chance or malpractice, and, as they will generally operate in an open office environment, special precautions are necessary to protect key business data.

Advantages of a minicomputer As we said earlier, today's mini-computer is as powerful as the mainframes of ten years ago and can be obtained at a fraction of the cost.

1 So the first advantage to be recognized is that minicomputers provide a cheap and powerful means of acquiring quite sophisticated data processing facilities. For example, it is possible to purchase a configuration that will support up to 16 terminals with ample backing storage for an amortized charge that is less than the annual cost of a middle-range executive.

2 Because of the lower capital costs involved, the pressure for high machine utilization is not as severe as exists with a larger installation, and idle time becomes less of a burden.

3 It is therefore not unusual to find a minicomputer dedicated to one task and not treated as a general work engine so much as an integral part of a single business or office system. One could, for example, dedicate a minicomputer to the inventory control system and not be concerned with other applications.

4 One feature of a minicomputer that recommends it for integration with normal office procedures is that it does not require a separate working environment with expensive air-conditioning and temperature controls; within reason, a mini can be set up in any part of the organization.

5 Furthermore, minicomputers do not call for specialist operating skills, and user staff can be readily trained to carry out fairly basic caretaking tasks. Once programs are up and running you do not need computer staff, and if you use software packages from the beginning you will not require systems development staff either.

Minicomputers were designed with multi-user on-line processing as a standard method of operating and thus provide the average user with relatively free access to computer power which will not be achieved so readily with a centralized machine not under the user's direct control.

Disadvantages of a minicomputer In taking this route, the user has to settle for the technical limitations of minicomputers, although these may cause no inconvenience in practice. There will be a limit to the amount of storage that can be hung on to the machine, and its capacity to handle terminals may be fixed at a level that could cause future problems. So what you have to be sure of is the impact of likely future demands on the computer in terms of growth in volumes of records and transactions and in the number of potential users of the system. If this estimation is done casually or you are misled by the low cost of the equipment, you may find, too late, that the computer has been under-specified and will not do your work without enhancement, if that is possible, or replacement, which could be expensive.

You should also bear in mind that the relative cheapness of the equipment may not be reflected in the cost of the programs needed to run the system. If you are not using software packages and wish to develop a bespoke system, using either internal or external staff, the cost of these programs may approach the capital cost of the machine. Ideally, these alternatives will be properly costed at the justification stage and you will know then how much more expensive it will be to have a unique system.

Advantages of a mainframe computer If the team's assessment of existing and future requirements, including expected growth, show that a minicomputer may not have the muscle to support the inventory system, or if a preliminary examination of other potential applications shows additional benefits, the answer may be to look at a mainframe computer.

1   The principal advantages of a mainframe are that, by definition, it will have greater potential capacity, will be faster and will offer more varied facilities.
2   Generally, most mainframes will also have the requisite software tools and aids that will enable the user to exploit these more sophisticated technical features, and will probably have a wider range of application packages than a minicomputer.
3   Mainframe computers are usually designed in modular fashion, allowing expansion of capacity and facilities within one model or a move to a larger model in the same family of machines. Thus, in theory, problems of growth can be accomodated readily with mainframes by selecting an entry point in an equipment range that affords the greatest upwards flexibility.
4   Most mainframe suppliers have been in computers for a very long time and have an extensive international customer base and a great deal of data processing experience which can be made available to new users. In particular, a mainframe supplier is more likely to have direct knowledge and experience of

your industry or activity than the average minicomputer supplier. These advantages will be apparent in the training, maintenance and support arrangements and in the amount of 'handholding' the potential user can rely on.

Disadvantages of a mainframe computer

1   Unless you are particularly well-endowed with funds, you will consider the higher costs involved with mainframes as a potential disadvantage. These higher costs arise not merely because of the additional technical features provided but also from the ancillary expenditure that will be incurred. For example, the machine will probably require a separate physically controlled working environment, with air-conditioning and temperature control. It may also call for a dedicated power supply. Maintenance charges, normally fixed in relation to the purchasing price, will be higher, and you may have to provide room for the supplier's engineers.

2   By virtue of its sophistication, a mainframe installation will require professional computer staff, and by the time you have recruited operators and systems development staff you may be committed, on an annual basis, to salary costs equivalent to the price of the machine. You may have also acquired, without realizing it, a host of new management, structural and staffing problems.

3   While it is relatively easy to get into computing, it is rather more difficult, if not impossible, to withdraw once management has made a commitment to a mainframe machine, to the associated staff and to a systems development programme. This argument applies equally to minicomputers, but it is much more of a problem to disengage from a larger machine on which many of an organization's activities may ultimately depend.

The higher costs involved in acquiring a mainframe computer encourages an emphasis on high utilization to make the maximum use of the asset. One result is often the development of systems that may be only marginally justified, on the basis that the facility is available and might as well be used. This can lead to a situation in which you need extra capacity or a larger machine to continue to support these marginal applications. If inadequate attention is given not only to identifying benefits but also to ensuring that they are achieved, the in-house installation rapidly becomes a net cost drain on resources.

Utilizing a package

Whether you choose to use a computer service bureau or to install your own machine, you may wish to consider the advantages and shortcomings of using a ready-written software package for your proposed application. Packages are available for virtually all standard computer systems and our feasibility study team would have no shortage of potential packages in the field of inventory control. Indeed, there are probably many hundreds of packages in this common area, some of which will be tailored for particular types of industry; for example, there are systems for manufacturing, for wholesalers, for distributive trades, for construction companies, and so on.

Advantages of a package approach Irrespective of the features of individual packages, which the study team may not have time to examine, there are some important advantages that adoption of a package approach can offer a potential user.

1 Using a package will enable you to implement the proposed computer system faster than designing and developing tailor-made programs.
2 Assuming the package is commonly used, it will represent the distillation of more knowledge, experience and technique than you could possibly bring to bear on your in-house project. Why re-invent the wheel?
3 Being in common use, development charges will have been spread across many users and so the price or rental of the package will almost certainly be less than the costs of in-house development.
4 Early implementation, lower costs and concentration of expertise mean that expected benefits from data processing can be obtained sooner by using a package in preference to a special development.
5 A package user does not have the potential burden of data processing staff to contend with, although there will be a clear advantage in having a staff member who understands what the package does.

Considering the theoretical advantages that a package approach can offer, I find it very difficult to understand, in a slightly different context, why so many local authorities, health authorities, public utilities and the like have tended to develop the same systems, time and time again. Just think of the colossal waste of national resources on separate development of rating systems or billing procedures, not to mention the range of machines involved.

Disadvantages of a package approach
1   The arguments most often advanced for such separate development are that the use of a package means that you have to forfeit some internal requirements and that each organization has unique characteristics which have to be acknowledged in its computer systems.
2   Any adaptation or customization of a package will add to the original cost and may not be initially apparent in constructing the economic case.
3   There is a danger that commitment to a package severely limits the individual organization's ability to adapt to its operating environment over the years, unless the package itself can be changed, which may not be popular with multiple users.
4   The design and structure of a generalized software package may result in the profligate use of computer resources such that, for example, it might call for a bigger machine than would be necessary with a custom-built system.

The costs/benefits equation

In the evaluation of alternative strategies – bureau or in-house, batch or on-line, package or bespoke systems – there may be a host of arguments and prejudices to resolve which may have little to do with the technical or commercial implications of the options under review. Nevertheless, the common denominator is always money and the validity of a chosen course of action should always be tested against the net contribution it makes to the aims of the organization. If, in preference, weight is given to non-financial factors then the organization should at least be aware of it and be prepared to accept the effects upon potential costs/benefits.

In carrying out justification studies on computer applications, we should make every effort to consider, and where possible to give a value to, all the costs and the benefits associated with a particular course of action. It is not an easy task and it is one which is frequently obfuscated by technical issues or by managers taking refuge behind statements about 'levels of customer service' or 'improved control information'. There are four main areas of varying doubt and uncertainty:

- Tangible costs
- Intangible costs
- Tangible benefits
- Intangible benefits

Tangible costs

In theory, it should be relatively easy to identify the types of costs that will be directly incurred in following a proposed strategy, but it is surprising how often significant items are omitted from an evaluation. For example, I have come across a number of cases where the costs of preparing existing records for conversion to a computer, i.e. setting up the files, have ignored the amount of *additional* clerical effort required and concentrated solely on data processing costs. Assuming that your staff are not under-employed (in which case you should question the need for a computer), some expenditure in terms of overtime or extra hands will be required.

Even if all categories of direct cost are properly identified, there remains the problem of accurately estimating what those costs should be. Obviously, some guidance can be obtained from potential suppliers of equipment or services, but you will be required to make a guess for some items and sensibly you should allow for variations upwards in your 'guesstimates'. If you are projecting costs forward over a period of time, you should also include an allowance for inflation, whatever the current government may say.

The following categories of direct cost should be taken into account for an organization considering an in-house computer.

1 The costs of buying or hiring the hardware making up the data processing installation, including transport and installation charges, covering:
   - computer, peripheral, communication and data preparation hardware;

- user support equipment, e.g. adding machines for check totals, rapid reference filing systems, etc.;
- accommodation for equipment;
- air conditioning, reserve power, fire protection equipment;
- furniture, telephones and office support equipment;
- maintenance costs associated with the above.

2   The estimated costs for developing and implementing systems or alternatively the costs of using packages. These estimates should cover the following items.
- Systems and programming costs:
  - recruitment and training;
  - salaries and allowances, including overtime;
  - stationery and consumables;
  - computer time for program development and testing;
  - travel and transport;
  - data preparation;
  - unbundled software; aids; packages; documentation.
- File preparation – file preparation costs are frequently under-estimated. Typically they will include:
  - clerical support costs;
  - stationery and consumables;
  - accommodation;
  - data preparation (internal or external);
  - computer time.

3   You should also estimate the costs for converting to the new computer system, taking account of the need for a period of parallel running of old and new procedures which will involve computer time, hand-holding and possibly extra staff.

4   The computer project may also involve direct expenditure on support provided by an external organization, such as a consultancy or software house, or even other professional advisers such as lawyers or auditors.

5   It is always difficult, at the justification stage, to estimate with any confidence for the annual processing charges that will be incurred once the system is in full production. Nevertheless, an attempt should be made to assess such items as:
- computer time;
- data preparation and/or collection costs;
- data control costs;
- stationery and consumables;

- transport and communication costs;
- new staff in user areas.

It will be clear that this type of checklist should be compiled even if you intend using a bureau service instead of your own equipment. To some extent the job may be easier if you can obtain guarantees on certain costs or at least agree a budget with a bureau.

Intangible costs
Intangible costs represent the 'forgotten' area, but any comprehensive evaluation must, at least, identify the factors involved and make some attempt to assess their likely effect, if only in subjective terms.

1 Although the direct costs of meetings and discussions can be evaluated in terms of salaries, etc., involved, there can be a significant element of intangible costs arising from lost opportunities, disruption, etc.
2 In general, computer systems are more formal than the clerical systems they replace. Even with careful design, customer relations can be adversely affected and this could involve an intangible cost in terms of:
   - additional effort to offset loss of goodwill;
   - dealing with complaints;
   - lost orders;
   - extra marketing/liaison duties.
3 Although interactive terminal systems have frequently improved clerical staff morale, the introduction of computer systems frequently leads to:
   - reduced job satisfaction;
   - lowered staff productivity;
   - increased staff turnover.
   In order to minimize these risks, extra effort will be required.
4 Computer systems are, in many cases, relatively inflexible and are slow to respond to changed circumstances. Ad hoc analyses are difficult, slow and expensive to produce and, in some cases, may not be possible. Thus instead of producing *better* management information, it is possible in certain conditions that management may be less well informed.
5 Another facet of the inflexibility of computers is that when change is required to systems it can involve:

- delay;
- high costs;
- disruption;
- difficult user relations;
- adverse customer relations.

It will not be possible to anticipate these indirect costs, but the cautious user will spend time thinking about what could possibly go wrong and preparing some form of contingency plan, with an associated cost budget.

Tangible benefits
Tangible benefits comprise the benefits to which a financial gain or economy may be directly and quantifiably attributed. They will typically include the following:

1   Staff reductions – these may comprise:
- reducing the number of staff or managers;
- lowering the skill requirement of staff required;
- reducing overtime;
- avoiding hiring additional staff to cope with growth;
- absorbing growth within existing staff limits.

    Economies claimed in this area require very careful examination, since they are frequently of a theoretical rather than practical nature and are difficult to achieve unless properly planned.

2   Equipment reductions – these may be significant and can include avoiding the purchase of new or additional equipment. When claiming equipment economies relating to existing equipment, the value claimed should be based upon the replacement value and not necessarily the original price.

3   Claims for space economies can be fallacious unless the space can be usefully employed or turned into a direct cash benefit. However, avoiding the need for additional space *is* a justifiable economy.

4   Improved cash flow represents a direct and quantifiable economy. Note that this applies to controlled payments, as well as reducing the average age of debt.

5   Credit control – as well as reducing the average age of debt, improved credit control can reduce the number and value of bad debts written off because of improved accuracy and timeliness of the information available.

6 Improved operations can include:
  - more effective use of assets and plant;
  - more effective use of space, e.g. automated warehouses;
  - reduction of stock and/or work in progress;
  - reduction in scrap, e.g. trim-loss programs;
  - more effective distribution systems;
  - more effective purchasing;

  all of which will contribute to profit or reduce costs.

7 It is not uncommon for secondary economies to emerge from an operation which was originally justified on different grounds. All potential applications should be closely scrutinized for such benefits. An example is the improved recovery of bank charges arising from the introduction of a computerized customer account system.

The important point about direct benefits is that they should be demonstrable and aimed at improvements to the profitability of the enterprise through extra business, reduced costs or larger profits. Estimates of benefits should be made by, or in conjunction with, the managers who will be expected to produce them, and there should be a clear plan setting out how and when these benefits are to be achieved. A common mistake is to compare the costs of the proposed system with the costs of existing procedures and claim the reduction, if there is one, as a direct benefit. This begs the question as to whether the present system is the most economic and effective way of carrying out the work; closer examination may reveal opportunities for improvement that do not require the use of a computer.

Intangible benefits
In the absence of specific direct benefits, many users have based their computer justification heavily on intangible advantages which they have been unable to quantify.

1 The classic case is the almost traditional sales argument that a computer will lead to 'better management information'. While it is true that a computer can contribute to the production of more accurate or timely information, the important issue is what use is made of that information by managers. Unfortunately volume is often confused with quality and usefulness.

2 Another common claim is that the use of a computer will

improve or extend the level of customer service. This is equally difficult to demonstrate. There are examples, such as inventory control, where the link can be clearly drawn between improved operational performance, i.e. fewer stock-outs, and a better customer service, i.e. more satisfactory orders. However, the key issue is, again, the determination of users to exploit the opportunities presented by the computer rather than the availability of the computer itself.

3   Cases have arisen where, if the enterprise is to continue, there is no alternative to the use of a computer and the question of tangible benefit is of secondary interest. If clerical staff cannot be obtained in sufficient quantity or quality to continue a task, the task must either be discontinued or automated. Examples abound in scientific research, and global communication has also reached this stage. In the commercial field an example was afforded by the banks, who could no longer attract adequate staff to cope with the maintenance of customer account ledgers.

As a manager reviewing the costs/benefits evaluation of your feasibility study team, you would be well advised to scrutinize their estimates carefully and to pay special attention to claims of intangible benefits.

Presenting the financial case

Practice in presenting the economic case for using computers varies from organization to organization, and does not always reflect their normal procedure. Some companies that have quite stringent standards for the evaluation of other capital projects may be inclined to casualness or a lack of discipline in producing the arguments for and against computers and representing them in financial terms. In other cases, where rigid accounting practices are observed, the full weight of argument in favour of the project may be diminished through lack of factual evidence.

In piecing together the evaluation and in presenting the case, the following points should be considered.

1   Factors that apply to costs should also be applied to benefits, to ensure consistency; for example. the allowance for inflation should be included in both sides of the equation, as should any provision for VAT, which is often ignored.

2 Recognize your shortcomings as an estimator by overbudgeting on costs and under-estimating savings. Your other errors will probably at least restore the balance.

3 Some economies, such as a reduction in inventory, will occur only once and you should make sure that they are properly dealt with – either you take them into account as a capital sum in the year of saving or you register them as an annual yield on capital at a rate agreed with your accountant.

4 Each organization has its own methods of costing capital projects and opportioning overheads and the same standards should be applied to computer projects, otherwise the results may be misleading.

5 This applies particularly when considering the cash flow implications of a project that may last several years and call for the allocation of funds that could be used elsewhere. You should show both the annual and cumulative positions for costs, benefits and the net position. Be suspicious of any project that does not break even within three years.

6 The point at which you spend or receive funds is important and should be taken into account when considering alternatives, using a technique like discounted cash flow which recognizes the time value of money.

6   The development process

It must be remembered that there is nothing more difficult to plan, more doubtful of success, nor more dangerous to manage than the creation of a new system. For the initiator has the enmity of all who would profit by the preservation of the old institution and merely lukewarm defenders in those who would gain by the new ones.

Machiavelli (1513)

Introduction

The acquisition of a machine is only a small, to some the least, part of the process of developing and implementing computer applications. The probability is that if you do not know with reasonable clarity what you wish to do with it and you do not exercise adequate control over the development process, you will join the rather full ranks of generally dissatisfied and bitter computer users – no matter how big the machine.

The history of data processing is littered with examples of systems that took an excessive time to develop compared with original estimates, cost several times more than was budgeted and proved to be more or less unsatisfactory when they were implemented. Our most recent experiences suggest that, in spite of improvements in the education and training of both managers and specialists, similar mistakes continue to be made, most often but not invariably by first time users.

In attempting to come to grips with these problems, general managers are frustrated by the jargon and the lack of familiar information with which to judge and control the process, and are frequently appalled by the time and costs involved in converting what seems to them to be a straightforward and well-understood procedure into a computer system. Invariably, the 'computer' becomes the focal point of criticism and resentment. In some cases the hardware, or more likely the software, *is* severely at fault; however, most analyses reveal that inadequacies or omissions on the part of management, users or specialists are the prime cause of failures. Consider the following example.

An engineering company wished to mechanize the analysis of orders received and to compare trends in actual sales against the annual forecast. On the surface this was not a difficult data processing task, nor were the statistical techniques involved particularly complex. The company had access to a bureau service which it already used on package systems, but had no computer staff.

A working party was established and a young and extremely able graduate trainee, with some knowledge of computing and statistics, was appointed as systems analyst. Programmers were supplied by the bureau. The managing director prepared a comprehensive brief relating the proposed system to the business as a whole and outlining associated problem areas. The project was estimated for completion within six months, which at the time seemed generous.

The uncompleted project was abandoned 18 months later, after considerable expenditure of time, effort and computer costs. Furthermore, the poor development history generated great bitterness between the prospective user and bureau staff and reinforced an anti-computer lobby in the company.

An independent review of the circumstances revealed that the following factors contributed to the expensive disaster.

1   The terms of reference were far too wide and had expanded the original intention to set up an order book analysis and monitoring system.
2   The attempt to accommodate these requirements led the system to spill over into production programming and re-scheduling of individual orders.
3   There was a demonstrable lack of clarity and discipline among the prospective users as to their exact requirements, right up to and through the programming and program test stages.
4   It was a major initial mistake to appoint a novice, however well qualified, to carry out the systems analysis and design.
5   This error in manning was compounded by three changes of systems analyst (when the trainee was promoted and another left the company) and several changes of programmer.

6   Project monitoring by the user and by the bureau was wholly inadequate and for long periods nobody knew what was happening and which stages had been reached.

7   There was no systems testing stage at all.

8   Users frequently added to or changed analysis codes without telling the computer staff.

All together it was a most extraordinary collection of errors and inefficiencies on the part of management, users and specialists.

A long-suffering management or a prospective user hearing such tales of woe is entitled to ask why data processing should be different from and less controllable than any other function of the organization.

- What makes data processing so special?
- Why does the development process take so long and cost so much?
- Why do data processing practitioners seem helpless to control their own activities?
- What can management do about it?

What makes it so special?

There are a number of factors to consider here.

- The nature of the technology and the specialists' response to it.
- The impact of the technology on the structure of an organization.
- The user reaction to the facilities on offer.

The technology

Early computer work was very much the province of a relatively few enthusiastic individualists with a scientific and technical bias. The application of computers to more general business and administrative data processing did not take place until the mid-1950s, mostly fostered by accountants familiar with the use of unit record equipment. The subsequent phenomenal growth in the number of computers installed, in the range of applications and in the variety and complexity of technical features available has had quite serious repercussions.

1   Demand for computer staff has always outstripped the pool of trained and experienced personnel available.

2 In spite of tremendous efforts by computer manufacturers, public and private bodies and commercial concerns to provide training facilities, there are still many computer staff with only a basic training and little experience.

3 Many software aids are designed to de-skill the programming function, while others are so complex that they require full time specialization. The result is that many computer staff are experts at doing one thing on one machine or in one area; in no sense can they be called general data processing practitioners.

Consequently, we have a new and complex technology, with a history of explosive growth and an incredible future potential, which is inadequately manned by practitioners, including in their ranks a proportion of inexperienced staff that is too high for the comfort of the average user.

The impact of the technology

The special nature of computing is also demonstrated by its lack of respect for conventional practices and organizational boundaries. Some applications cut right across the organization structure and may lead to the demise or merging of departments. While in some organizations this may be the effect of computerization, in others it may be the prime motive; in other words, senior management may use computer technology to integrate systems and to bring about fundamental changes in the structure of the business. Thus, whether it is by accident or by design, the introduction of computer technology can have a far reaching effect on an organization, its management style and the roles played by management and staff.

It is therefore not altogether surprising to find that computers and computer staff may be viewed with suspicion and possibly seen as a threat by other members of the organization. Most development projects encounter resistance in some form and it only needs a failure or an example of technical mismanagement to encourage scepticism and positive opposition. There is a natural resistance to change, and if the appointed agents of change are relatively inexperienced in their own disciplines and perhaps unfamiliar with general business practices, then the process of developing new systems is fraught with difficulties.

User reactions

One of these difficulties is the tendency for requirements to vary during the course of the project. It is a common complaint by computer staff that users never know what they want and frequently change their minds, often when the project is well advanced and changes are difficult to implement. This is probably inevitable.

Typically, at the start of a project, the computer expert may know little or nothing about the requirements of the prospective user or, for that matter, about the relevance of the procedures under review. The prospective user may be similarly ignorant about computer technology and may have difficulty in conceiving his systems in data processing terms. There is clearly a communications problem and the gap is not always successfully bridged. However, as the prospective user learns more about the facilities available from computers and, more significantly, becomes accustomed to thinking in systems terms, he begins to refine and alter his requirements. If this happens late in the development process, or even after the system has been implemented, it may be difficult or even impossible to accommodate his wishes.

Why does it take so long and cost so much?

Some users are fortunate that systems are implemented more or less on time and within a reasonable level of cost. However, it is a fact that the majority of applications are late and invariably cost more than expected. We can identify several factors that contribute to this poor record of performance, among which are:

- the accuracy of estimating time and cost;
- the difficulty of establishing user requirements;
- the communications/education problem;
- the need for policy decisions.

Estimating time and cost

For all but the simplest applications, it has to be recognized that systems development is by nature a lengthy process, to be measured in terms of months rather than in weeks. This is a reflection of the amount of work that is normally required:

- to analyse existing systems in order to establish information flows and problem areas;

- to conceive and elaborate the design of a new system, taking account of users requirements;
- to consider and adapt the various technical features of the computer facilities available to the organization;
- to document the design of a new system in forms that are suitable both for achieving user acceptance and as a guide to the computer programmers;
- to program and test the new system;
- to train staff and implement the application.

In addition, a multiplicity of resources and contributions is required from systems analysts, system designers, programmers, operations staff, data collectors, user management and staff. Computer systems development is in every sense a project oriented activity, with the emphasis on planning, coordination and progress control, although it has taken data processing managers a long time to reach this conclusion.

The starting point is a realistic target date. Senior management, for reasons which appear sound to them, frequently set dates for the implementation of systems that have little to do with the amount of work involved – 'I must have this system for the start of the next financial year' being a fairly typical instruction. Such dates are often set without consultation and before the poor computer manager has even had a chance to estimate the work content or to assess his resources. Even if his estimates reveal a lack of time or deficiencies in the number and quality of staff, he may fail to persuade management to alter the schedule or to supplement his resources. Pointing out that the decision on target dates was falsely based offers no inducement to a determined and ill-informed manager to change his mind.

Computer managers tend to compound this problem by not being very good at estimating. This is not entirely their fault. If one accepts that the development process is one of identification and gradual refinement of users requirements, then it is harsh to expect precision about the solutions to a problem before the problem has been adequately elucidated. For example, it is possible to be fairly accurate about the amount of programming required for a given system – there are many proven techniques for estimating programming work content. However, this level of precision depends on a detailed definition of the system which simply does not exist at the start of a project; the computer manager consequently has to make 'ball park' guesses about programming, which are usually wrong. His accurate re-estimates, after the system has been designed, are often regarded as an admission of error rather than a demonstration of professionalism.

However, proximity to the activity does not give automatic precision in estimating. The first stage of any project – systems analysis – is often difficult to assess because it involves not only investigation, which should be measurable, but also extensive discussion and consultation with users, which can be prolonged, argumentative and possibly inconclusive. It is sometimes more fruitful, if unscientific, to set an arbitrary deadline by which certain agreements have to be reached.

Establishing user requirements

The time taken to establish user requirements is a major influence over the time span of the project. If insufficient attention is paid to this activity in the early stages, it is probable that later stages will be frustrated by changes or procrastination initiated by users. The following case illustrates the dangers for the unwary in making a superficial assessment of user requirements.

A finance house wished to use a computer for the recording, control and accounting of its transactions. It had no machine and no experienced computer staff and had no wish to build up a large development department. One of the directors knew of a system being operated by another company in a similar line of business and was persuaded that, with modifications, it would meet their needs.

The finance house bought the system, ordered the configuration to run it and hired a software house to adapt the programmes. The software house advised that the system would be ready in six months and, apart from periodic steering meetings, was allowed to carry on with the work, largely unsupervised.

As the project developed, and it became clear that the system did not meet all their needs, users asked for more and more modifications to the package. It was also found that the system did not incorporate the level of accounting controls demanded by their application. As the system got bigger, they realized that the equipment configuration was inadequate and more equipment had to be ordered.

The target date came and went. Management's confidence –

in the system, in the equipment, in their suppliers and in their own ability to get the system running – was practically destroyed. The overt penalty of the initial under-assessment of requirements was:

- a systems and programming estimate of about £15,000 turned out in practice to be an actual cost of over £100,000;
- equipment costs were almost doubled;
- the system was implemented nine months after the target date.

This case also illustrates a general point about the advisability of modifying packages. We have found many cases where the total cost of doing so was far in excess of what would have been incurred by a tailor-made system.

The communications/education problem
We have already touched upon the problems of communication between the computer expert and the user manager and staff member, and it would be unwise to underestimate the influence that a failure to communicate may have on the duration of a project.

The computer man sees the solution as being principally one of educating the user in the significance of the computer. We consider this to be a rather limited view, confusing ends and means. On the other hand, the user is more concerned with obtaining a sympathetic and constructive understanding of his problems and the certainty of a decent level of service in dealing with them. Unfortunately, far too many computer experts are poorly equipped to meet the users half way in this dialogue. Many systems analysts do not have the depth or breadth of general business knowledge that enables them to win the user's cofidence from the beginning. Sometimes they do not have the functional knowledge of the area under review, thus adding to the frustrations of the user. If you are setting up a production control project, expecting a systems analyst with no previous knowledge or experience in that area to deal with hard-nosed production men, you are inviting unecessary and potentially disastrous problems.

Policy decisions
A significant source of delay in many projects is the time taken by senior management to give a ruling on matters of operating policy

that arise during the development of a new system. Such issues may be confined to the structure of the system, and the substance of the decision may be less important than the fact that a ruling is given, e.g. the establishment of stock control parameters. In contrast, though, other decisions may have implications beyond the new system and may affect other company functions. For example, a complex pricing and discount structure may have no logical basis and, if rationalized, would greatly facilitate the design of the system. However, such a change could affect many aspects of marketing, customer relationships and profitability and can rarely be taken at face value.

It is unlikely that all such policy matters will be identified and anticipated at the inception of the project, so management has to ensure that a suitable mechanism exists for dealing with them as they arise.

Why are computer experts unable to control their activities?

We have had the privilege of meeting many excellent computer managers who not only have a high degree of technical competence but also the innate or acquired ability to manage their function in the organization efficiently and effectively. To be sure, they still have their quota of projects that overrun or turn sour, but one is unlikely to find that mismanagement of computer activities is the cause. Some of these men go on to prove their worth in other functions at general management level, in which case their employers are fortunate to have recognized their value.

However, the general level of ability to manage the computer function is in need of a great deal of improvement and in this respect the computer expert is only partially to blame.

Lack of management experience
Many senior computer staff have achieved their positions through technical excellence at lower levels; others have advanced by length of service and familiarity with the workings of the organization of which they are a part. This is a not unfamiliar pattern with other functions. However, on average, most computer experts are young and lack any experience of line management; for example, they are often totally ignored when it comes to management training and development. They may also lack the broad under-

standing of business requirements that transcends the 'nuts and bolts' of systems design. It is therefore hardly surprising if they find it difficult to cope at a senior level. It is not uncommon to find managers of computer services, with budgets in excess of £1 million, who have no other line experience nor any management training.

Project management
At a lower but no less important level, we have found only a partial understanding and experience of the responsibilities of project management, despite the fact that these responsibilities might involve development costs of tens of thousands of pounds. There is ample evidence from case histories:

- that planning techniques are rudimentary;
- that estimating is loosely founded on slim previous experience;
- that control over progress is often highly subjective and unscientific ('How are things going then?'); and
- that user relationships are poorly handled.

Although established project management techniques and suitable training courses are available, computer departments seemed determined to go their own individual ways. The results are often uncontrolled projects.

What can general management do about it?

Your responsibility, as general managers, towards the application of computers and to the computer function is no less than your responsibilities to other parts of the organization and to other managers. Each requires a clear statement of objectives, positive support and the opportunity to perform. In so far as computer expenditure may represent a considerable investment in equipment and development costs, you should ensure that the rules and standards for returns on investment are no less rigorously applied.

It is evident that general management cannot ignore the problems of computing or hope that time and money will resolve them. There are certain actions to be avoided and some very positive steps that should be taken.

1 First of all, your job is not finished when you have presided over the decision to computerize and have authorized the

expenditure. The responsibility for the successful implementation of those decisions remains at the highest level and cannot
be delegated.

> A major insurance company called for an audit of its com-
> puter function after a growing body of complaints from users
> and several failures to implement systems became apparent.
> The review disclosed conclusive evidence of poor computer
> management and inadequate technical judgement, but was
> also severely critical of the role of senior management. In
> spite of frequent attempts to obtain directions and to
> appraise management of his problems, the computer man-
> ager had been largely ignored and allowed to go his own
> way. The result was a rather aimless and ineffective pursuit
> of technical challenges that added nothing to the interests of
> the business and set back the programme of developments
> for at least three years.

It is a natural corollary to this responsibility that it should be
advertized within the organization by making it clear that the
computer project has top level support and involvement.

2   You must ensure that good people are committed to the project, both at steering level and to any working party or secondment required. You and your colleagues must resist the
temptation to allocate the staff who can most be spared. In all
probability they will not be good enough nor will they carry
sufficient weight within their own functions.

3   In our experience, systems that are designed with the full
participation of the users tend to work better and be more
successful than those which are not. If a prospective user says
something will not work, that is a guarantee that it probably
won't. You must insist on the involvement of users, to the
point where the user underwrites and accepts responsibility for
the achievement of the agreed benefits.

4   To the extent that you are able to influence overall systems
strategies, insist on simplicity and flexibility in design rather
than elegance and technical virtuosity. Systems tend to last
longer if they are uncomplicated.

5   Satisfy yourself that the computer function is properly
organized and adequately staffed, and that sensible and
uncomplicated techniques exist and are used for planning,

controlling and documenting projects. If you cannot allow time for a regular monthly review of the function with the manager, make sure a senior colleague does it for you; perhaps you could look at it once a quarter.

6 Systems development is an evolutionary process and it is possible to establish review points at which progress can be checked and, more importantly, the status of the project can be evaluated in terms of the original objectives and the decision taken whether or not to proceed to the next stage.

Some managers are concerned that they will be confused or misled by the jargon and technical phraseology. Computer staff do little to dispel this impression and some encourage it, perhaps as a protection. The fact is, it is totally unnecessary. There are few computer problems of interest at senior management level which cannot be perfectly adequately explained and explored in plain business language. It is an excellent discipline and sound training for the computer manager and his senior colleagues to follow normal business reporting practices.

The classic approach

We have seen several approaches to the stratification of the development process and they all tend to follow a similar pattern which recognizes the evolutionary nature of systems design. They also identify similar types of output on which decisions about subsequent stages are made:

- A statement of business or user requirements, followed by
- a systems specification, leading to
- detailed computer programs.

To illustrate the nature of the development process and how it can be used as a means of discipline and control, we examine the classic five-stage approach to systems development, covering:

- Feasibility study
- Business requirement specification
- Systems specification
- Programming
- Implementation

We also indicate how this structure can be linked with a steering or project control reporting system, as illustrated in Figure 6.1

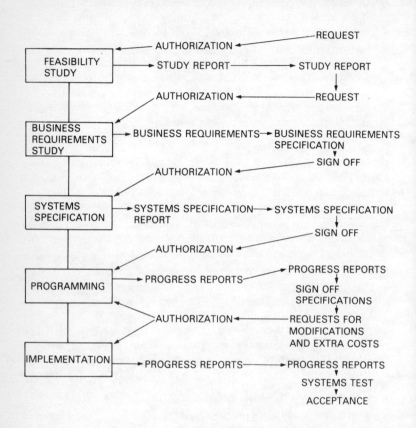

Figure 6.1 Five-stage approach

The feasibility study

The first stage, variously called the feasibility or justification study, will usually have been mounted because the organization has a particular problem area in which computer systems might help. The purposes of this stage are:

- to review and document the information flows in the area under review;
- to identify current and future problems that existing systems create or cannot cope with;

- to challenge constructively the necessity for each aspect of those systems;
- to identify the user requirements that are not being met;
- to form an initial judgement on the scope for improvements, weighing the relative merits of new or revised manual and/or computer procedures.

Ideally the survey should be carried out in close conjunction with user staff, who should be invited to subscribe to the recommendation. Findings and recommendations should be formally recorded in a survey report, preferably to a standard format, and should be sufficiently documented to give management a clear choice.

Business requirements specification
The survey report should enable management to decide whether to authorize a requirements study. This will be longer and cost considerably more than the initial survey, which might only have taken a few weeks.

The objectives of this stage, again carried out with the participation of the prospective user, should be:

- to evaluate alternative means of achieving the desired improvements, balancing feasibility, practicability and costs;
- to determine the overall shape of the preferred system;
- to establish first estimates of the likely costs/benefits of developing and running the proposed system;
- to identify resources required and the timescales involved;
- to prepare a systems proposal (the user requirements or business requirements specification), together with a justification for the work involved.

At the end of this stage, general management ought to be in a position to decide whether or not to continue or to redirect the project.

The systems specification
If management decides to go ahead, you enter a more expensive stage of development, designed to establish the full requirements of the proposed system. The output must include.

- detailed systems specifications from which computer program specifications can be prepared; and
- detailed user manuals that describe the interface between the computer system and user procedures.

At this stage, one is concerned with the detail of input and output and the way in which the system will operate on a regular basis. It is therefore essential to include the user in discussions and in the design of the system he is expected to operate. For this reason, the specification stage may last several months, depending upon the complexity of the system and the quality of analysis in the previous stages.

An important output of this stage is the first valid estimate of the amount of computer programming involved and the likely efficiency of the computer operation. The estimates for programming may be alarmingly high compared with previous guesses, but they are certainly more soundly based. However, management still retains the choice:

- to go ahead as planned;
- to abandon the project; or
- to modify aspirations and seek a cheaper solution.

Many organizations feel that they are totally committed at this stage, in spite of prohibitive costs, merely because the structure of their development has not allowed for review points at successive levels of clarification of requirements. They assume, wrongly, that this is the point of no return; in practice the point of no return occurs much later, after commitment to programming.

Programming
Programming also calls for a level-by-level approach. Ideally, your technicians should first of all prepare the program specifications for the whole system before a word of coding is uttered. There are well established programming techniques available to encourage and assist programmers to do this and to gain more knowledge and certainty about the programming work content and the way in which the load should be scheduled.

After specification, detailed coding and testing of the programs can be initiated, subject to an overall coordinated project plan. The user has a lesser role to play at this stage, although, inevitably, there will be queries on the specification and some changes may be necessary. However, it should be understood that any changes by the user after the programming has started can cause disruptions to the system out of all proportion to the modification requested.

Implementation

The programmers are responsible for testing the logic of their programs, individually and when linked together, but it is the user's responsibility to oversee the systems testing which initiates the implementation stage.

With the help of computer staff, the user must prepare test data that will rigorously explore the new system in an operational environment and that will also set standards for accepting the system. The time required for systems testing is difficult to estimate and may be the most harrowing period of the project. It must not, however, be evaded or skimped, because the errors it will find will otherwise inevitably crop up during live running, to everyone's consternation.

Wherever possible and practicable, there should be a period of parallel running, where the results of the new system are compared with the existing methods, before the organization finally commits itself to the computer. Obviously, if the new system embraces several related procedures or heralds a new departure from current practices, it may be difficult to make complete comparisons.

Improved development methodologies

The approach to the development of systems described above – the 'classic approach' – has a number of shortcomings which create particular difficulties when designing large, complex systems.

1 Because it is firmly based on the analysis of procedures, it is often difficult to break free from the tendency to re-create on the computer what is happening in existing systems. No matter how rigorously today's practices are challenged and how firmly emphasis is placed on future information needs (What?), rather than on the mechanics of processing (How?), the outcome is often only an elaboration of current systems.

2 The process of development can be long and tedious and, as we have seen, often results in computer applications that fail to satisfy the users.

3 The perennial user/DP communication problem is not eased by the quantity and quality of documentation that is used to represent the system, which is usually narrative in form and uses the physical representation of computer devices to illustrate the system.

Throughout the 1970s there were several innovations that attempted to overcome these shortcomings and, at the same time, bring a greater degree of professionalism to bear on the problems of analysis and design. Perhaps the most significant development was the concept of data analysis, which is based on the premise that, while procedures in an organization may change, there is a permanence about the nature and the content of the data on which those procedures, or any replacement system, will operate. Through data analysis it is possible to represent the activities of the whole organization, or some subdivision of it, without being circumscribed by the structure of current procedures. Identifying the discrete elements of data enables the analyst to build a model of the organization, or sub-unit, that forms the framework for the creation of a database that will service information needs. Shortcomings in the representation of computer systems have been overcome by the development of techniques that use logical relationships between data to demonstrate requirements, which users understand, rather than the physical identification of computer devices or processes, which users may have difficulty in relating to their operations.

These developments in structured methodologies and latterly in information engineering techniques have proved extremely valuable in the analysis and design of complex systems. What is more important, they have won the support of users, who understand the processes of computerization more readily when they are expressed in terms that relate clearly to the activities being performed in an organization. However, these techniques have not replaced traditional methods, which remain viable for the majority of standard computer developments. Potential users can at least take comfort in the knowledge that systems development methodologies continue to improve and, in harness with the facilities increasingly available with fourth generation languages and prototyping techniques, that systems more closely attuned to their needs are more likely to be developed.

In the next chapter we deal with the problems associated with planning and controlling new systems development projects, and the mechanisms by which management can monitor performance and exert influence over events.

7   Keeping control of projects

The Chief Executive should regard systems design as another of
the delegated responsibilities over which he has the ultimate
authority. It is not always seen in this light.

F.W. Latham and G.S. Sanders,
(*Urwick, Orr on Management*, Heinemann, 1980)

Introduction

In the years since their inception, the surveys of data processing
problem areas carried out by Urwick Dynamics reveal the concern
expressed by computer managers with the difficulties of meeting
deadlines for computer projects. Over the same period there has
been an equally significant decrease in anxiety over staff recruitment, which seems to imply that a lack of personnel was not the
prime reason for missed target dates. My own limited researches
suggest that it may have more to do with the productivity and
experience of existing computer staff than with the availability of
such resources. In particular, there continues to be a dearth of
senior computer staff who are able to estimate, plan and control
projects with any degree of confidence. One frequently hears of
projects which are several months late and way over budget, while
the system that is implemented on time and within cost is a rare
occurence. It has reached the stage where failure is accepted as
normal and where a six-month delay on a two-year project may be
considered an achievement.

We have examined some of the reasons for this state of affairs in
the previous chapter. I would now like to concentrate on one
particular area that general management often assume, wrongly,
to be the sole preserve of the computer expert. This is the management of a systems development project from inception through to
implementation. The falsity of the assumption arises not merely
from the tendency for delegation of responsibility to become

abdication but also from a belief that computer staff invariably have the knowledge, training and pertinacity to manage their own skills. Unfortunately, many data processing practitioners have been inadequately schooled in the planning and control of time and resources and badly need the support of experienced managers.

Any deficiencies rarely stem from a lack of ability, as the intellectual quality of many computer staff is exceptional. In part they arise from the absence of commonly accepted professional disciplines in a field that favours the individualism of the craftsman in preference to mass production techniques. Because of the nature of computing and the extreme specialization of the trainee that is fostered by early dedication to one machine or one language, it is difficult to acquire a truly professional training. It should come as no surprise that surveys have revealed that on average less than 0.5% of data processing budgets is allocated to training in computer skills. Without the proper training, computer staff have to learn 'on the job' and as a result costly mistakes may occur which could have been avoided with more forethought on the part of both general management and the computer executive. Some organizations, mainly those with a major commitment to computing, take the trouble to construct staff training programmes and to develop their management skills at senior levels, but it is not a common practice.

Knowing that a great deal of progress has been made in computerizing project planning and control procedures in recent years, especially since the widespread introduction of microcomputers, I enquired among colleagues about the availability of suitable software packages for use on computer projects. It turned out that one colleague had been closely involved in a study of this requirement for a very large, multi-computer user. His survey of project control packages revealed about 120 offerings that would operate on a variety of machines, from microcomputers to mainframes. However, few of them were directed specifically at computer projects, though all claimed, with some justification, to cover the essentials.

The principles of planning and control

In the previous chapter we described the development cycle as an evolutionary process in which the system was progressively explored, level by level, until a solution in the form of production programs was achieved. We stressed that each level management should demand the opportunity of re-evaluating the implications of a decision to proceed to the next level, bearing in mind the increasing difficulty of beating a retreat once you have committed resources. Whether you regard each of the phases in this evolution as separate entities or treat them as stages of a whole project, the principles of planning and control which should be applied remain the same. The approach described in this chapter offers no miracle cure to the common ailments of computer projects, but it has proved successful in minimizing complications in the vast majority of cases where it has been applied. Many of the techniques will strike familiar notes with engineers, architects and similar professionals, who are frequently called upon to plan and coordinate the activities of divers resources.

This approach is described under the following headings:

- the analysis of the project into the jobs to be done;
- estimation of the work content of those jobs;
- planning the work and allocating resources;
- controlling performance and reporting progress; and
- controlling change.

Additionally, we must not lose sight of the fact that project management operates broadly on two levels: one is concerned with the internal control of project activities; the other relates the project to the overall objectives of the organization.

Analysing the project

Notwithstanding the overt simplicity presented by clear terms of reference and objectives, most projects other than those lasting only a few weeks can look immense and rather complex to start with, and a novice project manager may be uncertain where to begin. The result may be a period of unproductive exploratory work or concentration on matters of detail before the problem has been properly delineated. I believe that the best way to deal with a big problem is to break it down into a number of smaller problems, as these usually turn out to be easier to resolve. This approach to project management offers a technique for analysing the problem based on a simple hierarchy of definitions which perpetuates the concept of a level-by-level analysis of the project.

According to this technique, a project will consist of a number of stages, each stage requiring a number of activities to take place and each activity comprising a number of tasks.

1 A stage will coincide with one of the levels described in the previous chapter, i.e. programming is a project stage.

2 An activity is a group of related tasks which is under the control of one person, although many staff may be involved. Normally it should not exceed three months elapsed time. An activity will have a clearly defined start and finish and the end product will be known in advance, e.g. preparation of program specifications will be an activity within the programming stage and the end product(s) will be program specifications.

3 A task is a specific job within an activity, performed by one person. No task should exceed ten days work content, although it is conceivable that the elapsed time for the task may be longer. In any event a task will have a stated beginning and end and an identifiable output. For example, preparing the specification for a nominated program will be one task within the activity known as preparation of program specifications.

In each of these definitions we have stressed that there should be clear start and finish points, that the duration or work content should be prescribed in advance and that the completion of the work should be signalled by an identifiable end product. The completion of an activity will be marked by a project milestone. Identification of milestones is a simple technique for focusing attention on key events in the duration of the project and they will normally coincide with the completion of an activity, although there may be several subsidiary milestones to augment control during an activity of long duration.

It may already have occured to you that it is possible to have a standard hierarchical framework of stages and activities, whatever the nature of the computer application. For example, we know in advance that the programming stage will at least have the following activities:

- studying the system specification;
- deciding the programming strategy;
- defining file structures (which will be common to all programs in the application);

- preparing program specifications (for each program in the application);
- program writing; and
- testing.

We should also know that within the program-writing activity there are standard tasks to complete, such as flowcharting, coding, desk checking, compiling, etc. It should not take much intellectual effort to interpret a specific application, say stock recording and control, in terms of this hierarchy of jobs to be done. However, there is an additional dimension to be considered which reflects the way in which the system is conceived in processing terms. For example, the stock recording and control system is in effect a collection of subsystems comprising, say:

- a set of input programs;
- updating programs;
- output programs; and
- enquiry programs.

Nevertheless, the same hierarchical technique can be used for identifying the activities and tasks for each subsystem.

Some computer specialists baulk at the prospect of this type of pre-planning and are anxious, naturally, to get to grips with the computer and the activities they most enjoy – problem solving, systems design, programming, manipulating the software, and so on. However, experience has shown that projects which are front-end loaded in terms of planning effort tend to progress more easily through the later detailed stages and to be more successful. For instance, one of the most important results of a proper analysis of the jobs to be done will be to identify those areas in which there is an element of innovation or where special skills are required which the organization may not possess; for example, if you have long experience of successful implementation of batch systems, this is no guarantee that a move to an on-line enquiry system will be painless or that your staff will be able to accomplish it without additional expertise, although they may be tempted to think they can. The implications are not solely technical, although you will need to acquire knowledge and skill in on-line procedures, screen layouts, etc.; there are also the potential problems arising from the creation of a new user interface with the computer, involving acceptability, confidence, training and methods of work.

Estimating

Identifying the jobs to be done to complete a project is a necessary forerunner to the difficult process of estimating the amount of work involved. There is no value in precise estimates of work if tasks or even whole activities have been overlooked at the pre-planning stage. If your organization has an established data processing function there will be some past experience of development performance on which to draw when formulating estimates for new projects, although this may not be a good guide if you have a record of missed or late deadlines. The personal competence of the estimator ('How long would I take?') is also an unreliable basis for determining the productivity of resources, the identity of which may not even be known at this stage.

For some activities, such as programming, we have begun to accumulate experience and guidelines that enable estimators to be more confident of their guesses, but these parameters are not yet at a level of general acceptance which establishes them as industry standards. Furthermore, there are other areas, such as systems analysis work, where it is much more difficult to be precise about the work content because of the number of imponderables that may be involved, e.g. time taken to reach agreement, the quality of user staff allocated to the project, etc. Nevertheless, the least we can do is to approach the matter in a disciplined and methodical manner.

1 Begin by making a broad estimate for each activity which should be based on the judgement and experience of the estimator.
2 Then estimate the work content for each task within the activity, bearing in mind that the definition of the task includes a limit of about ten days work. If the estimate suggests that more time is required you may be dealing with a job that could be usefully broken down further.
3 In estimating the work content of a task, take into account such factors as:
   - previous systems development experience;
   - the innovatory content;
   - the type of skills/experience required;
   - the degree of difficulty of the task;
   - the inter-dependence of tasks;

- · the extent to which performance may be influenced by external factors such as dealings with user staff, liaison with suppliers, contact with union representatives, etc.

  If you are in any doubt about the validity of an estimate, seek a second opinion. In fact, it is probably good practice to involve more than one senior person in the estimating process.

4 You should ensure that estimates include allowances for the time required to document the work and to review progress and results as the activity develops.

5 Having estimated each task within an activity, accumulate a total and compare it with the broad estimate made initially. If there is a major discrepancy in either direction, re-examine your assumptions to establish where the main points of difference occur.

6 Arrive at a total of task estimates for the activity and accumulate with the totals for other activities.

The sum of estimates for each activity makes up the total work content for the project stage. To this amount should be added an allowance to cover project management and direct supervision, say 20%, and a contingency factor of, say, 15% to provide flexibility in response to unforeseen events or delays. These allowances are for the discretionary use of project management in planning the project and are *not* intended to be divided up among individual tasks or to provide a cushion for flabby estimates.

The discipline and credibility of the estimating process is assisted if it is formally documented rather than jotted down in rough. Established data processing departments may have a standard estimating procedure, and I would advise any potential user to ask to see how the estimate for his own work has been compiled. The process we have described is illustrated in the sample document shown in Figure 7.1.

Planning

The disciplines of identifying activities and tasks and estimating their work content are of course all part of the general process of planning a project. What we are concerned with in this section, however, is the approach to matching these jobs, and the work they represent, to the resources that the project manager has available. Ideally, these resources should be known, in terms of

	DATE
ACTIVITY TIME ESTIMATE	

PROJECT NAME:					PROJECT CODE
ACTIVITY:				ACTIVITY LEADER	ACTIVITY CODE

TASK OR MILESTONE	ESTIMATED DAYS	DAYS TO DATE	ACTUAL DAYS	TARGET DATE	COMMENTS

Figure 7.1 Activity time estimate chart

the pool of skills and experience that can be drawn on, and should be available for commitment on a full-time basis; nothing is more likely to erode project performance than reliance on part-time resources. Unfortunately, circumstances are rarely ideal and the project manager may find that the estimated total manpower requirement cannot be met from existing personnel within the envisaged time-scale or that the need for certain special skills will introduce training or recruitment into the project. This may call for a review of the estimates or for a revision of the implementation date; in any event it will emphasise the need for close monitoring of progress in the early stages in order to validate the planning standards.

Procedures adopted for planning vary between organizations. Some companies have constructed elaborate networks and identify and sequence the various activities involved in launching projects, but it is surprising how few survive the first. In my view, the reason for this is that once you technique to identify the activities, you will hav main problem and subsequent control of those activities does not warrant the sophistication of network planning. Other organizations use variations of the Gantt or bar chart to record both the plan and its achievement, and I believe this is a clearer and more understandable way of representing project progress to management. The activity bar chart is a feature of the approach I am describing in this section, and takes the form illustrated in Figure 7.2. There will be summary bar charts at higher levels which show the plan for the various stages and for the project as a whole.

The construction of a plan utilizing this approach involves the following steps.

1   Record the main activities on the activity bar chart, bearing in mind the guidelines that:
    ● one person is clearly responsible;
    ● duration should not exceed three months elapsed time;
    ● the activity should end with a milestone, although there may be interim milestones.
2   Plan the work content of each activity on the basis of a 3½ – 4 day week to allow for occasional holidays, sickness, training and other contingencies. Take note of the incidence of public holidays, factory closures, annual holidays, etc., where these are known and will affect elapsed time.
3   Allow 2 – 3 weeks for all important decisions involving management or users, especially if users have to 'sign-off' systems.
4   Identify and emphasise the milestones and make it clear that they are there to be achieved. While tasks may overrun and additional resources may be called for, the milestone should be regarded as inviolable and should never be missed, without early warning and a very good reason.
5   Make staff and users aware of the plan and the importance of keeping to it. There is no reason for secrecy, especially towards the personnel on whom the success of the plan ultimately depends.

Planning is both the mechanism for identifying what has to be done and the means of anticipating problems. Too often plans are regarded as set in concrete and people are reluctant to change them. This is a misconception; the existence of a plan provides the ~wledge with which to respond to factors affecting the project in

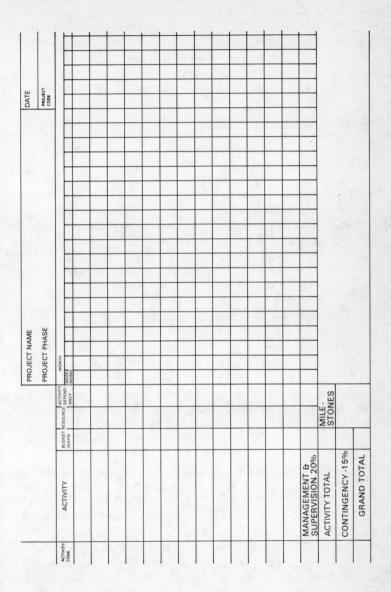

Figure 7.2 Activity bar chart

order to minimize their adverse effect. Without a plan, actions might be taken that would be wrong in themselves or would have a knock-on effect on subsequent activities. Thus, plans should be subject to regular review but not necessarily frequent change. The bases for review are the results of the week-by-week execution of the tasks that make up the principal activities of the project.

Project control

In the early days of computing it was not unusual for a programmer to be given a brief statement of a problem and to be sent away to write a program to solve it. As likely as not, at some unspecified point, his supervisor would ask how he was getting on and the programmer would usually respond encouragingly. Thus, performance on an imprecise task set by the supervisor would be assessed subjectively by the programmer and accepted at face value. Unfortunately there are still some data processing departments that operate in this fashion, and many programmers have been trained without attention being given to more precise methods of control of progress.

An advance on this subjective approach is the pseudo-precise assessment of progress, typified by the comment 'I am 80% through the program', which is in common use in many computer installations. The problems really begin when not only is the assessment of progress in error but also the amount of time left to recoup the situation is minimal. All too often the rational assessment of the achievement and the remaining work, which should have been a feature of the planning process before a word of coding was written, is promoted by the realization of imminent disaster.

The sensible way to control work positively is to plan it in detail, to allocate it in chunks that are capable of achievement in defined periods of time, and to specify how that achievement will be measured. Thus, we can ask the question 'Is the planned task complete?' If the answer is in the affirmative there should be concrete evidence of achievement, such as a report, a flowchart, a set of codes and so on. I emphasise again that there should be clear start and end points for a task and tangible evidence that the task has been completed.

In the approach we are examining, the project manager will be aware of the activities planned for the next three or four months. Within each activity he will know the tasks which have to be completed and the resources that have been allocated. Like any production man, he will wish to maintain positive control of work on a week-by-week basis. Similarly, his managers and the user will require reassurance about the project at, say, monthly intervals. The techniques available to him within this approach are:

- short-term scheduling;
- progress monitoring; and
- project reporting

Short-term scheduling
At prescribed intervals the project manager should prepare a list of tasks to be accomplished within the next scheduling cycle. The frequency of this schedule and the amount of 'look ahead' involved will depend on the confidence of the manager and the amount of work in progress outstanding. However, we have said that ideally no task should exceed ten days duration and on that basis, with several tasks in progress, it is likely that a project manager would make weekly reviews and look ahead at least two weeks. What is critical is that he should know what everyone is doing and be aware of any imminent task completions or milestones.

We should perhaps amplify the constraint imposed by the insistence that task duration should be limited to ten days. Obviously there will be some jobs, which sensibly must be treated as whole entities and desirably allocated to one person, that exceed this limit. For instance, the project manager may wish to allocate a complete program, estimated as six weeks work, to one individual. However, it would be foolish to allocate the work and six weeks later expect to see the end product. Quite apart from slippage and the dangers of unbalanced application of effort during that period, there is a need for the technical contribution that a supervisor can and should make to the development of the program if it is to fit within the overall strategy for the project. Thus, in scheduling the work, the project manager will identify points at which a sensible review of progress and technical content can be made.

Progress monitoring

This will usually, but not invariably, coincide with a weekly review of progress against the plan for the current activity. Progress against each task is checked off against the budget for the activity (see Figure 7.1) and the effect on the plan calculated. Particular attention should be paid to tasks not completed, or in danger of overrunning, and the reasons for the shortfall thoroughly explored. Early warning of problem areas is essential. At the risk of over-burdening you and the project manager with paperwork, I suggest that at this stage you need to record overall progress on the activity separately and in a form which enables full project reports to be generated on a monthly basis. This can be accomplished using the type of document illustrated in Figure 7.3, on which the project manager should record:

- actual effort against budget;
- estimated time to complete;
- any revision to the budget;
- estimated completion date;

and any suitable and printable comments on progress. If as a result of the weekly review there is any suggestion that the activity bar chart (Figure 7.2) may have to be revised, then something is seriously wrong and immediate action should be taken. I am amazed how often shortfalls are reported without a flicker of remorse, received with hardly a word of recrimination and reacted to sluggishly.

Some years ago I was asked to comment on the reasons why a particular project was several months late. It turned out that there were many factors that had contributed to the failure of the project, of which perhaps the most significant was the complete inexperience of the computer staff in both systems work and project management because of their previous dedication solely to programming (at which they were highly competent). However, one of the more intriguing aspects was that at fortnightly progress meetings (a good point) run by the user (a better point), progress was recorded, although nobody was delegated to act upon the results. Thus, a program would be reported as being behind schedule but, because the target date was away in the future, the shortfall was merely noted. At subsequent meetings the shortfall remained the same, or more likely increased slightly, until, as the deadline approached, it was

CODE	PROJECT	ACTIVITY	TOTAL DAYS	RESOURCES	START
					END

No.	TASK	TARGET DATE	EST. DAYS	PERSON		WEEKS ENDING												COMMENTS
					PLAN													
					ACTUAL													
					ACCUM. ACT													
					EST. TO GO													
					DIFF.													
					PLAN													
					ACTUAL													
					ACCUM. ACT													
					EST. TO GO													
					DiFF.													
					PLAN													
					ACTUAL													
					ACCUM. ACT													
					EST. TO GO													
					DIFF.													

Figure 7.3 Activity progress chart.

realized that the backlog was now immense and there was no alternative but to declare a new implementation date.

Situations such as this can be avoided by a degree of anticipatory progressing effort on the part of the project manager and a determination to nip overruns in the bud rather than allow them to develop into major arrears.

Project reporting

It is all too easy for computer staff, wrapped in the technicalities and complexities of a major system, to consider that they are the only or the most important party concerned with the success of the project. The actual situation reveals a diversity of interests, as illustrated in Figure 7.4, especially when there may be several activities moving in parallel. Thus, within the computer department there may be reporting relationships between activity team leaders to the project manager and between the project manager and the executive in charge of the computer function. There is a much more fundamental link between the project and the prospective user, who may or may not be closely involved in the current activity but who has a right to know what is going on. Then there is general management, who not only want reassurance that a particular investment is being profitably pursued but also want to know that the computing function is being properly managed.

These differing requirements call for a variety of manipulations of the same planning and performance data and, like most reporting structures, imply a selection and distillation of content as you move up the management tree. At the very least:

- project managers should provide monthly progress reports to the head of computing and to the users;
- the head of computing should provide a summary of project progress and a review of the computing function to management on a monthly basis.

The hierarchy of reports involved in an ideal situation is illustrated in Figure 7.5. The representation of the efficiency and effectiveness of the whole computer function and the contents of these reports are discussed in a subsequent chapter.

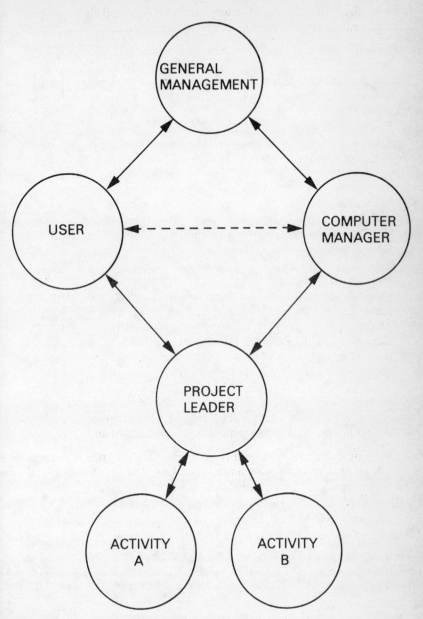

Figure 7.4 Project structure

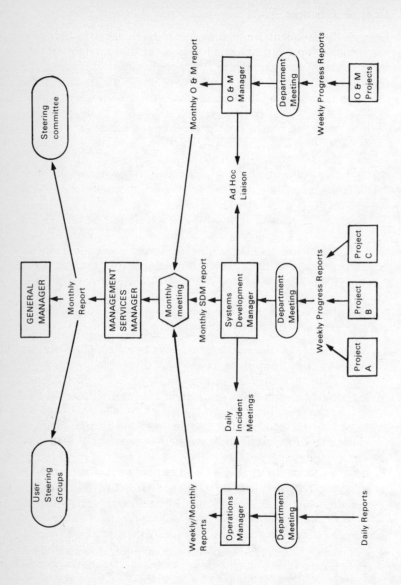

Figure 7.5 Project reporting structure

Control of changes

One of the frequent complaints made about users is that they cannot make up their minds; another is that having done so they are constantly changing them. It is not altogether surprising that managers and staff who are unused to dealing with computers find difficulty in expressing their needs in a form that immediately and completely satisfies the dictates of good data processing practices. If they could, we would not need systems analysts to act as go-betweens in developing systems. Nevertheless, there are points at which a change of mind or a new requirement can be incorporated without great difficulty, and a well constructed systems development technique will be designed to give this flexibility and to trap errant needs, right up to the last minute.

There will come a time, however, when no matter how strong may be the case for change, it would be foolish to accede to it for fear of jeopardizing either the structure of the system or the adherence to a deadline. This will usually be the situation once programming is well advanced and it would be difficult or costly to revise the system.

From the point of view of project control, there are really three disciplines to observe in responding to requests for change.

1 To acknowledge the existence of a 'frozen zone' within which it would be folly to entertain changes.

2 To ensure that a formal mechanism exists for processing and authorizing changes once the system has been officially 'signed off' by the user. In other words, the user should be disciplined to justify his request for change and the project manager should be expected to confirm whether or not, and with what effects, the changes can be made.

3 Thirdly, to ensure that any changes that are not accepted are properly recorded for the first (next) formal review of the system in operation. For instance, the better installations adopt a standard practice of carrying out post-implementation reviews at regular intervals to ensure that the system is operating satisfactorily and is continuing to meet the needs of the user. These reviews might take place after six months, after 18 months and, as a major re-examination, after three years operation. In between appraisals, the unactioned requests for change are filed together for resurrection at the next review.

It is up to general management to arbitrate in circumstances where the user and the computer department cannot agree, bearing in mind their overall concern that the investment which the project represents should bear fruit within the parameters set by the justification study. Excessive change, that might call into question the quality of the systems analysis work, may create a situation in which the project has to be re-evaluated in the light of new requirements.

Project management

It will be apparent from the above that the project manager is a rather special type of person. He requires the competence to plan and control a technical function but has also to be aware of the users and his interests. Indeed, in some projects, he may be allocated the responsibility of coordinating non-computer resources and activities, for example the host of O & M-type activities essential to the preparation of the user environment and staff in order to receive and operate the new system. He may even be allocated user personnel as part of the project team. Many computer staff who become project leaders are not only light on supervisory experience within their own function but have also rarely had the wider exposure to management of multi-resourced teams and the responsibility for performance to an external customer that many large projects demand. The tendency is often for the computer team to become isolated from the end user and to concentrate on the parts they know most about, while the user is left unaware of progress unless some commitment is required from him, such as the provision of suitable test data. The ideal project manager will not only keep his customer fully appraised of developments, in language that he can understand, he will also encourage the user to participate in the project. User involvement is essential when designing the system and it is always possible that technical complexities can be eradicated if a user is aware that his demands are creating difficulties that might prejudice other more important features of the system.

A user had requested that the system should cater for the production of certain infrequent statistical returns. This requirement introduced complications in file structures and in certain associated programs which began to emerge as testing proceeded. After struggling to achieve clean programs, the worsening situation was reviewed with the user, who admitted that the reports could be produced quite easily by clerical means and that he had only asked for them to be computerized because he was told to 'think of everything' from the beginning. Quite apart from the implication that systems analysis had been casual, it was also apparent that there had been no communication between the user and the project for several months.

In an attempt to achieve a closer integration of computing within the organization, some companies have veered towards appointing a non-computer person as the project manager, on the basis that managerial and functional experience are more important and less easily obtained than technical competence. There is merit in this approach, although there are obvious dangers that, by default or intent on the part of the technicians, the project manager may acquire a false understanding of technical matters and project progress because of poor communication within the team. Where a non-computer person is made project manager, it is essential that his immediate subordinate has the requisite technical skills to support the manager, not only in the detailed design and development of the system but also in the planning and control of the project.

I know of some cases where, instead of appointing a user executive as project manager or selecting a senior computer man, the organizations have opted for what I can only describe as a professional project manager. These individuals have been either existing members of staff or specially recruited people who owe allegiance to none of the principals and report direct to general management.

I saw this working extremely well while on an overseas assignment. The client had been attempting for some time to implement a fairly complicated payroll package and had made little progress because of constant conflict between the user and the computer department. In desperation, he engaged a subcontract project manager who proceeded to re-form the project team with subcontract staff and a reduced representation from both the users and the computer department, whom he insisted were under his day-to-day control. There were some initial problems, but the clamour of dissent gradually subsided and, to the client's relief, perceptible progress was made. The project was still late overall in being implemented but had not fallen further behind and, in some areas, had achieved the original target dates.

In forming the project team and developing the system, these managers regard the user and the data processing department alike as potential providers of resources which, once allocated, are managerially their concern. It is an interesting development which probably has greatest value for large projects in large concerns, but the choice of individual is critically important. He must be sufficiently knowledgeable to satisfy both the computer expert and the prospective user and have enough presence to carry clout at management level – sounds like an expensive person . . . or possibly a consultant!

The role of the user

In the following chapter we will examine the role of users, both existing and prospective, in the development and management of computer systems, but at this stage it is perhaps worth recording the contribution that the user can make to project control.

1 In the first place, authorization of a project depends on the potential user agreeing that the proposal meets his requirements and that he can obtain specified benefits from implementing the system. At this crucial point the user should also satisfy himself that the plan for the project is rationally based and that arrangements for monitoring progress are adequate, including provisions for user participation in development and project control.

2 It is almost inevitable that, as the development unfolds, the user will wish to vary his original requirements or add new ones and will be tempted to insist on changes. This prerogative must be exercised with care and discipline, and in the knowledge of the effects the changes may have, otherwise the fabric of the project may be threatened.

3 During the life of the project the user must insist on being fully appraised of the progress being made, of any problems that arise, even if they are technical, and of the commitment expected from the user department.

Perhaps the most important objective is to eradicate any feelings of 'them and us' and to strive for a true partnership in the development and introduction of a change that is designed to affect the whole organization.

Guidelines

The aim of this chapter has been to underline the principles applicable to the planning and control of computer projects. As managers, you will be aware that they hardly differ from the approach adopted for many management tasks. In authorizing your computer project, however small it may be and no matter how many staff may be involved, you should at least ensure that similar disciplines are observed. In particular, you should be satisfied that the following minimum requirements are met.

1 That the terms of reference and objectives for the project are clearly stated and understood, together with any cost or time constraints that are integral to the project.
2 That the man appointed to manage the project has the requisite personal skills and access to resources that will enable him to fulfil his commitments.
3 That adequate procedures exist and are used to analyse the jobs that have to be done, to estimate the resources required, to plan and allocate the work and to control performance.
4 That satisfactory arrangements are introduced to ensure user participation and effective management control of the project.

Computer projects are highly volatile; if they are ignored they get out of hand very quickly and either blow up or set the most unpleasant booby-traps for the unsuspecting manager.

8   The exercise of user power

Introduction

Some years ago I was present, as an observer, at what I was assured would be a routine meeting between data processing staff and the end user on the progress of the current project. The computer department was represented by the systems development manager, the project leader and the principal systems analyst. The user had fielded heavier guns in the shape of the divisional general manager, the head of the department mainly affected by the project and two or three section leaders. It quickly became apparent that this would be no ordinary meeting as the project leader unfolded a tale of unrelieved gloom, culminating in a request for a further authorization of funds. (This organization followed the practice of submitting formal quotations to users for both development and operating expenditure.) There followed a question and answer session of growing intensity, with the computer staff attempting to defend unsuccessfully a largely untenable record of under-achievement and escalating cost. The exchanges became heated, abusive and recriminatory, but I was totally unprepared for the climax, when the general manager and the project leader rose to their feet and, but for the intervention of their colleagues, might have come to blows. The meeting was abandoned and there followed a bitter exchange of memoranda that led ultimately to the cancellation of the project with the computer department. The user, however, pursued his requirements with the aid of a software house and eventually implemented his system satisfactorily.

The possibility of physical confrontation, demonstrated in this case, is not what I mean by the exercise of user power and it must be emphasised that this incident is unique in my experience. Nevertheless, the circumstances and behaviour that prepared the ground for this outburst are not uncommon.

1 Firstly there was ample evidence of a lack of communication between the parties concerned with the project, so that the latest bad news came as a complete surprise to the prospective user.

2 On the other hand, previous poor experience with the performance of the computer staff should have alerted management to the possibility of delays and excess cost at an earlier stage, but the user staff charged with liaison had been remiss in carrying out their responsibilities.

3 Both user and computer management were at fault in allowing divisive attitudes to develop among staff who should have had a close day-to-day working relationship.

4 Whenever computer departments charge for their services they automatically invite comment on value for money and comparison with alternative sources of supply, especially in organizations that operate with decentralized authority.

5 In the end, the user felt sufficiently confident of his need for computer support that he could justify turning to an external source to implement his system.

In this case the general manager was fortunate in having the authority to take an alternative course of action; this option may not be available to the average user who, because of the spread of computing, may be relatively lowly placed in an organization. What then is the nature of user power and in which circumstances and by what means should it be exercised?

I am not unaware of the almost limitless opportunities presented by computer technology to man – to extend his capacity for learning, to develop his environment, to broaden his intellectual and artistic horizons and to make feasible what our ancestors could only dream about. Nevertheless, so far as the application of computers to business, commercial or administrative processes is concerned, I have a more pragmatic view. A computer is an asset to be exploited in support or extension of the objectives of the organization and, unless this can be accomplished efficiently and effectively, and with demonstrable benefit, you might be better off without one. The user, before he becomes a user, is just as much bending his back in support of the aims of the enterprise as he is afterwards; the advent of computers, far from diminishing his stature, should be directed at enhancing his abilities to contribute to those aims. A computer may offer opportunities to revise the ways in which some activities are performed, or even remove their raison d'être, but, unless the user is in harmony with such changes, they are unlikely to be successful.

For me, therefore, the essence of user power is that the user should be effectively in control of computing, wherever it may lie organizationally, and he should retain the initiative in deciding how it should be applied. If there is any doubt as to whether the user is exercising this power correctly and in the best interests of the organization, then it is the responsibility of general management to intervene.

User experience

I suspect that this view would not be shared by a majority of in-house computer personnel, whatever they say when marketing their services. Historically, users have tended to come a poor third in the success stakes behind 'the profession' and 'the art', and it is hardly surprising to find that they are becoming more militant and vociferous in demanding a better deal. They are assisted currently by major developments in technology, which have made a greater variety of cheap hardware and software facilities available, and by a marketing policy which has dramatically reduced the costs of making mistakes.

It was not always so. The early high cost of entry into data processing and the scarcity of the requisite skills to apply computers combined to encouraged organizations to centralize the service. Furthermore, there was a prevailing view that the computer provided the means for radically changing the structure and operation of the organization and that this revolution in control should be directed from the centre. Although many of these early machines were initially introduced for a particular application, e.g. manufacturing control or financial ledgers, it was not long before the concept of integrated management information systems began to dominate the systems development strategies of most companies. So the average potential user, waiting patiently in the queue for the first big job to be computerized, now found himself perhaps further back because his application had a low priority in the long-term plan. If the initial systems caused problems during development or implementation, these added to the delay and frustration experienced by those in the waiting list. Furthermore, as each new system became operational it required a commitment to maintenance which reduced the resources available for new developments. Estimates of the commitment of resources to application maintenance have varied between 30 – 60%; in any event it has been too high and has severely limited opportunities for new developments.

If the user was fortunate in being near the head of the queue, he may not always have been happy with the outcome. He might have experienced some or all of the problems we have described elsewhere:

- difficulties in communicating requirements to computer staff;
- delays in designing the system;
- excess costs, over which he had no control;
- varying degrees of chaos when the application went live;
- realization that the system did not meet his needs;
- discovery that nothing had been documented and modifications were out of the question;
- recognition that the benefits on which the system was justified would not be achieved.

He may also have realized that the system was no longer his; it belonged in some sense to the computer and his role had been diminished.

Some organizations, from an early stage, insisted that computer services should be charged out either at a cost or at a pseudo-commercial rate that was designed to promote efficiency and to create funds for re-investment. Thus, a prospective user might be advised that it would cost £50,000 to develop his system and approximately £5,000 per annum to operate it. Being a captive market, he probably has no basis for comparing or challenging these figures, but he should be able to relate those costs to expected benefits. However, the probability is that the development period will overrun and excess costs will be incurred. Quite apart from arguments over who collects the bill for the additional cost, the organization may have lost out on some or all of the anticipated benefits. The frustrations of users are increased when they seek a modification or enhancement to an existing system. 'When Mr X (the systems development manager) comes to see me (a divisional manager) his eyes light up like a cash register. No matter what I ask for it is almost always a six month job and invariably costs *y* thousand dollars.'

It should come as no surprise that many users have acquired cynical attitudes towards computer staff and are generally dissatisfied with the level and quality of the service they have received. The exceptions are those cases where, by dint of personality or management style, the user has been given or has assumed the dominant role in systems development. This arises, for instance, where the philosophy of the organization favours a decentralized management structure, with profit responsibility vested in local units. In these circumstances, unit managers have the implicit right to challenge the validity of a policy of centralized computer services and many have done so quite successfully. Others have received a temporary set back to their plans.

A manufacturing division of a major industrial group had made use of central computer services for a number of years. The pattern of applications development was fairly typical. First of all, standard accounting procedures were introduced, followed by a stock recording and control system. There followed an attempt to computerize production planning and control procedures that was only partially successful. All the systems were operated on a batch basis at the computer centre, which was over a 100 miles from the plant. Local managers were not satisfied with the quality of the systems development nor with the level of service provided by the computer centre, which always seemed pre-occupied with machine enhancements, conversion exercises, software upgrades and experimenting with new facilities. One good thing that emerged from these central activities was the introduction of an on-line enquiry facility, but otherwise improvements were marginal.

With their agreement and some assistance from the centre, the division reviewed its future requirements, especially in manufacturing planning and control, and came up with a comprehensive specification based on on-line facilities. The central computer service was asked to quote for the development work, to indicate what extra equipment would be required, centrally and locally, and to estimate the annual processing charges to the division. The results were quite horrifying:

- one-off costs, incorporating development and equipment, involved several hundred thousand pounds; and,
- annual operating costs were also expected to be in six figures.

Furthermore, the development would take over three years to implement.

Divisional management expressed their opinion of these estimates in no uncertain terms and set about finding an alternative approach. Utilizing their own systems team, they drew up plans to introduce two minicomputers and to utilize manufacturing control packages provided by the equipment supplier. The outcome was a proposal that:

- could be developed and implemented for a third of the original cost;
- enabled the first package to be operational within six months and the whole project completed within two years;
- offered compatibility between the local minicomputers and the mainframe if it was necessary.

On the face of it, an extremely attractive and cost effective solution for the division and for the group. However, the centralist lobby was very powerful and they argued that the loss of a major customer would seriously undermine the economics of the central installation, which was being enhanced, and would put up the costs to all the other divisions. Separate development would dissipate the benefits of a group approach to computing, among which was numbered the concentration of skills and expertise that were difficult to acquire. They also reduced their quotation substantially!

It came as no surprise when the project was shelved pending further investigations.

It remains to be seen how long the established patterns of user/computer department relationships will survive the impact of cheap computing facilities and the parallel development of software techniques that enable users to take advantage of them.

The impact of technology

The traditional computer manager operating a central service is under siege. Not only has the pace of recent changes in cost/performance factors threatened to undermine the economics of his existing installation, which is perhaps only a few years old, but he is also faced with a rising clamour from users demanding their own facilities. Agreeing to these demands would reduce his customer base and erode further the viability of a central service. These changes not only affect existing users, but they also lower the threshold at which organizations can consider acquiring computer facilities.

There are several factors at work here.

- The economics of computing are changing because hardware costs are falling rapidly, whereas personnel costs are rising at a rate where maintenance of clerical systems becomes a luxury.
- There is no shortage of software aids, simple programming languages and, above all, standard application packages to help the user get off the ground quickly and relatively painlessly.
- Users and potential users tend to be much more knowledgeable about data processing than previously and are more confident of their ability to exploit computers.
- Above all, users want to manage their own systems and are less prepared to have them controlled remotely.

First time users are clearly much better placed to take advantage of the opportunities presented by these changes than organizations with a relatively long history of computer usage. New users do not have a prior commitment to a long-term computing strategy; there is no investment of hundreds of man-years in programs to write off; and they do not have a data processing unit which may have a vested interest in the status quo. For the existing user, these changes have reopened the whole question of centralization versus decentralization, and organizations have reacted differently to this challenge.

1 Some companies have persisted with a predominantly centralized policy but have encouraged the use of terminals and the development of on-line systems. Although this approach makes computing power more accessible to the user, it may not enhance his control over his systems and he is still dependent on the centre for the provision of development resources.
2 Other organizations have introduced a network of minicomputers connected to and dependent upon a mainframe, giving the user control over input/output and job initiation, with possibly a limited facility for local processing. Notwithstanding the improved facilities that this approach offers, again the user remains in the hands of the centre for development resources.
3 In other cases a more liberal policy has been developed which

allows the introduction of minicomputers or micros for dedicated applications, subject to central approval of capital expenditure, a common supplier policy and the central provision of programming resources. Under this regime, the lot of the user is vastly improved as he will almost certainly have a local systems analysis capability, as well as control over computing facilities.

4   In an increasing number of cases, the cheapness of microcomputers has enabled users to acquire them within their revenue budgets, almost regardless of any attempts at central coordination.

5   The ultimate relaxation of central control exists where individual units are given a relatively free hand to determine their local computing requirements, subject only to normal standards for justifying capital expenditure.

Although access to and control over computing facilities may have significant psychological benefit for users, the source of computing power is relatively unimportant. The critical issue is whether or not they are in a position to influence or determine systems design initiatives and to exercise positive control over the development process.

Mechanisms available to users

Over the years, several mechanisms have been devised to enable the user to exert influence over the application of computer techniques in his area, some of which are managerial while others involve him deeply in the procedural elements of systems development. Unless you choose to do it yourself, you will have to exploit one or more of these mechanisms in order to preserve any semblance of control.

Steering committees

Steering committees are much maligned institutions, not so much because they are intrinsically inadequate for the task but because they have been ill-used by management and computer staff alike. The mere mention of the term is likely to provoke a wry smile from the general manager and gales of laughter from systems analysts. The pattern of disillusionment is pretty well established.

The committee is set up initially to oversee the case for a

computer and invariably attracts the senior executives who are most anxious to stake a claim on any planned computing resource. At this stage, the committee is usually chaired by the chief executive because all the pundits say that it should be. The committee meets regularly, deliberates on proposals, seeks and is guided by expert advice, and finally concludes that a computer would be a good thing. If he is not already on the payroll, an expert is recruited to launch the project and the committee's role becomes that of a 'ways and means' committee, convened to sanction the detail of expenditures and actions already agreed in principle. Some time later the committee becomes involved in the detail of the first application and the growing problems of managing computer projects, leading eventually to consideration of day-to-day operational problems.

While this has been going on, the composition of the committee will have changed. Often the first to depart will be the chief executive, who has many more important tasks to perform, but he will leave the committee in the safe hands of the senior executive who is concerned with the first major application – quite possibly the financial director. At this point the other senior executives begin to lose interest but sensibly appoint one of their subordinates to maintain a foothold on the committee. Gradually, the interval between meetings lengthens and the seniority of those present spirals downwards until, inevitably, the committee loses credibility and is constitutionally ill-formed to arbitrate on the many important issues that can arise. At this point, we find that the most influential member of the steering committee is usually the computer manager. Enough said . . .

The problems arise because we are trying to use one institution to fulfil several different roles:

- as a capital sanctioning authority;
- as a policymaking body;
- as a forum for the debate of systems requirements; and
- as a line executive responsible for the computing function.

In my opinion, the only valid role for a steering committee is to act as a policymaking body. The responsibility for sanctioning capital expenditure is correctly a board function, although in practice it may be guided and advised by some form of executive or management committee that represents all the company's operations. Any debate of systems requirements should be confined to those parties with a direct interest in the application, and it can be perfectly well accommodated by other means. As for attempting to manage the computing function by committee, the mind boggles.

If a steering committee is to function principally as a policymaking body, it should concern itself primarily with the following tasks.

1 Ensuring that a long-term plan for the exploitation of computers exists and is adequately resourced.
2 Considering and, if appropriate, authorizing new projects or major expenditures that are consistent with the overall computing strategy.
3 Monitoring the general performance of the computing function in meeting the objectives of the computer plan.

To perform these functions adequately, the committee need meet no more frequently than every quarter and it should certainly demand the attention of all senior executives, whether users or prospective users:

User steering groups

By far the more important vehicle to the average user for getting his own way is the user steering group, but it is surprising how many organizations see it as subsidiary or subservient to our mythical steering committee. In practice, the user steering group provides the ideal opportunity for users.

- to explore the inadequacies of existing procedures;
- to begin to construct a framework of future systems that will satisfy or excel the objectives set for their function;
- to explore how these objectives can be achieved by computing techniques;
- to determine the relative contributions of the user and the specialist;
- to cement a working relationship between user and computer staff;
- to establish the parameters by which the contribution of computers will be measured;
- to monitor performance of a joint operation;
- to act as an authoritive body for seeking executive approval for major claims on the organization's resources.

Such a group should meet at least monthly and its decisions, except where overall computing policy is affected, should be regarded by the computing function as directives.

Working parties.
Working parties are a common phenomenon in computer projects, especially in the public sector, and arc usually sct up to work with computer staff during the investigation and data collection phase, as well as to act as a sounding board for the early design concepts. It is up to the user to ensure that such working groups are properly manned, not necessarily with the persons who know most about what goes on but with staff who have the intellectual flexibility to discriminate between what is important and what is a trivial manifestation of the existing procedure. All too often, user staff allocated to a computer project are those who can be most easily spared and are not the people who can contribute best to the definition of a future system. If you adopt this approach, you can hardly complain if more able computer staff assume the initiative in determining your future requirements. My advice is to put your best brains to work with the computer boys because it will put them on their mettle, it will ensure that the system which eventually emerges will have the support of user staff who can command respect, and it will go some way to guaranteeing the success of implementation.

Secondment
Some organizations have seconded user staff to the project team on a full-time basis, usually because of the complexity of the application or to meet the need for expert functional knowledge. This frequently happens, for example, where computers are being applied to production planning and control, whether or not the computer department can claim the requisite experience. The problem here, as with all secondments, is to ensure not only that the best people are released for the development team but also that perhaps two years away from his parent department will not impair the professional and career prospects of the person concerned. Nevertheless, full-time representation on the project team during the crucial analysis and design phases can be enormously helpful to the user. Not only has he a direct opportunity to influence the shape of the system but also his representative, if he

is doing his job properly, will be feeding back an understanding of data processing which helps prepare the ground for implementation.

One of the more successful approaches to secondment that I have come across is the one adopted by a large and highly successful international bank. At the insistence of the head of management services, users are obliged to nominate a line executive with a minimum of x years service in their function to serve as a joint leader of the project team until the proposed system is implemented. Because computing is now so critical to banking operations, there is an implication that in future, without this type of experience, the ambitious young banker will be less well equipped to make progress in the bank. The role of the seconded banker varies with the phases of the project, embracing:

- detailed involvement with the investigation and interpretation of the procedures under review;
- personal identification with the costs/benefits evaluation;
- contribution to the non-technical aspects of design;
- planning and control over the marshalling of user resources and management of the systems testing phase;
- preparation of user manuals and training courses;
- chairmanship of the fortnightly project progress meetings.

The success of this approach depends greatly on the personalities of the seconded individual and the senior computer man as they have to work in harmony and with respect for each other's contribution. Although I have reservations about one or two aspects of this approach, I am happy to say that it seems to work very well.

Project management

An extension of the practice of secondment is the appointment of a user representative as the project manager. This is a tricky situation as so much depends on the individual and on the job he is expected to carry out. Except in the most unusual cases, it is unlikely that a user project manager could fulfil the responsibilities of technical and design leadership, although he may know or acquire sufficient data processing background to contribute to development. His main contributions are likely to be management skills, coordinating ability and a positive commitment to achieving the objectives set for the project. From the organization's point of view, the appointment of a user as a project manager should remove one problem, namely the constant bickering between user and project leader over progress and cost, as these elements will now be under direct user control.

One of my clients had had a patchy record of achievement in developing and delivering very large real-time systems, although, once finally implemented, the systems worked well. When the next big application came along, management appointed a senior user manager to lead the project, hinting broadly that success would help his career. Eighteen months later the project was implemented before the target date and under budget. My regret is that I had not been party to the decision.

The development process
As we have described in a previous chapter, if you adopt a staged approach to the development of computer systems, you have also to accept certain disciplines. They include:

- clearly stated terms of reference and objectives before a stage is authorized;
- the authorization process itself which requires commitment on the part of management;
- a formal signing-off process that commits the user.

These disciplines can work to the advantage of the user who is anxious to obtain the best possible system. He should play a full part in constructing terms of reference and in setting objectives for the project before any commitment is undertaken. He can resist the authorization of a stage if he is dissatisfied either with the previous work or with the activities that are proposed for the future. Most important of all, he should not sign off any stage, particularly the business requirements specification, if he has any doubt that his requirements have been correctly understood and are catered for in the proposed system. Things can still go wrong during systems and programming work and he should take similar care in agreeing to subsequent stages.

User-based systems analysis
In response to user discontent and complaints that their unique requirements are being ignored, some organizations have fostered

the devlopment of systems analysis teams that are attached to or part of user departments. I believe that this is an excellent development and should be encouraged as, properly constituted and controlled, these teams should produce systems which are much more relevant to the user's needs than applications that may be developed remotely. It also facilitates the appointment of a user representative as project manager who, being a trained systems analyst, is particularly well placed to control all aspects of a project.

One financial institution I worked with had taken this development to the stage where 80% of data processing resources were fully assigned and accountable to the user. The central computer function was virtually confined to the provision of highly specialized technical support and the production service – not unlike a computer service bureau in many respects. Perhaps the more important outcome was that the erstwhile central computing staff developed a high degree of loyalty and commitment to their individual users.

Internal audit

A resource potentially available to users in the struggle to obtain effective computer systems and an efficient data processing service, which is not much used outside financial institutions, is the internal audit department. Properly constituted and briefed by management, this unit should concern itself with the identification of inefficiencies and waste, and the growth in computer systems provides particularly fertile ground for such investigation. Unfortunately, too often the unit is relegated to physical stock checks and monitoring the petty cash, and is rarely involved in major operational studies. However, if your organization is committed to computing on a large scale, you should recognize that there will be an increasing number of procedures which are known in detail by fewer and fewer staff, most of whom will be the computer staff who design and run them. The implications for maintenance and security, in its widest sense, are significant and you would be well advised to consider the need for some unit to keep abreast of the developments and to carry out periodic audits. However, many internal audit functions are ill-equipped for this work, largely through lack of proper training. This need could be readily satisfied by inviting your external auditors to lend a hand.

Education and training

As a consultant, the clients I enjoy working with most are those who have, or have taken the trouble to acquire, an understanding of the area under review, no matter how technical the content. This understanding is usually revealed at an early stage by the type of questions asked and in the attention paid to the detail of investigations. This approach places me and my colleagues, if we are working as a team, under pressure to produce better results than might emerge with a more languid client. It is much more rewarding to satisfy a hard-nosed client, of which I have known many, than to respond adequately to a disinterested one. The same circumstances prevail in project development, where you will find computer staff reacting favourably to a knowledgeable and interested user and adversely to one who is obtuse or passive during critical periods of development.

As the heading suggests, part of the remedy lies with the intelligent use of education and training facilities to enhance or encourage the user's contribution to the project. Far too little attention is paid to this activity, which often deteriorates to a half-day session on 'What is a computer' or hasty task training sessions when conversion is imminent. I believe that the quality of many systems would be improved and implementation would be much smoother if a planned programme of training was considered as much a part of the project as the design and programming activities. By all means have the introductory sessions but also include, at relevant points, participative working sessions on:

- The development process
- User contributions
- Project progress and problem areas
- Functions of the system

using external services, if necessary or appropriate. The user should know the areas in which he or his staff require training and he has the right and the obligation to insist that it is provided.

Guidelines

Past experiences of applying computers to business and administrative systems have generally not been happy ones for users. The users have had to wait too long for systems and the results have not always been satisfactory. In addition, the quality of production services has left many users wishing they had continued with manual procedures, with which at least they felt in control of what was happening. By and large, computer departments have been slow to respond to user dissatisfaction, but their hands have been forced by the dramatic fall in the cost of hardware and the realization by users that they can to some extent help themselves.

Whether you plan to remain a customer of a centralized service or intend going it alone, with or without help, you have plenty of mechanisms available to you to influence the structure of the systems and to exert control over the project.

1 First of all, you should ensure that the direction and progress of the project is subject to formal management and user control, through such means as:
   - a steering committee;
   - user steering groups; and
   - a procedure for authorizing and signing off project stages.
2 The content of new systems and questions of acceptability and ease of implementation should be resolved by direct representation of users through all stages of development, preferably through working membership of the project team. Whether or not the user should have total control of development through a user project manager will depend very much on the nature of the system and the quality of staff available.
3 Perhaps the most effective way in which the user can exercise his power over the development of the system and its subsequent operation is by building up his own systems analysis resources. I would favour this approach, whether or not it met with the approval of any central computing function.

Computers are a means to achieve an end and not an end in themselves. The pursuit of technical excellence is of no consequence and no value if the user cannot fulfil his objectives satisfactorily within the organization.

9   The use of computers in planning and control

Introduction

The concept of the computer as the centre of the planning and control functions of an enterprise began to take shape from the moment the general data handling and processing capabilities of computing devices became apparent. As a concept it was not difficult to formulate, but the experience of the 1960s and 1970s suggests that few organizations have been successful in developing fully integrated systems that depend on and are controlled by computers. This shortfall has been partly due to the complexity involved in elaborating and implementing this concept, as well as the prohibitive costs of hardware and the design effort required.

Complexity

Any organization, be it a business enterprise or an institution, is a mixture of formal and informal processes, old 'Spanish' custom and practice and, probably, battling personalities. Furthermore, these ingredients are constantly changing or becoming more or less significant as a result of the influence of both internal and external factors such as, for example, the appointment of a new managing director or the demise of a product or technology. The situation is therefore not only complex but also dynamic, and even if it was possible to identify and comprehend all the relationships that make an organization work and fulfil its purpose, the model would be essentially historic and quite possibly valueless as a basis for the design of a fully integrated planning and control system. It would be rather like a football manager planning a whole match as a series of set pieces and ignoring the opposition, the weather, the crowd and the vagaries of referees. Consequently, most successful developments have followed from a concentration on the principal functions of the organization and the identification of the major information flows connecting these functions.

Costs

Although, in general terms, the availability of suitable hardware has tended to exceed the ability of users to exploit it, the high costs of equipment in the past have been a further discouragement. In addition, the associated investment required to investigate, design and program a total system could be of the same order as the equipment cost and may be less controllable.

> A major insurance company set out to develop a total system utilizing a comprehensive database. The project was two years late in being implemented, involved over 50 man years of design effort and led to an excess expenditure of over £600,000. A second machine was also required.

Not all cases are as dramatic as that one, as we know, hardware costs are falling all the time, especially with the advent of cheap mini and microcomputers, which have had a beneficial effect on the economics of applying computer techniques to areas previously ignored by computer staff. For example, according to one advertisement in a national newspaper, it is possible to obtain a quite powerful microprocessor, with associated input/output and storage facilities, plus a pre-written stock recording and control package, for considerably less than the wage cost of employing a clerk.

While hardware is becoming cheaper, the balance of investment is swinging towards the software required, both to run the machines and to perform user functions. Notwithstanding the development of cheap, powerful computers and the availability of much improved software, it is unlikely that the fully integrated system will become a commonly observed feature of computer usage. In fact, the very cheapness of some devices encourages users to dedicate them to single applications, like the stock control package referred to above. As we have seen in a previous chapter, this technological breakthrough complements and encourages the growth of user power and facilitates user control over their own functions, which to some extent works against efforts to integrate systems.

To what extent, therefore, is it both feasible and practical to apply computers to the planning and control functions of an organization? Can the investment be justified in terms of the likely benefits that can be identified? If it is feasible, practical and cost effective, how can we ensure that it is successful? In this chapter, I propose to look briefly at the nature of the planning and control problem, to review the ways in which computer facilities can be brought to bear and to examine the lessons of experience gained from attempts to computerize major functions.

Levels of planning

You will have realized by now that I prefer to think in hierarchical terms and, for the purposes of this examination, I propose to follow what I believe to be commonly accepted definitions of business planning and control. These definitions distinguish three levels of need which are applicable to all types of organizations:

- Strategic
- Tactical
- Operational

Whether or not you have a computer or access to computer facilities, you will have to apply some effort in these areas if your organization is to survive and prosper.

Strategic planning

Strategic planning is primarily concerned with the long-range survival and growth of the organization and typically has a time frame of five years or more. Ideally, strategic planning follows from the setting or clarification of the organization's objectives and an analysis or reassessment of strengths, weaknesses, opportunities and threats. It also seeks to identify or predetermine future trends. Much of the information on which this type of planning is based is unstructured, informal, external and possibly non-numeric, e.g. anticipating future government intentions, predicting rates of inflation, estimating future markets. Inevitably, prognostications become more speculative the further you move away from the present.

The contribution offered by computer systems varies enormously from one organization to another. Where the computer is already used extensively for administrative and operating procedures, it may be possible to produce analyses or summaries of current and historical data held within the existing information system in order to provide a starting point for any future estimates, making use of appropriate statistical forecasting techniques. A more sophisticated approach involves the construction and manipulation of a planning model such that many different alternative strategies can be examined before the organization has to commit itself to any one approach. Given a computer of sufficient size and power – and it does not have to be your own – management can ask 'What if . . .' type questions and determine the model outcome of different courses of action. Most computer manufacturers offer this facility as a software package and many proprietary systems are marketed, but if these are too general or rigorous for your purposes, there are tools available that enable users to construct their own models on an interactive, evolutionary basis. For example, some accountants have constructed simple but effective cash flow models using a microcomputer, without the aid of modelling experts. Indeed, there is some justification in arguing that the explosive success of the microcomputer in recent years is largely due to the development of 'spreadsheet' software which, though generally applicable, has been enthusiastically exploited by the accountants.

Tactical planning
Characteristically, tactical planning is dealing with shorter time scales, usually a minimum 12 month period equating with the annual budgeting cycle, but possibly looking forward two or three years on a rolling basis. It is primarily concerned with the exploitation of the strategic plan in terms of resources, individual markets or products, organization development, manpower and operations. Typically, the information on which this form of planning is based tends to be structured, quantifiable, formal, largely internal and derived principally from the operation of the main functions of the business; for example, the utilization and productivity of administration and productive resources and other operating performance characteristics.

If computers have been applied successfully to these functions, and if the data is available in a usable form, which are rather important prerequisites, management can obtain considerable support for their tactical planning; in translating a sales forecast into a gross production capacity requirement, for example, or in assessing manpower needs in response to given increases in the volume of work. The problem is often how to select from the mass of data that usually accumulates within computer systems and is presented to management in a raw form. Again, most computer suppliers and software houses provide software package facilities that can assist in this planning and budgeting exercise.

Operational planning and control

Planning at the operational level is designed to give effect to the aims and objectives set out as a result of the formation of strategic and tactical plans. Operational plans are usually functionally oriented and unfold in timescales that demand close management control; thus, typically we are concerned with the sales plan, the production programme and the planning of revenues and expenditures, where we will be monitoring progress on a month-to-month basis.

This level of planning is based firmly on known and often predetermined data that describe the operation of the main functions of the organization. There is a close identification between what happens in practice and what you intended should happen. Hence, the prevalence of month-end reporting, concentrating usually on departures from some budgeted standard, for example:

- the flow of orders;
- the volume of shipments;
- the inflow/outflow of funds;
- the workload, however expressed.

Most computer applications will perform some functions that relate directly to this level of operational planning and control, and will be designed to provide information that enables management to monitor performance and to modify their short-term plans.

The control loop

Planning is a fruitless activity unless the execution of plans is monitored and controlled. In order to achieve these aims, some feedback of results is essential. This is particularly the case where the main purpose of planning is to provide a mechanism that can respond flexibly to changes in the environment. Schematically, the planning and control cycle at all levels owes much to the concepts of control engineering, as illustrated in Figure 9.1. The plan specifies what actions should be taken and the results of those actions are fed back for comparison with the plan. The plan for the next phase is adjusted to take account of the results of the previous phase.

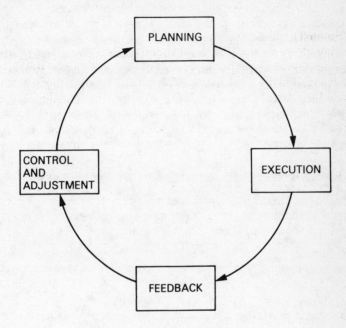

Figure 9.1   The control loop

The sensitivity of the plan to the feedback, and the timeframe within which to react, will obviously vary with the level of planning involved. At a strategic level, the announcement of some government initiative might materially affect the long-term plan, but investigation of its implications and agreeing changes to the plan could conceivably take several months without any risk to the organization. In contrast the need for prompter analysis and response is much clearer at the level of tactical planning. For example, an increase in the rate of interest or fluctuations in the foreign exchange rates may force an immediate consideration of inventory policy and a demand for relevant data about current stocks, outstanding commitments and the sales order book. It would be a good test of your computer systems to see how readily this information could be assembled and in what form. The probability is that the data are spread over several computer files, can only be obtained with difficulty and will need some manual processing before the results can be used with confidence. The next problem arises when, having decided what actions you want to take, you have to implement those decisions in the computer systems so as to have an immediate effect on operations. For instance, you may wish to alter certain stock control parameters or vary your procurement commitments. It may not be possible to accomplish these changes without a great deal of inconvenience.

The sensitivity of the plan is even more critical at the operational level, where the impact of a change must be interpreted and acted upon very quickly. For example, if a manufacturing company receives a cancellation of a major order from one of its principal customers, management needs to know promptly:

- what the effect on the workload will be;
- what commitments to suppliers have been concluded;
- what the effects on cash flow will be; and
- how the changes can be implemented.

A less depressing problem, but essentially no easier to deal with, would be having to respond to a new large order where you might be required to quote firm delivery promises.

This type of problem, where large volumes of data have to be sifted or manipulated in relatively short periods of time, has provided the impetus for many computer applications and, hopefully, will have been anticipated in constructing the files and designing the system. You are even better placed if your systems are on-line, even if this merely gives users the facility to enquire on records. The problems of the interface between users and computer systems, in terms of the impact on planning and control, is well illustrated in the efforts made to apply computers to the complexities of production systems.

The case for using computers

There is a strong prima facie case for applying computers to manufacturing planning and control procedures if it can be demonstrated that one or more of the following features are present:

- large volumes of data;
- complex procedures;
- a degree of urgency;
- increasing staff costs.

The features of the computer that can be exploited in manufacturing control procedures are its ability to handle such large volumes of data, at high speeds, effortlessly and with consistent accuracy and at an increasingly favourable cost compared with continued reliance on clerical resources.

As we have seen, the availability of powerful microcomputers and minicomputers provides the opportunity either to decentralize data processing operations or to dedicate a machine to one application. Unlike the situation that existed even as recently as the early 1980s, these machines are supported by reliable software that includes sound production control application packages. In this field, the choice is very wide; on the last occasion I checked there were over 200 packages on offer.

Large volumes of data
It is a distressing fact that to manufacture a complete product frequently requires many hundreds of documents and clerical transactions. For an engineering firm these include parts lists, operation layout sheets, works order documents, stock record transactions and payment recording.

Before they installed a computer for planning and control procedures, one manufacturing firm was regularly generating 3,000 pieces of paper per day in shop documentation alone. It does not require many products and components to make the handling of this data a formidable task, even for a large clerical force.

The virtually unlimited storage capacity of modern computers – limited generally by what you are willing to pay – provides the basis for solving this increasing problem in a growth firm.

Complex procedures
Apart from the large volumes of data that have to be handled, production control procedures are usually very complex to operate because of the number and variety of linkages with other systems. There is also a high degree of duplication and transcription of data which makes the process susceptible to clerical errors. However, if

these complexities can be programmed, the computer has the ability to follow intricate instructions, effortlessly and consistently, and to perform all tasks with accuracy.

A degree of urgency

It is frequently necessary for these complex procedures and large volumes of data to be manipulated under severe pressures of time, e.g. major amendments to production programmes. It is under these conditions that the system may break down or be circumvented, often with disastrous results.

The high speed of computers, combined with their accuracy, is a considerable asset to a company when coping with rapidly changing conditions. For example, it might be possible to undertake several production re-scheduling operations in one day whereas it might take weeks to complete *one* revision manually.

Increasing staff costs

The susceptibility of staff salaries to inflationary pressures, together with a steady decrease in hardware costs, has markedly changed the costs/benefits equation in favour of equipment. Furthermore, computers do not take time off to have babies, do not expect annual holidays and do not complain about increasing volumes of work. There is also a growing realization that staff are as reluctant to undertake boring, repetitive clerical jobs as factory workers are to be tied to an assembly line.

Application to planning and control

The areas of manufacturing planning and control to which a computer can contribute effectively are illustrated in Figure 9.2 and may be broadly grouped as follows.

1   Planning activities – these are the processes by which demands made upon the company for its products or services are converted into detailed manufacturing and supply requirements. Typically, these will include such tasks as receiving and processing new orders or changes to existing instructions, and any forecasting activity which is designed to anticipate future sales, e.g. planning the production of seasonal products before the nature of demand is known.

2   Authorization and execution – these are the activities that

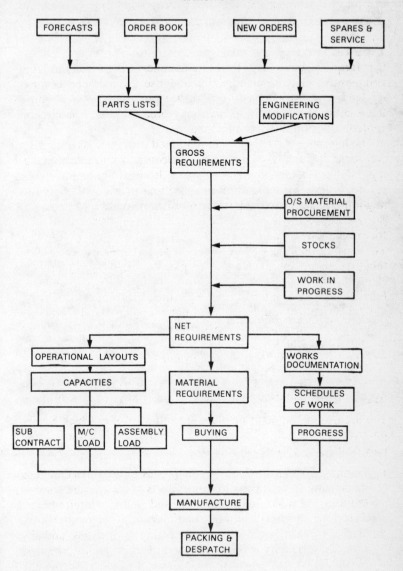

Figure 9.2 The main supply procedures

facilitate the conversion of known or forecast requirements into the schedules and documentation that authorize and initiate procurement action and production. They will include the issue of purchase orders, manipulation of inventory, issue of work to the factory and day-to-day control of production.

3   Feedback activities – these are the processes by which achievement of the various aspects of the plan are recorded and used to update the operating position. They include evidence of output, notification of materials and services flowing into, through and out of the factory, and are essentially quantitative in nature.

4   Control activities – control information is that amount of useful data which enables management to assess qualitatively the past, present and future position, and provides the basis for initiating any preventive or remedial action which may be necessary.

As you will note from Figure 9.2, there is a host of related functions that lie outside the mainstream of manufacturing planning and control but which have to be coordinated in line with production activities. Thus, for a manufacturing planning and control system to be integrated and truly effective, we need to computerize activities which would not normally come within the realm of production control. For example, we need to include selected sales and purchase department procedures and to take an overall view of the logistics or supplies management function. In designing such a system it is also important to recognize that the 'control' elements will be limited by the relative merits of human and computer response to particular situations. For example, I am not yet convinced that a computer will ever be as effective in coping with a machine breakdown as the man on the spot, real time processing notwithstanding.

To enable these procedures to operate effectively on a computer, a considerable amount of preparatory work is necessary; in particular, you will require comprehensive and accurate basic data and reference information. For a manufacturing company this data may include:

- Bills of material
- Process layouts
- Manufacturing and material procurement batch sizes

- Stock control criteria
- Machine tool performance
- Costing data
- Customer reference information

In addition, there is the express requirement to ensure that this basic data is maintained in an up-to-date condition once it has been set up in computer files.

The advantages to be gained

Although it is probably quite clear that the applications of a computer to these procedures may yield considerable benefits, it is worth recording some of the more important features of a computer-based system.

1   A revision of control methods – a major problem in many manufacturing companies is the domination of the 'shortage' list. Much of the production activity is initiated by a 'sucking' action from final assembly, owing to an inability to plan work effectively at earlier stages. The characteristics of a 'suck' system of production control are:
    - the inability to forward load the factory with any accuracy and a tendency to overload to ensure that work is always available;
    - excessive work in progress;
    - uneconomic batches, either programmed initially or as a result of split batches;
    - difficulty in implementing changes and identifying priorities before they become shortages.

    The application of a computer offers the chance to operate a 'blow' system of production, whereby the correct amounts of work are injected into the factory and up-to-date control over their progress becomes feasible. It is remarkable how closely these concepts coincide with those used so successfully by the Japanese, as embodied in Kanban and 'just in time' control mechanisms, and exploited in a range of excellent software packages available at all levels of computing.

2   Reduction in cycle times – where the computer undertakes major clerical tasks such as order explosion, initiation of material procurement and the preparation of works docu-

mentation, it is possible to reduce to a minimum that part of the manufacturing cycle which, though essential, is non-productive. The time saved can be used to improve delivery promises and to provide greater flexibility in response to changes.

3   Flexibility – in an advanced system, the speed of the computer's operation and the completeness of the information available to it allows the company to delay finalization of production plans until the last moment. Such 'controlled fluidity' provides more scope for re-scheduling activities than can be attained by manual means.

4   Supplies management – the facilities offered by computer techniques present a company with the opportunity to exploit the concept of supplies management by which the total logistics system (the planning, procurement, production and distribution of products) is integrated.

The possibility of achieving this level of control and the benefits to be derived from better stock management, more economic utilization of resources, more accurate and up-to-date information and the potential for staff reductions, have proved a major attraction to a number of companies. However, even in the mid-1980s, fewer companies have entered this field than one might have expected and this reluctance must in some measure be due to the lack of success which earlier users have had with this particular application.

Problems to be overcome

There are several reasons why computer-based manufacturing control systems have failed to realize the full benefits which are apparently possible. Hardly any of these reasons are related to the technical features of computer equipment, although it is certain that the horizons of early applications were limited by not having random (or selective) access facilities. Factors which we consider to have had a major influence on the development of this type of application are as follows.

1   Complexity – there is no doubt that some companies have seriously under-estimated the complexity of production control; others, recognizing the complexity, have settled for something

less than a fully integrated system, e.g. they have concentrated their attentions on stock recording and control and on bills of materials processing. In many companies it is often difficult to unravel the real requirements of the system from the collection of formal and ad hoc procedures which have developed over a period of years. It is also frequently difficult to persuade management that the procedures which are supporting a profitable enterprise are in any way unsuitable or in need of change.

2   Readiness for change – for a computer-based manufacturing control system to be fully effective, a company should already have achieved a high level of procedural and operating efficiency. It is not sufficient to assume that the introduction of a computer system will act as a catalyst in achieving this level. Many companies have ignored facts or have been misled in assuming that they are ready for this kind of change. In practice, it has been found in a number of cases that the situation is unsatisfactory in important respects.

- The organization structure and associated procedures have not been sufficiently well developed, e.g. the absence of any concept of material control, the confusion of stock control with stock recording.
- Essential basic data has not been available or has proved inadequate or inaccurate.
- Essential (non-computer) preparatory work has been overlooked or skimped, e.g. establishing lead times, verification of parts lists and stock records.
- The discipline and accuracy necessary in the supporting non-computer procedures has been of a low level.

3   The communications gap – there is evidence of a signal failure on the part of both computer staff and of management to understand each other's requirements. The success of any data processing system depends in the last resort on the ability and willingness of non-computer staff to make the system work. In many companies, a lack of understanding of the facilities offered by a computer, and perhaps an innate fear of automation itself, has made the development of a complex system extremely difficult. The relatively limited use so far made of such features as data collection terminals and shop-floor visual display units, which can be essential for certain aspects of

feedback and control, may be due to reluctance to involve employees directly in major system changes.

4   Large investment in development required – the greater complexity of manufacturing control applications, the general inadequacy of basic data and the difficulties of creating informed cooperation all tend to lengthen the time required to implement revised systems. Systems development for manufacturing control requires a larger investment in staff than other commercial applications, and many companies have been reluctant to recognize it. Consequently, there has been a tendency to attempt too much in too short a period with too few staff, many of whom have been inexperienced in manufacturing procedures.

5   Project direction – the management control of data processing departments has in general been placed at too low a level in the organization structure. For applications as far reaching as manufacturing control, this has proved a major drawback. The computer manager has frequently to 'sell' changes to senior management and is poorly placed to lend authority to the implementation of major changes. It is now more generally recognized that development projects will be more successful if they involve users and have the support of senior management.

We have found these factors to be extremely important in modifying the success of complex planning and control systems. It is also clear that, in the past, the bigger organization has stood a better chance of overcoming these problems, particularly where a large preparatory investment is involved. Smaller companies have been less fortunate, partly through lack of staff of the right calibre and a restriction on the amount of time and money which can be devoted to such projects. It is also important to recognize that companies installing micros or minicomputers are likely to have less depth of management experience and skill than companies buying mainframes. Assistance for the smaller company almost certainly lies with the use of application packages, even though this will involve some sacrifice of requirements.

In this respect, the small-scale user is remarkably well attended by the software houses providing manufacturing control packages on microcomputers. I have seen quite elaborate systems operating on one multi-user microcomputer and even more sophisticated packages offered for networked machines. Furthermore, the entry point for the small business is much lower now; a modest production planning and control system can be introduced for between £10,000 and £15,000, including the costs of hardware.

Furthermore, the past few years has seen a significant expansion in government aided schemes to promote the use of computers, especially in manufacturing industry. The schemes provide free or heavily subsidized consultancy support at the early feasibility stage and, in some cases, generous grants for subsequent implementation. In any event, there is nothing to be lost in enquiring at the start of your project if your organization will qualify for such assistance which would make specialist advice available, at a low cost, when it is most needed.

10 Management information systems

Introduction

Throughout this book, the phrase 'management information system', or some variant of it, has been used as if it was uniquely associated with computers. This is of course absurd; managers required information and sought means of obtaining it long before computers were invented or before we had experts to tell us how important it was and how we misunderstood its purpose. The current vogue is to urge management to acknowledge information as a resource which is as critical to the well-being of an organization as capital, manpower and technology. I would not disagree with this view, but I would suggest that you treat this concept cautiously when it is promoted by equipment salesmen or by your own computer staff, as the chances are that it will cost you a pound or two.

Although there is no logical dependency between information systems and computers, there is a fairly obvious connection. Most computers are installed initially to take over or support the principal operating or administrative procedures of an organization, such as billing, accounting, payroll, sales administration and aspects of production and inventory control. Once you begin to use a computer to trap the main data flows through an organization, it is clearly possible to operate on those data to produce information in ways that would have been difficult or impossible using manual means. By and large, the output from most computer systems will reflect what was available under clerical procedures, but with the added advantages arising from the computer's ability to search, sort, manipulate and test large volumes of data at high speeds. Thus, computer systems will usually also present information to management in terms of summarized results, variances, exception conditions, forecasts, prompts and so on, provided that these requirements are identified during the design of the systems. Unfortunately, this is not always as simple as it would appear. Prospective users often have great difficulty in articulating their future information needs, particularly if they are unfamiliar with computing facilities, and as a result they usually opt for what they are getting at the moment. Once computer systems settle down and users gain confidence in operating them, they begin to refine their requirements and ask for more or different information. The competence of the system to meet these demands depends, firstly, on whether the data are available in the system and, secondly, if it is technically possible to access them. The ease with which users' developing needs can be accommodated will determine whether or not you think you have a good management information system, attention thereby being focused on the technical aspects of information handling. This may be a false assessment that could lead you into considerable expense on equipment and software, while ignoring the quality and purpose of the information itself.

The nature of information

It is not the aim of this book to enter into a discourse on information theory; if you feel you need an intellectual basis for considering your organization's requirements, there is no shortage of books on the subject. What we are concerned with here are the practical problems of defining what information is required, determining how those requirements should be met, and preserving as much flexibility as we can in the means we adopt.

Defining information needs

What usually happens in practice is that systems analysts will ask user managers to state their information needs during the initial investigation and the early stages of design. Unless these managers have had previous exposure to computers, they are unlikely to know what the possibilities are and will tend to ask for the reports they already receive from their existing system. In the absence of initiatives by the user, the systems analyst may make suggestions based on his understanding of the function, but this may lead merely to an increase in the quantity of information produced rather than improvements in quality. Furthermore, the inherent disciplines of most organizations, which are geared to control on accounting principles, are likely to be perpetuated in new computer systems such that information is produced at fixed intervals, usually monthly, although it is evident that managers have to operate effectively in between reporting cycles. If the time taken to produce reports is at all lengthy – say 10 – 15 days – a line manager may not have notice of problems until long after it is possible to take remedial action. In practice, of course, what happens is that subsidiary systems ('little black books') develop which enable managers to keep track of events and respond to them promptly.

We have referred implicitly to two important characteristics of management information that are rarely considered in designing computer systems.

1   Firstly, we have linked information to the kind of decision that managers have to make in order to carry out their job.
2   Secondly, we have introduced a time factor that conditions both the availability of information and the manager's response.

Organizations that observe techniques based on or akin to management by objectives will be familiar with disciplines that focus on the results to be attained and the actions to be taken to achieve them. A similar technique facilitates an understanding of the nature of the information required by managers. This is based on the identification of the key decisions that a manager has to make to fulfil his function in the organization. The information he requires to arrive at these decisions must be the key or essential management information, and it must be available in the right form and at the time that the decision has to be made.

Thus, a simple definition of a management information system is that it should provide the information necessary for managers to make decisions. You will note that this definition says nothing about computers being the source of that information, although, for an increasing number of organizations, this is likely to be the case. However, the information required for some types of decisions will never reside in computer systems.

Identify decision areas
In the previous chapter we referred briefly to the hierarchical nature of planning and control, distinguishing needs at strategic

tactical and operating levels. This basic structure can assist with the identification of the types of decision facing managers and the likely sources of information.

Strategic decisions Strategic decisions in this context are those which affect the medium- and long-term plans of the organization and are the type that would be made in such areas as:

- opening/closing a factory;
- re-locating a major administrative centre out of London;
- developing a new product or service; or
- entering a new geographical market.

The information needed to reach this type of policy decision is required mainly to evaluate alternative strategies and to minimize the risks involved. Some of this data will be quantifiable and may be obtainable from computer systems, but there will be a high proportion of unstructured information and some subjective judgements involved in reaching a decision. The time frame within which a decision has to be made may also be quite long, up to two years in those cases where feasibility studies are necessary.

We were asked to review the information available for strategic planning purposes to the six most senior managers in a very large organization with a long history of highly successful computerization. There was virtually no major administrative, operational or technical activity that was not supported in some measure by a computer application. Among sophisticated facilities available to managers were on-line random enquiry facilities, personal computers with access to central databases, and a bevy of research assistants for special projects.

It was quite clear that there was an excellent framework of functional management information systems, but no facility to combine this information at the highest general manager level. It was also apparent that the nature of much of the information required by general managers for strategic planning could not be provided from the functional applications, notwithstanding their excellent design. There were also two critical findings that altered the orientation of the consultancy assignment. One was the conclusion that a whole level of general management activity was not needed; this disposed of the information requirement. The other was that changes in technology and operating characteristics had introduced new information requirements that no existing computer system could provide.

The contribution of computers at this level is debatable. It is most unlikely that computer systems will contain much data that will be pertinent to this type of decision, although in the case of new markets the evidence of trends that provide the starting point for a study may have emerged from a routine system. On the other hand, the availability of computer facilities and relevant software may be very helpful in researching alternative strategies. For example, if your current computer systems include routines for constructing and modifying sales and manufacturing budgets, those same programs could be used to 'model' the establishment of a new factory or a new market. In any event, there is now a vast range of modelling software available at all levels of computing and it is surprising how much can be achieved with a microcomputer and good spreadsheet software.

Tactical decisions Tactical decisions are those related to the formation and execution of short- to medium-term plans that are designed to give effect to the overall strategy of the organization. In relation to the four examples of possible strategies quoted above, for instance, we would expect to see a tactical plan for the provision or training of the necessary manpower. The decisions associated with the construction of that plan and those arising from it would be based on hard information, some of which might be found in existing computer systems.

For example, in order to construct and implement the (tactical) manpower plan for the establishment of a new factory, we would need to know:

- the number and type of skills required;
- the phasing in of the workforce;
- our current stock of skills;
- the flow of new entrants;
- the training needs;
- productivity and the learning curve effect;
- wages/cost structure, and so on.

If we have any personnel, payroll or costing applications on our computer, we may be able to find relevant information enabling decisions to be taken. However, it is most unlikely that these systems would have been set up in the first place with this requirement in mind. Thus, one of the problems in providing information for tactical decisions is that, in the design of computer systems, it is difficult to anticipate what often amounts to a future unspecified project requirement.

On the other hand, some tactical planning and decision making is predictable and relies on analyses and projections of historical data. Whether this data is available from the computer will depend on the extent of computerization, i.e. how much of the organization is covered and whether or not arrangements have been made to secure it. Even if it is available, it may not be easy to obtain, although again the time frame for decision making allows some flexibility. Clearly, the contribution that computer systems can make to decision making at a tactical level depends on the extent to which you can predict your information needs in advance and can provide the mechanisms for interrogating computer data. My experience suggests that most well-established computer users have recognized this requirement in the design of new systems while, at the same time, wrestling with the difficulties presented by routines which were not developed with these objectives in mind. First time users or organizations reaching a point of total re-design and re-equipment have a tremendous advantage over the veterans, as we shall see when considering database management systems.

A major public utility acquired a new chief executive with a strong commercial background and a commitment to performance-oriented management. After a suitable interlude, and a detailed appraisal of the organization, he decided on an extensive programme of re-structuring which radically changed the management structure and concentrated attention on a revised range of both financial and physical performance factors. Although the organization had fairly extensive computer systems covering operational activities, it quickly became apparent that these would not provide the data required to plan and control the development of the authority. Rather than delay the introduction of the structural and management changes, the chief executive wisely went ahead and relied on temporary procedures to provide information while computer systems were re-designed, using database techniques.

Operational decisions Information for operational decisions is concerned with the identification of deviations from the established operational plan. This information is used to monitor the current activities of the organization and to draw the attention of managers to areas where action is required. More than any other kind of decision, the emphasis at an operational level is on control rather than planning, although short-term plans may be adjusted as a result of these decisions. At this level there is a heavy reliance on predetermined standards of performance and a recognition that decisions must be made in relatively short time scales.

For example, if a customer exceeds his credit limit, it is important either to take prompt action to obtain payments, to place a 'stop' on further business or to initiate both actions. On the other hand, to preserve goodwill you might wish to treat the matter differently. In any event, there is a requirement to know when a deviation occurs and to have immediate access to other information that might be relevant to making a decision. Similarly, if a stock item hits or falls below its re-order point, this fact should be signalled to inventory control who will decide whether or not to re-order, in what quantities and from whom.

In both examples, the need for the decision was triggered by a predetermined criterion and the nature of possible action was also to some extent determinable in advance. In which case, you ask, why doesn't the computer take the decision and initiate the necessary actions? The answer is that it does in many organizations, but you have to be absolutely certain of the consequences of automating even quite low-level decisions. For instance, although the presence of predetermined re-order points in a stock control system may be based (hopefully) on some rational analysis of usage, it may be quite wrong to re-order if, by looking ahead six months, there is evidence of a severe fall in demand that would leave the company significantly over-stocked. In terms of the structure of computer files, it may not be possible for the stock control system to do this easily and, in any event, users may prefer to retain a long-stop role when such decisions are made by computer.

A large chain of department stores maintained several warehouses and sub-depots for replenishing stocks at shops by imprest on a weekly cycle. The inventory at the warehouses was administered centrally with the aid of a comprehensive stock recording and control system based on mathematically derived parameters. Among other tasks, the computer generated orders for items that had reached a re-order point, but we found that the stock clerks were reviewing all the requisitions and cancelling or amending most of them. As many thousands of orders were involved this seemed a rather strange practice. So far as we could see there was nothing wrong with the inventory model, but it became clear that the problem was that the basic parameters had not been revised for three years and were initiating orders that the clerks knew instinctively were wrong. Even after the parameters were brought up to date, it was a long time before they would relax their inspection.

There is no doubt that computer systems can contribute substantially to the provision of information for decisions taken at the operational level. In spite of experiences like the above, it is equally clear that, with increased confidence in computers and more finesse in defining the rules for decision-making, more and more decisions will be automated.

Technical factors

From the point of view of the average user manager, there appear to be two types of decision he is called upon to make for which he requires the necessary information. There are those decisions, essentially to do with control, which are part of the routine performance of the function he manages and which are characterized mainly by correcting or acting upon deviations from a prescribed plan. With care, many of the lower-level decisions in this category are capable of being delegated to a computer. Some of these decisions have to be taken promptly, i.e. within the working day, whereas others can be dealt with in the normal processing cycle, e.g. once per week or once per month.

Occasionally this kind of decision verges on the second type, which is characterized by an interrogative approach:

- 'If I do X what is the effect on Y?'
- 'Before I authorize X, I need to know factors Y and Z.'

Even here, well-constructed systems may be able to anticipate ancillary information needs and provide mechanisms for finding the appropriate data. In my opinion, it is the difficulty of providing this second type of information that many users have in mind when criticizing the quality of their information systems. The fact that it would have been totally impossible with manual methods is considered to be irrelevant. It is also probable that their needs and their management perceptions have become more sophisticated as a result of exposure to computer systems, and what they are criticizing is their own past failure to deal imaginatively with questions of computer system design. On the other hand, it could be argued that the high cost of the most desirable technical features severely limited their ability to anticipate future requirements, even if they had recognized their significance.

The pattern of development

It is not difficult to understand how we have arrived at a situation where user managers in an organization that has used computers extensively for, say, 15 years are complaining about the availability of information. The following pattern of development is fairly typical.

1   The first application may well be one that has been supported in the past by unit record equipment (punched cards and tabulators) or accounting machines. It is significant how often an accounting procedure becomes the first computer system and the computer installation becomes closely identified with the accounting function.

2   Because of the relative inexperience of both users and computer staff, and an understandable caution on the part of management, the first application will probably stay close to the existing system in terms of processing features and reports generated. Computer files will tend to be almost exact copies of clerical records.

3   By the time the next application comes along, both users and computer staff will have more experience and competence and there may be new technical features to be exploited. Although the second system may be better designed, it will probably still largely reflect existing practices and records and stand very much in its own right as a computer job. If there is any connection between the first and second application, the link will usually be formed by passing a data file between the two systems.

4   However, as the years roll by, no matter how successful we are, we will find that we have accumulated a large number of

independent, although possibly linked, systems, each of which has its own files and array of management reports. Because of enhancements to the computer installation or software, we may also have indulged in, or been forced into, re-writing or converting some of the earlier systems.

I recently had occasion to review the development of computer usage within a highly successful computer user in the public sector. Among the facts that emerged were that there had been five changes of equipment in 16 years, if you count the original unit record machines, and that several key applications had been subject to three major modifications or re-writes during that time without changing the fundamental approach to processing. As a result, the largest and most complex system, accounting for over 30% of capacity, was still influenced by punched card processing concepts.

It is also probable that many of these systems will be batch oriented, although we will have introduced on-line facilities for the most recent systems.

5   By this time, users will have enough experience and confidence to have refined their needs and to seek, where appropriate, more advanced technical solutions, e.g. on-line updating instead of a weekly batch process, and on-line enquiry facilities to supplement fixed interval reporting. They may also have begun to ask for information which they know should be resident in the computer, because of the range of converted systems. However, it will probably become quickly apparent that, because the data are spread through several files, this information will be difficult to extract or, because of different updating cycles, will be quite misleading.

6   If the new information requirement is to be a feature of future processing, it may make sense to develop an interrogation/extraction routine or acquire a package. Many installations have adopted this approach. On the other hand, if the need is for random, unstructured access to the mass of data available in the computer, it is highly unlikely that an efficient system can be developed for conventional computer files.

For these and other reasons, many established computer users have turned to database management systems to provide the flexibility denied them by traditional approaches to data processing.

The database approach

Adopting a database approach on a mainframe can be extremely expensive in terms of hardware, software, resources and implement-ation time, and you should be certain that the arguments for doing so are valid and can be justified in an objective fashion. The reason for caution is that it is possible for suppliers and computer staff to advance very good technical reasons for this approach, although the benefits may be greater for them than for the organization as a whole. To illustrate this point, your sales force could argue that the allocation of a Rolls Royce instead of a fleet car would make them more effective, whereas you may know that, being 'order takers' rather than sellers, they can fulfil this role by far less exotic means.

Definition A database is a collection of related data stored together, with the minimum of duplication, to provide a common pool of information in order to serve one or more applications. In popular terms this means a single computer file for the whole organization, although in practice it will mean a number of separate databases each serving a group of related applications.

It is perfectly acceptable to have a database co-existing with conven-tional file structures that deal with different applications; indeed, experimentation with one application is often a good way to sample the benefits of a database approach. Thus, we may find organizations with different needs following a variety of approaches to database.

- A life assurance company may have a single database or policy file.
- A building society may have two separate bases, one dealing with mortgages and one with savings. Alternatively, it could opt for a single database founded on membership of the society in whatever capacity.
- A manufacturing company may have several databases covering sales, production, engineering and personnel.

Obviously where more than one base is involved, it may be necessary to provide a bridge between them for some processing or interrogative purposes.

The need As we have indicated, the reasons for considering a database approach are a mixture of technical factors and user requirements.

1   Conventional file structures involve the duplication of data. For example, employee details may be repeated several times in

records used for different purposes in applications covering payroll, personnel information, welfare schemes and pension funds. In a manufacturing organization, the opportunity for repetition is enormous, with the same component number appearing dozens or even hundreds of times in different files. One obvious effect is that storage space is wasted by the repetition of the same information, whereas a database approach will be designed to eliminate such redundant data.

2 A more significant problem from the users' point of view is that although almost identical records exist, the separation of files and applications can mean that they are updated at different times and are thus not always consistent with each other. For example, it is possible for a stock record to be showing one cost whereas the costing file will be holding a different value.

3 Because several applications may use the same files, a description of the files and record formats is embedded in the computer programs that operate on them – for example, the number and content of data fields, field names, record lengths, etc. If you wish to amend or add to the file or record structure to suit one of these applications, or to accomodate a new one, you will have to change the parameters for every program that utilizes the file, and every program will have to be amended. This could mean altering dozens of programs, re-compiling and testing them, and hoping that you have not caused other problems. These problems will account in part for the anguish with which a computer manager will greet another user request for change and why it may take an apparently disproportionate amount of time to introduce what appears to be a simple change. One of the great advantages of a database approach is that it provides the facility to insulate your programs from the data and allows modification of the structure of the base without the need to change existing programs.

4 A natural corollary to a database management system is some form of enquiry facility, or query language, that provides the means for multiple access to the data and the facility to seek information on random issues.

It is perfectly feasible for the ambitious user to develop the software necessary to set up and maintain a database, and some have done so, occasionally successfully. However, for most users, the sensible approach is to use the software provided by the equipment supplier or by a reputable software house. Database facilities are now available at all levels of computing, including for many microcomputers. I would suggest that any organization considering a computer for the first time should adopt a database approach in preference to conventional data processing file structures. This strategy will not only facilitate the building of computer systems, it will also provide manipulative facilities that are more in tune with the requirements of modern managers.

Problems for existing users In the case of existing computer users it is often a question of 'If I was heading for Brighton, I wouldn't have started from here.'

1   The principal reason is the potentially high cost of converting from a traditional to a database approach and the upheaval it can create. The costs accrue from many areas.
  - The cost of the software, which can be relatively low.
  - The cost of additional hardware to accommodate and access the database management system and to ensure that processing efficiency does not suffer.
  - The staff costs for designing the structure of the base and the on-going cost of maintaining it securely. For example, a database administrator is required to ensure that all changes to the base are properly disciplined, documented and implemented.
  - The time and cost required to convert existing computer programs to operate under a new processing regime.

  These costs can be quite high for an organization that has already invested a good deal in computer systems, and management would be remiss if they did not scrutinize the claimed benefits very closely. For example, I know of one case where a proposal to move to a database for all existing procedures involved one-off costs of £500,000 over two and a half years. The existing data processing budget was £1.0 million per annum and would increase by about £100,000 as a result of the change. It was a very long time before management agreed to the conversion, and then only because of increasing pressures to provide improved information.

2   It is often difficult for management to identify the direct benefits to the user from a database approach, especially when most of the arguments advanced appear to offer most advantage to the data processing department:

- better use of facilities;
- ease of change and maintenance;
- an exciting new technique to attract and retain the interests of the computer expert.

This often arises because the first time the user manager hears about a database and its advantages is when a proposal from the computer department lands on his desk. Just when he was beginning to understand about computers, he is plunged into a new and baffling area of jargon and expertise that places him once more at the mercy of the technician.

3 The problems of investigating and designing the structure of the database are also significant and may occupy both expert and user staff for a considerable time before any recognizable progress is achieved. This is not only because of the need to determine the data elements, their relationships and the format of the base, but also because of the information processes they are designed to serve. These problems are minimal if you are designing a base for a single application, but very much more complex if you are trying to encompass multiple needs.

Thus, an existing user, no matter how successful the computer applications have been, will be beset with more problems and incur greater costs than a first time user in opting for a database approach, particularly if the intention is to convert across the board. However, some organizations have decided instead to introduce database techniques gradually, with new application areas, and to convert existing routines only when they would have come up for re-design under normal circumstances anyhow. Another approach is to link the database concept with the major changes of equipment or supplier that crop up from time to time. In this way, the organization can take advantage of falling hardware costs and absorb some of the price of conversion in costs that would have been incurred anyway.

In the meantime, what can organizations do to improve the information content and services available to users and general management?

Improving information systems

Whether or not there is a general dissatisfaction with the information system, there is a great deal that can be done at company level and at individual user level to improve the effectiveness of most computer systems, especially those which have been around for some time.

1 If you have not already done so, your organization would benefit from a formal review of management practices and decision-making processes, concentrating on the information that managers require to carry out their jobs. This means identifying key decision areas and the types of decisions that managers have to make. The outcome of this study would be a framework of information requirements which may be in some instances quite different from the information currently provided.

2 With this management information framework in mind, existing systems, both computer and manual can be assessed in terms of their contribution to the achievement of this 'blueprint' of requirements. It also provides the basis for evaluating new systems proposals or amendments to current applications.

3 A particular feature of this approach should be the objective assessment of the time factor in making decisions, as I am convinced that some managers and many systems analysts are obsessed with the immediacy of information and pay scant attention to the user's ability or need to act upon it promptly. In one example, an on-line database approach was justified partly because of the service it would provide to an insurance claims manager in settling claims, where it was recognized that client service was very important. Most claims, the easy ones, could be settled within days, but the few tricky ones often took months to clear because of the amount of investigation involved. Even so, the computer system was geared to provide information for the difficult decisions as if they had to be made within 24 hours.

4 We have stressed elsewhere the importance of reviewing computer systems periodically after they have been implemented. We have suggested reviews after six months, after 18 months and after three years, although it is the principle of post-implementation review rather than the timing that is important. These reviews provide the ideal opportunity to review not only the performance and effectiveness of the system but also the quality and usefulness of management reports. I

would be very surprised if after the system had been running for some time you did not discover that:

- some reports were no longer required;
- some reports contained the wrong data, or too much data, or were inaccurate or too late;
- many relevant reports were either not used by managers or were subject to manual processing in order to make them useful; or
- some emergent needs were not being met.

Making changes to the reporting methods can be accomplished more readily and at less cost than designing a new system.

5 I also feel that many users do not sufficiently exploit the data content of existing files and systems and are inclined to design a completely new routine when a 'quick and dirty' approach might be just as effective in meeting an information requirement. For example, a manufacturing company needed a long-term assessment of the forward production load in order to take planning decisions about plant capacity, labour, shift working, etc. The computer department's solution was a new system that precisely analysed the forward load in terms of standard hours for every machine centre. The development of the new system was planned to take several months and involved the collection of a large volume of parametric data. However it was realized that by constructing work load profiles for a few key products and machine centres and utilizing existing order book information, a less precise but adequate statement of capacity requirements could be prepared that was sufficient for planning needs. A program to do this was prepared in three weeks.

It should be apparent that the benefits of reviewing the information provided by computer systems may be equally obtainable by examination of clerical procedures, many of which will have been in operation for considerably longer than computer systems and quite possibly ignored in previous improvement plans.

Information centres
In those organizations which have largely kept in step with the advances in hardware and software technology, whether or not all their systems are founded on database techniques, there have been significant attempts to respond to the developing information

needs of the end user. One of the more interesting approaches has been the concept of the information centre.

Typically, an information centre provides a meeting place for the user, the computer and the professional adviser. Using terminals or personal computers, together with query languages, report generators and maybe fourth generation languages, the user is encouraged to make use of data in existing systems and to create mini-systems to meet his particular requirements. This approach has been successful in many environments, but it requires adequate technical resourcing, for hand-holding purposes, as well as a generous attitude towards the provision of equipment. Cynically, one might suggest that it benefits the equipment supplier, whose market is extended, and the computer manager, who retains control over potentially errant users while appearing to enhance the facilities available. Nevertheless, any move to provide the user with access and a measure of control over computing must be beneficial in the long run.

Guidelines

Management should not be seduced into believing that management information systems and computer systems are necessarily synonymous, although there may be an increasing interdependence as more of an organization's operations are converted to data processing systems. Faced with pressures that you feel may be relieved by access to better information, you should at least make the following assessments.

1   Relate information needs to the nature of the decisions that managers have to make and, where possible, automate the lower level decisions. For the rest, ensure that both clerical and computer systems are oriented towards the production of information that is relevant, accurate and timely in terms of the time allowed for decision making.
2   Subject information needs to frequent scrutiny in order to eliminate wasteful activities and to exploit the latent opportunities often available within existing systems.
3   If you are a first time user, or an existing user contemplating a new application, seriously consider the advantages of a database approach, bearing in mind that it will involve more complexity and higher costs initially but might eventually provide a

much more flexible framework for varying or adding to information requirements.

4 If you are a well established user and are tempted to move towards a database, be wary of the costs involved and be careful to choose the right moment. Pay particular attention to the costs/benefits evaluation as there is a tendency to underestimate the costs and not to think through the benefits.

5 Information systems, whether or not they are founded on a database, depend on a man-machine interface to be wholly effective; experience has shown that we have not fully appreciated the problems that this can create. Man is flexible, intuitive and inclined to unstructured ad hoc reactions, whereas the computer displays the opposite qualities.

6 Many computer specialists are wholly unfamiliar with the purposes for which information is required, although they are often highly skilled in providing the means. While they may understand the mechanics of operating procedures, they do not usually have the background and experience to appreciate the less structured environment of management decision-making. Greater emphasis needs to be placed on two-way communication between users and specialists.

Finally, you should ensure that managers not only recognize their information requirements but are also capable of exploiting the information when it is available. Inadequacies in overall performance may stem from the quality of managers and their ability to make the best use of the information rather than from any deficiencies in its content or the system that provides it.

11   Computers as the agents of change

Change is not made without inconvenience, even from worse to better.   (Richard Hooker, 1554–1600)

Introduction

Whether we like it or not, and I confess that I do not, computer and related technologies have resulted in significant changes to the nature and meaning of work and will do so increasingly in the future. Work, in the conventional sense of an activity which is both financially rewarding and spiritually satisfying, is an important part of the life of the average man, occupying perhaps one half of his waking hours; as such, we cannot avoid being affected by these changes, which may be more insidious than apparent and quite impossible to reverse.

The use of computers is irrevocably linked with the search for efficiency, whatever evidence is adduced by case studies to suggest the contrary, and this search is often conducted at a feverish pace. Each invention or new advance seems to produce a leap-frogging of applications and, more importantly, to stimulate both the imagination and the confidence of prospective users. Thus, the explosion in microtechnology has spawned thousands of potential applications and encouraged belief in what previously had appeared to be the romancing of science fiction writers. As a result, we now talk in matter of fact tones about voice-actuated computing, fully automated offices and robotics in terms of 'When?' not 'How?' and 'Why?'. It takes a potential disaster, like five computers failing to talk intelligently with each other during the space shuttle launch, to remind us of how fine a line we tread between utter chaos and the brave new world.

However, the pace and direction of change in macro-terms is one thing; interpreting and exploiting change at the level of the individual organization is quite another. Organizations comprise not merely functional structures designed to carry out work but also collections of individuals and groups that have, or develop, aspirations, needs and objectives of its component parts. Thus, for change to be effective and capable of beneficial exploitation, it has to be perceived by all components of the organization, however dimly, as being in their best interests. Historically, there are many examples where change has been avoided or resisted, with the inevitable result that the organization has declined or disappeared. In the early 1980s the steel industry was an example of the former consequence but has proved not to be an example of the latter; at the conclusion of the debilitating miners' strike, we hope the coal industry will similarly survive.

In this chapter, I propose to look briefly at an area that has yet to be fully researched by organizational theorists and historians of economic change – the effect the computer has had on the creation of new types of organization and on the structure and operations of existing ones. In particular, I propose to speculate on the opportunities that have been overlooked or ignored for using the computer constructively to change the nature of management tasks. Inevitably, I will be considering the larger organization that makes extensive use of computing facilities, but there is no reason why our tentative conclusions should not be relevant to the potential problems of the smaller computer user.

Organizations created by computers

The most obvious examples of organizations created by the emergence of the computer are, of course, the companies that design, manufacture and supply data processing equipment. Some of these companies owe their origin to a prior commitment to punched card processors, whereas others have developed to protect a vested interest in the market for accounting machines. There are also many cases, particularly in the field of small business computing systems, where companies have been specifically created to meet a need that was not being met. These organizations provide the economist with fascinating material both about the interplay between technology and the market place and about the influence of competition. Sometimes it would appear that an organization's development and marketing strategy will be dictated by what its principal competitors are up to; at other times, it seems that the weight of investment in R & D will dictate the products, almost irrespective of market needs.

The mid-1980s have yielded a wealth of case material on the rise, decline and fall of computer companies. In between editions of this book, some microcomputer suppliers have been formed, grown at a rapid pace, overtraded, found that they did not have the financial resilience to withstand the intense competition and have finally disappeared. The same is true of many computer 'shops' and dealerships, and some software houses. The wonder is not that these enterprises foundered but that so many have survived. For example, there are around 700 different makes and models of microcomputer and over 1300 suppliers of software products operating in the UK.

By virtue of the nature of the products, i.e. general purpose computers, and their multiple uses, these organizations have had to identify closely with the objectives of their customers and to provide support and services that are almost unique in the supply of capital equipment. Thus, the computer supplier will undertake not only to manufacture and maintain machines to a fairly rigorous technical specification but also to help you to use it by assisting with the identification of applications, design and development of systems and general advice. Some go further and create specialized functions, directed at the support of particular industries or specific functions, in which you may find experts who are more competent than any professional you may employ. Of course, it is all part of creating awareness and stimulating the demand for the product – preferably their product – but I cannot think of many industries where the product has such a profound effect on the structure and operation of the organization.

There is a similar market/technology pressure on computer service bureaux and software houses, which are two further examples of companies that owe their existence and shape to the computer. Of these two, the computer bureau is particularly susceptible to change because it has to commit its fortunes to hardware facilities that could be rendered obsolete or uneconomic by the next advance in technology or product announcement. For example, the continued decline in hardware costs, the explosive development of the microcomputer and the predilection for on-line systems have all combined to erode the traditional customer base of the service bureaux, which has been the small user unable to justify his own installation. The bureaux that have anticipated the effects of these changes and have varied the range and costs of their services are the ones which will survive. In the same way that computer manufacturers have taken on responsibilities that extend beyond the supply of a reliable product, computer service bureaux have had to assume a hand-holding role that amounts at times to the fulfilment of line management tasks. Where its customers have several applications with the bureau, this commitment can involve it, as an outsider, to an extra-ordinary extent in their operational affairs, and a sizeable proportion of its resources may be committed to these responsibilities. Whether the bureau likes it or not, it becomes an integral part of its customers' operations and indirectly changes some of the management practices of its clients. With some notable exceptions, many computer service bureaux are ill-resourced to manage vicariously.

There are organizations that have been created principally because of the uses that can be made of computers and related equipment, and without these facilities they would simply not exist. Take, for example, the few successful computerized booking services for theatre and other leisure pursuits. They owe their existence to computing and communications techniques, as well as marketing flair, and without them could not provide a service which in some countries purports to be nationwide. Of much more consequence is the growth in specialized companies providing an information storage and retrieval service for research or professional reference. Some of these services have developed from library units that see their traditional market being threatened, but many have seen the commercial opportunities that improved international communications offer. I have no doubt that many more service organizations will develop once potential markets are identified and entrepreneurs can see how to apply computer technology to satisfy them.

The extension of services

There are many more examples of organizations which have been encouraged to extend or modify their services significantly as a result of computers, and which have reflected these changes in their approach to management.

1   The development of banking services, and particularly the provision of credit facilities on an international scale, could not have been accomplished without the massive investment in computers we have seen in the 1970s and 1980s. In many cases, the computer (or rather the complex of computers and allied communications facilities) have ceased in practice to be a service function and have become central to the banks' operations. Without these facilities it is doubtful if the volume of work could be handled using clerical resources, even if you could find anyone who could remember how things were done. It is a fact which has not escaped the attention of the trades unions involved, and has markedly altered the approach of bankers to the tricky questions of industrial relations. Inevitably, it also changes managements' attitudes towards costs/benefits evaluation, in an environment where you might expect a narrower view. If it costs a million pounds to duplicate a system what does it matter, if thousands of millions of pounds of business would otherwise be at risk. There seems to be a point in computer investment beyond which it makes less sense to quibble about the marginal cost when committed costs are already astronomic.

2   A similar environment exists in the airline business, which has thrived more than most on the services provided by computers and which is now so committed that chaos reigns if a system breaks down. As a result, the computing function is often represented at the highest management levels and its contribution is taken into account in forming policy much more than lowly administrative functions ever were before the advent of computers. Moreover, the very existence of a network of computers/communications which is international in character has enabled airlines to extend the services they offer customers into areas nor strictly related to transport. So, we find airline systems interfacing with hotel booking systems, package tour organizers, car hire companies and the like, and by virtue of assuming that role they take on new or different management responsibilities. In fact, tourism is an industry in which it is possible to conceive major changes arising through the use of computers and communication facilities, some of which are already beginning to take shape. However, the big problems this industry will face arise from the proliferation of small units with widely different interests and from the inherent difficulties in harmonizing largely unstructured information requirements.

3   Until quite recently, building societies had concentrated their computing activities on what amounted to a conversion of existing systems. In some ways it is difficult to see how these fairly simple procedures could have been differently approached. However, the national spread of the larger societies, with branches in every major town, supported by terminal networks, provides them with the opportunity to consider extending their services into the banking sector. Some societies have introduced cash dispensers, and there are many attractions for customers in a six-day counter service supported by cheque facilities. These ventures are beginning to change the operating characteristics of the societies, influence marketing policy and management and have stimulated mergers and rationalizations in an industry that at present still appears somewhat fragmented.

4   For many years it was popularly supposed that the use of computers in public administration would lead to some sinister conversations between computers that would cause many citizens embarrassment or grief. I was never convinced that this would happen, not because the technology did not exist, but through scepticism that computer staff in different public sectors would ever successfully achieve their limited objectives, let alone agree to some wider systems framework. I began to get worried when the Driver and Vehicle Licensing Centre finally went live and I realised that dogged perseverance might have its ultimate reward. Now I suspect that before long these computers *will* be holding animated dialogues and comparing notes, and public administration will acquire a new dimension. This is perhaps a situation in which the use of computer facilities to extend the services of organizations should be viewed with dismay.

Arguably, every computer user should be able to point to some area in which the computer has profoundly affected the nature of business operations, if only to permit growth where it might have been otherwise impossible. A lot will depend on perseverance, the imagination of users and computer staff and, particularly, on the commitment of top management. However, few companies have fully exploited the opportunities presented by computer systems to bring about radical changes in their organization structure and in the ways that management tasks are performed. As a consequence, many companies persist with a structure that may not have changed significantly in 20 years and expect it to cope with an operating environment that has changed several times in a similar period.

Exploiting change

The arguments for change, to which I subscribe, go something like this.

1 Computers are capable of taking on the routine data processing work associated with all operating, accounting and administrative procedures in an organization.

2 They are also capable of performing certain decision-making tasks that are normally carried out by junior and middle managers, provided the rules are carefully constructed and adequate precautions are taken to monitor the execution of those rules; for example, the development of expert systems and the early application of artificial intelligence.

3 Taking on the execution of routine procedures removes or dilutes, at the junior level, one of the major management tasks, namely the supervision and coordination of a workforce and the custodianship of one of the organization's functions.

4 Delegation of a whole raft of low-level decisions to the computer also removes part of the raison d'etre for many managers.

5 Releasing management and supervisory skills at lower levels should lead to one or more of the following results:
   - surplus management resources;
   - radical revision of job descriptions and functional responsibilities;
   - enhancement of the management task through concentration on higher levels of decision making and other activities;
   - redundancy.

   However we know from experience that these consequences are rarely pursued.

6 Furthermore, having committed these procedures to computer operation, we have effectively overridden the existing organizational or departmental boundaries. For example, consider

the computerization of a sales order processing system that covers the administration of the customer's order, the selection of stock items to satisfy it, the preparation of despatch notes and invoices and the calculation of sales statistics. Such a system embraces some of the functions carried out by the sales department, by inventory control, by the transport department and by accounts. To whom does the system belong? To any one of the departmental managers or to them all in some kind of commmittee? Or does the system become the responsibility of the computer manager in a managerial sense as well as a technical one? If one endorses the concept of joint responsibility, the position of the individual manager can become very confused. One can conceive a situation in which most functions supervised by a manager have been integrated into a number of computer systems, giving him a collection of different committee relationships with other managers and perhaps little direct responsibility. Where computerization is extensive the multiplicity of relationships can involve every function in the organization. Even so, we tend to preserve existing organizational structures and departmental boundaries, in spite of these quite radical changes in the pattern of control. We are reluctant to change the specification of individual management jobs and rarely recognize that wholly new types of managerial functions are being created.

7   In spite of the potential impact on structure, management jobs and staffing levels, few organizations take the trouble to plan their evolution, tending instead to adopt fairly negative policies such as reliance on natural wastage, or even actions to slow down the pace of implementation. I am convinced that this has happened in many administrative areas where the prospect of confrontation with clerical unions has daunted management.

8   Although computer systems may become crucial to the operating efficiency of the organization and have a direct bearing on managerial effectiveness, it is surprising how few organizations lay positive plans not only to give user managers a direct working knowledge of computers but also to introduce computer specialists into line management functions. After all, in terms of intellectual capacity and energy, you could not have better material.

A possible approach

The situation created by the impact of extensive computerization is not dissimilar to the problems facing an organization when it decides to establish a project framework to deal with a multi-task responsibility. There is a need to coordinate different functions and skills and to have a unified control over progress. It is also important to have one backside to kick if things go wrong and a singularity of purpose to make sure they go right. In the case of a computer system that straddles several traditional functions, it is more a case of ensuring that the process is not interrupted and that individual functional needs do not subvert the objectives of the system. It should be possible, therefore, to conceive a computer-oriented organization structure (See Figure 11.1) that identifies 'systems managers' rather than functional managers. In other words, a designated user manager would be responsible for the day-to-day running of a computer application, or a set of related systems, rather than for the coordination of the work of a group of staff. He may have staff or he may have none; the nature of the system would dictate the need for non-computer resources. Being the focal point for the management and performance of the system, he would have a highly specific interest in ensuring its production efficiency and its overall effectiveness in contributing to the well-being of the organization. Ideally, he would be the user representative seconded to run the systems development project at the outset and would be as familiar with its design and operation as any computer man.

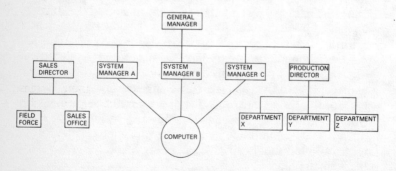

Figure 11.1 Possible organization structure

It is not necessary to wait for the complete computerization of an organization's procedures in order to introduce this concept. It could be applied successfully in any situation where a relatively self-contained group of systems could be identified. For example, all those systems and procedures that relate to the recruitment, training, welfare, remuneration, productivity and administration of employees, and that might currently be the responsibility of four departments (personnel, production, costing and wages), could be brought under one systems manager charged with the responsibility to manage human resource systems.

Consider also the structures commonly adopted for control of manufacturing in an engineering environment. Typically, the functions reporting to the manufacturing director will be organized in the manner illustrated in Figure 11.2. Parcels of work or particular specialisms are recognized structurally and in management terms because of the need to share the clerical burden in some logical fashion. All our management training is also geared to a hierarchical, span of control, job oriented structure.

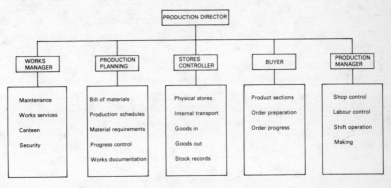

Figure 11.2   Typical production organization

If, however, we introduce a comprehensive computer system which deals with the processing and elementary decision-making involved in:

- breaking down customers requirements into a gross demand for components;
- apportioning available stocks of components and initiating make or buy orders for the unsatisfied portion;

- planning the use of factory capacity;
- scheduling production in terms of time and quantities;
- raising and progressing orders on external suppliers;
- progressing actual production;
- initiating despatch activities; and
- maintaining current and forward production statistics;

we could create a totally different structure, as illustrated in Figure 11.3.

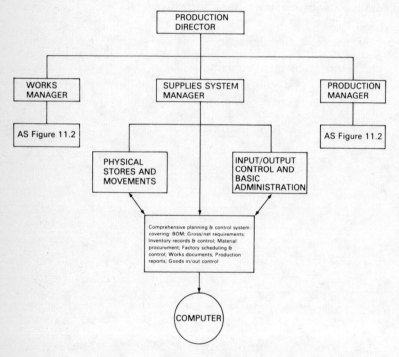

Figure 11.3   Alternative production structure

Capitalizing on the comprehensiveness of the computer system, we would be able not only to reduce manning, because of the elimination of clerical tasks, but also to change the management structure by:

- elimination of functions;
- combining functions;
- automating elementary decisions;
- providing a unified information structure; and
- removing a layer of management and supervision.

It should also be noted that by implication we have subordinated the production manager to the supplies manager, even though functionally they may appear as separate roles. Unfortunately, no organization to my knowledge has followed the logic of computer systems through to this extent, although I have seen some cases that approximate to it.

It is not difficult to apply this approach to other areas where we have reflected our working methods in the management structure. The upshot of a change might well be the need for fewer managers, or at least fewer staff exercising management functions, but it is almost certain that the remainder would have to be of a much higher and different quality. In this connection, I believe that most organizations could make better use of the talent that exists in their computing departments. There are some glittering exceptions where senior computer men have been pulled out of the data processing function, given line responsibilities, proved enormously successful and in most cases achieved board status. Timing is critical. If you leave them too long, they become hard-boiled specialists, too expensive or too secure to want to change their job, and if you take them too soon they may over-reach themselves. If they are totally ignored then the chances are they will move on to other organizations.

Guidelines

It is difficult to offer general guidelines for the exploitation of computers as an agent of change as so much depends on the management style and general ambience of the organization concerned. In some cases one can move fairly rapidly to bring about changes, whereas in others much more care is required, especially if you have a crop of managers who are well versed in existing practices. There is also the whole question of the responsibility of the organization towards its workforce, including managers, and the socioeconomic pressures that may moderate the pursuit of excellence. However, I can say that those senior managers who see the computer primarily as a means of instilling discipline and achieving changes that they have already identified not only misrepresent the purpose and value of computing, but also reflect poorly on their current approach to management.

12   Organizing for computer usage

Introduction

There are many thousands of computer users who may never need to establish a formal computer department as a means of ensuring that computers are operated efficiently and effectively. For example, organizations that place their data processing jobs with computer service bureaux should make sensible internal arrangements to oversee the flow of work and to formalize liaison duties, but it is unlikely that they will require a separate formal structure solely devoted to the computing function. Nor does the existence of an in-house installation necessarily imply that you need a computer department, many small business systems being specifically designed for integration with normal business or administrative procedures and for management by users. Nevertheless, there are many installations which, by virtue of the scale of computing involved and the number of staff committed directly to data processing activities, demand a more formal approach to organization structure and management practices. This requirement arises whether the computing function comprises several hundred staff or merely a dozen people, and is influenced primarily both by the recognition of computing as a corporate resource and by the need to coordinate the activities of specialists. Some computer departments have more employees and a larger expenditure budget than many small companies, but often have less management experience than the one-man business.

There are two ways in which I want to look at the question of organizing for computer usage. The first concerns the position of the department in the overall structure, and the inter-relationships which are thereby created. Secondly, I want to examine the problems of organizing specialists within the computer department itself.

Historical development

It seems strange to be talking in terms of historical development of an activity which has been in existence for such a short time. Nevertheless, in the evolution of organization structures for data processing one can recognize a pattern that reflects changes in the technological and managerial environment.

Functional attachment

To begin with, many data processing units were attached to the function that first promoted the use of computers or which had current control of the punched card installation which the computer was intended to replace. I doubt if any serious thought was given to this decision; it just seemed the natural thing to do. As we have indicated elsewhere, the accountants were among the first potential users to recognize the opportunities presented by computers. The accounting function had all the right characteristics: the user was numerate and disciplined; the procedures were constructed logically and well-understood; and there was an evident data processing load that was carried by accounting machines or punched card installations. It seemed appropriate that not only should the computer be applied initially to accounting routines but that the embryonic department should become part of the accounting structure. This situation applied with the majority of early users, and only rarely was the computer attached to other functions such as sales or production.

This approach, illustrated in Figure 12.1, had several effects, not all of which were recognized as being bad at the time.

1 First of all, the concentration on accounting routines effectively blocked any other applications for two or three years. This occurred even where the justification for the computer ultimately depended on the conversion of operating systems such as production and inventory control.

   A company in the aerospace industry acquired a large computer in order to computerize manufacturing planning and control procedures. It was decided that the first application should be costing systems, which placed control with the accounting function. Three years later virtually no progress had been made in converting production systems, but quite a number of accounting routines had been transferred to the

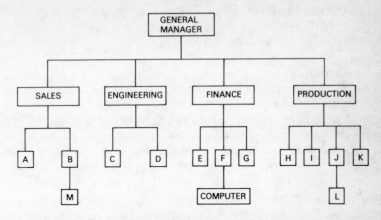

Figure 12.1 Functional approach

computer and, organizationally, the accounting function controlled the computer department. This provoked the manufacturing units to prepare a case for a second installation devoted solely to their needs.

2 The second effect, then, was to equate computing with accounting, and many potential users became frustrated and lost interest in obtaining access to the 'accountants' machine.

3 A less obvious result only became apparent when the non-accounting systems were eventually tackled. The experience and expertise of computer staff, accumulated from converting well-structured and largely unchangeable procedures, proved wholly inadequate when they were faced with more complex routines that demanded a creative approach to analysis and design.

4 Attaching a computer department to the accounting function often placed it organizationally at a lower level than its potential influence demanded. This was especially true if it was founded on an existing punched card installation. It meant, among other things, that the scope of the computer manager to influence senior management was often quite limited.

The application of the computer to accounting routines did not generally lead to world shaking benefits, and many potential users became sceptical of the contribution that computers could make in their areas. By and large, one could conclude that the close association between computing and accounting in the early stages of development was a barrier to progress.

Service function

An alternative approach was to establish the computer department from the outset as a service function (see Figure 12.2), providing data processing services to all potential users and owing line allegiance to none. This solution was welcome to users and to the computer manager, whose organizational status was dramatically improved. This approach was also adopted by existing users after unsatisfactory experiences arising from the attachment of the computer department to one specific function.

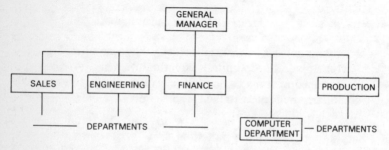

Figure 12.2   The service approach

However, this solution raises a number of important issues, not all of which have been satisfactorily resolved, even within quite advanced computer installations.

1   The first question is, if the computer manager does not report to a specific user, to whom does he report as a service function?

The answer, invariably, has been to press for the computer function to report direct to the chief executive, especially following the realization that the evident support of senior management was often a critical factor in the success of computer projects. Where the chief executive has been prepared to take on this additional direct responsibility and discharge it consistently, the outcome has frequently been beneficial to the data processing function and the organization as a whole. However, it is too much to expect every chief executive in every case to take on this job, especially if the result is merely to elevate tedious detail or squabbles between users to the status of executive decision-making.

To resolve this problem, many different approaches have been used with varying degrees of success. These include making the computer department responsible to:

- a main board member who has no other functional responsibility;
- an executive who has an existing service commitment to the parent organization, such as an administration director;
- a steering committee of senior executives.

Latterly, in some larger installations, the computer manager has been given the equivalent of board status and has joined the ranks of senior executives responsible for a major business function.

2. If the principal reason for establishing the computer department as a separate function is the recognition that its services have a universal application, how does the department decide between competing demands for those services? Should the computer manager have the responsibility of deciding priorities and arbitrating between requests from users?

Obviously, decisions about the allocation of priorities and the use of limited resources must be subject to some kind of procedural discipline accepted by the organization as a whole. Ideally, the organization should prepare a long-term computing plan which is weighted according to the estimated benefits that potential applications offer. This plan should set the objectives and constraints for the computer department, and any variation should need exhaustive justification. The implementation of the plan and consideration of any changes to policy should be vested in some form of executive steering group that represents the interests of all users. Some organizations have recognized this need and have been diligent in producing and controlling an overall computing strategy, while others have been less successful in achieving long-term consistency.

3. The separate identification of computing as a service function raises the question of how the function should be controlled managerially. This is clearly connected with the setting of objectives and guidelines within an overall plan; there has to be

a complementary mechanism that enables computer management to report on its custodianship of the resources of the function and on its service to a variety of users in the organization. This is in many respects a unique reporting requirement that does not apply to any other function.

The concept of management services

Once computing had been identified as a separate entity, it did not take long for the concept of a management services function to develop. Indeed, there is a sound rationale to the idea of combining under one control all those services that are aimed at improving the efficiency and effectiveness of the organization. This approach has the twin advantages of focusing related skills and providing management with a powerful resource for shaping or redirecting the organization in line with corporate plans.

Where management services departments have been created they have typically included such activities as:

- data processing;
- organization and methods (a function unfairly overshadowed by the emergence of systems analysis);
- operations research;
- clerical work study;
- internal consultancy;
- the development of user support services and information centres;
- latterly office automation.

However, as we shall see later, the ways in which these activities have been organized and used within the management services department have had an important bearing on the effectiveness of the function as an aid to management.

Decentralized computing

A contrary development has been the emergence of a decentralized approach to computing that may have been fostered by the management style of the organization and/or by the availability of small, cheap computing facilities. This in effect is a return to the attachment of computer units to single functions or, as in the latter cases, to individual operating units or geographically separate locations. This development is usually promoted to meet user aspirations or to endorse intrinsic systems requirements that call for a dedicated local approach. What it means for an existing, centralized computer function is a loss of control over most aspects of data processing, which the centralized function may resist; furthermore, it significantly changes management and reporting relationships. Too many organizations fail both to appreciate the implications of this approach and to think through some of the following issues.

1 In dispersing responsibility for data processing activities, you have to be extremely careful that the parent organization's control over the direction and cost of computing, which may have been hard won, is not entirely dissipated.

2 In other words, there has still to be some form of central coordination, if only to conserve funds and to avoid re-inventing the wheel in several locations.

3 There may be certain skills or experience that the centre will have accumulated and which it may be difficult or impossible to duplicate in the multiple locations, e.g. expertise in the understanding and manipulation of manufacturers' software. As a result there may be a continuing role for a central service in providing a pool of computing expertise to users who are otherwise independent.

4 Decisions on equipment and the shape of systems commit the organization for some time ahead, but eventually the next stage in computer developments will have to be evaluated. In a decentralized environment these decisions may arise at different times for each part of the organization, depending on their progress, and potentially quite divergent policies could emerge. Whether implementations of these policies would be in the best overall interests of the organization depends on what measures are taken to preserve an optimal approach to computing.

5 You have to ensure that decentralized control of computing does not in practice mean an absence of control, with the local units repeating the same kind of mistakes that are endemic with new computer users.

Although I have stressed the pre-eminence of the user's requirements in applying computers in organizations, I would be against any devolution of control which resulted in anarchy. It is vital that in adopting a decentralized approach, management is fully aware of its ramifications and makes arrangements to maintain a proper, if distant, control over computing policy. Control of capital expenditure and headcount are, as always, the final arbiters in such situations.

The position of the computer function

It will already be apparent that the position of the computer function in the structure of an organization is dependent on the contribution that data processing is expected to make to the overall objectives of the organization. If the intention is to use a computer for a single purpose and to integrate it as far as possible with an existing functional activity, there may be no need at all to allocate computing a separate role in the organization. On the other hand, if the aim is to create a source of computing power and technique that can be applied generally to a variety of tasks in the organization, it will be necessary to take a more formal view of the position of the computer function. Past experience suggests that the creation of a separate computer department has proved most successful where the following conditions prevail:

- the organization has paid some attention to its long-term computing strategy;
- specific objectives and key tasks have been identified for the computer department;
- a framework of management practice and reporting relationships has been defined.

Ideally, management control of computer activities should follow the practices observed by the rest of the organization, e.g. budgetary control, performance evaluation, etc.

Computing strategy

It is terribly easy to become academic or over-mechanistic about the development of corporate plans, and determining a computer strategy is no exception. The important requirements can be quite simply expressed.

1 How is computing expected to contribute to corporate goals?
2 How will that contribution be implemented in terms of hardware/software and systems development policies?

3 What are the financial implications?
4 What actions need to be taken in order to initiate and achieve the plan?

Most computer strategies take a 3-5 year view of requirements, and are usually re-examined annually to take account of any significant changes in the factors that originally influenced the formation of policy. For example, currently, I would expect any review of computer strategy to assess the merits of centralized or distributed computing, to find a basis for exploiting the increasing virtues of microcomputers, and to take note of developments in communications and office automation that could conceivably affect the plan. The relationship between the corporate plan and computer policy is illustrated in Figure 12.3, and typifies the difference between strategy planning and tactical planning referred to elsewhere.

Objectives and key tasks
Determination of an overall computing strategy will dictate the objectives and key tasks for the computer department. These may be expressed in terms of the acquisition of resources, the implementation of specific systems and the setting of quantified criteria of performance for the provision of services. Unless a computer manager is given express terms of reference, he will define his own – the nature of management being to abhor a vacuum – and they may not be wholly in keeping with the organization's needs. Too often, computer managers are placed in charge of a considerable volume of assets and in positions of great influence without any attempt to define their role and the results expected of them. Where tasks are identified, e.g. 'To provide a reliable production and development service to users', there is usually no thought given to the basis for determining if the tasks have been properly acquitted. It is obviously far better, for example, to define 'A reliable production service' in terms of such factors as:

- a minimum of x production hours per month;
- a $y\%$ availability for an on-line system;
- missed deadlines;

and so on. It is not difficult to agree parameters of performance and it makes the task of establishing management control easier.

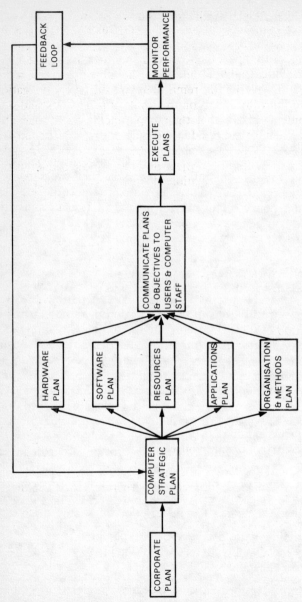

Figure 12.3 Computer policy framework

Management reporting and control
Computer managers have a dual responsibility when it comes to reporting on their activities. As with every manager, there is a requirement to report their performance in utilizing the organization's resources and in meeting the objectives set for their departments. Within this remit there are subsidiary obligations to report to individual users on the levels of production and systems development service that their departments have been able to sustain. We have indicated in the chapter on project control what we consider to be a suitable hierarchy of reports in order to provide information on project progress. In the same illustration we depicted reporting relationships which called for information that is more comprehensive than project status. Of these relationships, the most important is the obligation to report regularly on the custodianship of the computer function. Whether this report is made to the chief executive, to the board or to the steering committee, it should be prepared to a prescribed format and produced on a regular basis, preferably monthly. The report should at least record the following matters.

1 A review of the month's performance in operations and systems development, in units and value.
2 Budget/actual comparisons on hours, value, other performance criteria and established standards.
3 A review of the forward plan.
4 A summary of project progress.
5 Problem areas.
6 Policy matters requiring attention.
7 Decisions required.
8 Administration and resources.

If your computer function is part of a broader management services unit, similar reports can be generated to cover the other functions.

Accounting
All too often, when I ask to see the data processing budget for a computer department, I am told there is no such thing because computing is regarded as an overhead. Ignoring the obvious non sequitur, it seems to me to be wholly irrational for an organization to invest considerable sums of money in equipment and manpower

and then to abdicate responsibility for controlling the investment, probably in contrast to what it is doing elsewhere in the organization. The computer manager should be subject to the same disciplines as other functional heads and should produce budgets for capital expenditure and annual running costs.

The capital budget should indicate what enhancements to equipment, software or other facilities are planned during the coming financial year. The budget for annual running costs should distinguish between production expenses and the costs of systems development, and, where these functions have a seperate manager, each should be held responsible for his part of the budget. Thus the budget for a computer department might include the following main headings.

- Production
  - Equipment costs
  - Maintenance charges
  - Software rentals
  - Supplies
  - Staff
- Development
  - Staff
  - Development aids
- Administration
  - Management
  - Training
  - Expenses
  - Overhead
  - Clerical and secretarial

Some of the headings might be subdivided to show significant items. For example, equipment costs might distinguish between the central installation and network facilities, and staff could be further analysed to show the type of resource involved, e.g. operators, data entry, programmers, etc.

For purposes of overall control of computing, actual costs should be allocated to production jobs and to development projects on a month-by-month basis. Software is available on most mainframes to provide job accounting information on the use of computer facilities, and simple procedures can be introduced to collect data on the use of resources on development. This information can be used purely for monitoring the efficiency of the computer department, or it could also form the basis for a charging procedure by which users are invoiced for computer services. Whether or not you choose to introduce a charging system depends on the objectives you wish to achieve. There are several possible aims.

1 To encourage/discourage users of the equipment or particular aspects of the service. For example, you could use a weighted charging structure in order:
    ● to encourage the development of on-line systems;
    ● to discourage excessive report production;
    ● to discourage activities that affect efficiency, such as excessive magnetic tape mounts/dismounts.
2 To provide a pseudo-commercial service for internal users and to generate surplus funds for re-investment in hardware, software or staff.
3 Merely to act as a means of internal budgeting and costs control.

Unless the aim is clear, it will be difficult to establish the right cost structure and pricing policy.

Internal structures

Bearing in mind the relative newness of computing, it is quite surprising how many different ways have been devised for organizing computer resources. At the level where the computer function involves several hundred staff, a variety of technical expertise, control of major capital facilities and the management of budgets that may be in excess of £1.0 million, we clearly require a more formal approach to organization structure than for a small department.

Functional structures
The earliest structures devised for computer departments were founded on the distinctions between the various functions performed. As illustrated in Figure 12.4, this approach distinguished three main functions;

● Systems analysis
● Programming
● Operations

This method of organization caused a number of problems in the area of systems development. In the first place, the separation of systems analysis from programming introduced a communications interface between the two functions that was not always overcome by good standards and systems documentation. In addition, programmers working on a system had a dual responsibility: to the systems analyst in charge of the system; and to the chief programmer who managed their function. As often as not, when the systems analyst handed over the specification it became absorbed into the programming function and he lost a measure of control.

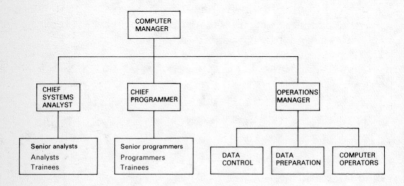

Figure 12.4　Functional organization

Project orientation

Recognition that computer applications were more successful if they were established on a project basis, thus giving the systems analyst control over all aspects of development, led to the introduction of project management techniques, which in turn influenced the structure of computer departments, as illustrated in Figure 12.5. Following this approach, the systems analyst is given day-to-day control of all project activities, including full supervision of programming resources.

One effect of this development was to raise questions about the need for a separate programming function, and particularly for a chief programmer. Various modifications to the basic project-oriented structure were therefore accommodated. In some cases, the production role of the chief programmer atrophied and he became responsible only for such issues as standards, document-

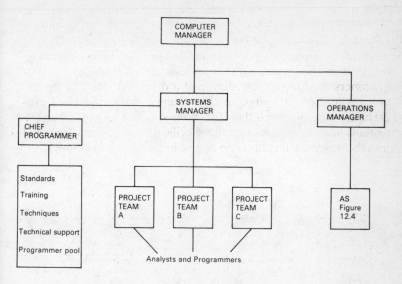

Figure 12.5 Project organization 1

ation, training, and so on. In other installations, depending on the computer, it became apparent that there was a need for the concentration of particular technical skills and software expertise, and a separate technical function was created, as illustrated in Figure 12.6, although it might consist of only one individual.

Obviously, there are different ways of organizing on a project basis. In some cases, a whole application area could be regarded as a project and the development function could be divided into, say, financial systems, production systems and commercial systems. Alternatively, the structure could be based on customer identification, such that there might be a team for division A, a team for division B, and so on.

Line and staff
As installations increase in size and technical complexity and the range of applications expands, we see the emergence of a greater distinction between production activities and the specialist internal services devoted to support tasks. Thus, for example, the structure has to be modified to include database functions and terminal network control, as illustrated in Figure 12.7. Depending on the

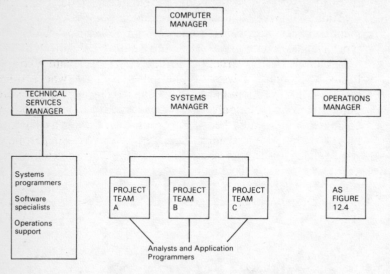

Figure 12.6 Project organization 2

importance of the database approach to applications, the database function can be part of technical services if it has limited applicability, or can be a separate general service function if the intention is to base all systems on this technique.

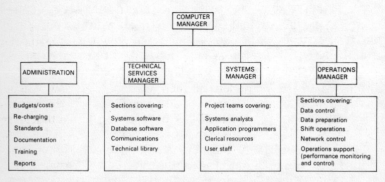

Figure 12.7 Specialist organization

Management services

In many large organizations the development of the computing function may have culminated in the establishment of a management services department, incorporating data processing. A typical management services structure is shown in Figure 12.8.

Variations on this structure include efforts to create a core of business systems analysts or internal consultants whose prime tasks are investigation and problem solving, the seeking of computer solutions being only a secondary role. In other words, the computer quite rightly becomes one of several tools available to management. More recently, management services departments have tended to acquire responsibilities for communications and office automation which might otherwise spawn new service functions. We have also seen the development of information centres designed to support users in the exploitation of both microcomputers and mainframe data processing systems.

Problem areas

Development of organization structures to exploit computing has created many problem areas for the technician and the general manager alike.

1 In the first place, most computer managers have had no formal management training and are likely to be at the top because of their technical excellence rather than their organizing or managing abilities. Consequently, we may create large and expensive structures that will be controlled by managerial novices.
2 Similarly, where several functions are involved, the function managers are likely to be even less experienced at this level than the computer manager, thus increasing his problems of coordinating their efforts as a management team.
3 Where they are left to their own devices, few computer departments have introduced formal management practices that would support their lack of experience, even though such practices may be common in the rest of the organization. Consequently we find few detailed job descriptions, inadequate reporting mechanisms, reliance on technical jargon to demonstrate activity, and only a passing recognition of budgeting or management accounting procedures.

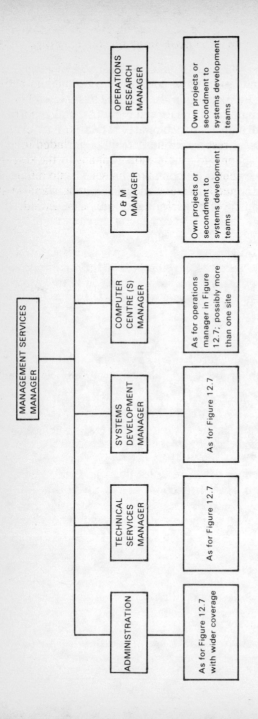

Figure 12.8 Management services structure

In some respects it is your responsibility as the general manager, to ensure that these circumstances do not arise. You should insist on a formal approach to organization and management, and seek evidence that it is supported by adequate control and reporting procedures. In particular, senior computer staff who may eventually have management responsibilities should be included in any management development programme that applies to the rest of the organization. In essence, the computer manager is no different to other managers. He needs to know and clearly understand what is required of him and know his performance will be measured.

13   Computers and industrial relations

Introduction

Some years ago I was present at a conference on computers and
trade unionism, part of which was addressed by Clive Jenkins
(general secretary of the white collar union ASTMS) on the subject of the threat to management and supervisory jobs from
extensive computer usage. Having captured the attention of his
audience with graphic tales, handsomely expressed, he paused
and, wagging a finger gently at the several corners of the hall, he
said quietly 'You're next . . .' The hush was almost physical,
broken eventually by people moving uncomfortably in their seats.

His forecast would be even more pointed today, with signs on
every side of the intrusion of computers into areas previously
secure by virtue of the costs of change or the difficulties of
achieving it. For a long time, based on early experiences, it has
been generally accepted that, although computer systems may be
designed to reduce the number of staff employed, these savings
rarely occur, some systems having actually led to other different
jobs being created. I believe the comfort sought in this conclusion
is illusory and that computers have had a profound effect on
employment, without attracting the obloquy that immediate job
losses might create.

To begin with, any successful system will improve productivity
and enable more work to be done with less and less reliance on
staff; whether or not you have a no-redundancy policy and rely
on natural wastage, you will effectively reduce the number of job
opportunities in the long term. Computers have also markedly
affected the ways in which residual jobs are carried out; such jobs
may still be open to change, including the less well-defined tasks
of supervision and management. It should come as no surprise
that employees continue to feel uneasy about the spread of com-

puters, although the fact that they seem disinclined to do a great deal about it must be a source of relief to management.

This is all the more difficult to comprehend in an industrial relations environment that has noticeably polarized in recent years, and at a time of great economic insecurity. This may say something favourable about the skill with which systems have been introduced, although I doubt it, complete ignorance of the human factors involved in computer applications being a common feature of implementation. I think it has more to do with the characteristics of many development projects, which have tended to concentrate on converting existing systems rather than on making radical changes, and which have had lengthy implementation cycles. Subsequent changes or new systems seem to create fewer shock waves and are accepted as natural progressions. A process of computing by stealth has thus taken place in many organizations, albeit unconsciously, and many staff are oblivious to the significance of the changes that have occured.

In this chapter, I wish to look briefly at two aspects of the impact of computers on people and jobs and the industrial relations problems that this creates for management. The first area concerns the human relations side of systems development and implementation, particularly what could be done to improve the fairly negative approach adopted by most data processing departments. The second aspect focuses on the industrial relations problems generated by the growth in both unionism and dissident activity among computer staff, and the measures management should consider to prevent or circumvent disputes.

Industrial relations during development

Generally the computer specialist has been more interested in machines than people and more concerned with problem solving than with the sociopolitical effects of his work in the organization. This attitude is influenced in part by the technical difficulties associated with the harnessing of a new technology and by the complexity of business systems, but it is also the product of naïvety and inexperience in the working environment. As a result, many computer applications are developed and implemented without much attention being given to the interests, aspirations and motivations of the staff who have to operate the systems. Typical of the mistakes that are made are the following.

1 By and large, junior staff are not encouraged to participate in the development process and are often introduced to their new roles only a matter of weeks prior to cutover to the new system.
2 Training and preparation is often minimal, such that questions which should have been raised at the earliest stage are faced when it is too late to introduce changes.
3 Changes to job content and working relationships often have profound significance for the people doing the work, although they may have no logical impact on the system. In creating a man/machine interface, we are probably introducing a wholly new relationship for most clerical workers, but little attention is paid to the psychological difficulties this may present.
4 Little attention is paid to the ergonomics of the new working environment, either in selecting equipment or in designing a system that is dependent on an interactive man/machine dialogue, e.g. visual display layouts that are easy to use rather than technically efficient.

These shortcomings, which are relatively easy to overcome in the formative stages of systems development, can result in prolonged implementation periods, frustration and resistance on the part of the operatives, and the erosion of the objectives of the system. The view I have expressed elsewhere is that the initial stages of development are essentially selling and confidence-boosting processes that should be directed at creating an environment that is receptive to change. The ground gained in these early stages should be consolidated by a planned effort to understand and elucidate how each individual affected by the system will have to operate in future. Quite clearly this requires an elaboration of the techniques of systems design into areas with which the average systems analyst may not be familiar. Whether each analyst is trained in these non-computer skills – behavioural science, job enrichment, ergonomics, etc. – or whether you rely on attached specialists, is a matter of cost and convenience. Any expenditure in these directions would be vastly superior to the average situations, where the problem is not even recognized. An example of the effect of some of these shortcomings is illustrated by the following case.

> While carrying out an audit of the effectiveness of a well-established computer installation in the engineering manufacturing industry, I chose to follow through the development and implementation of a new system that had been in live operation for two weeks. Briefly, the system was concerned with preparing instructions for delivery of products straight from the end of the production line or from stock. Part of the system involved the parallel printing of despatch notes on a terminal located in the despatch office. When I visited it, the office was manned by a single elderly warehouseman sitting opposite the terminal, which occasionally spluttered into life. When I asked him what was happening, he said that he didn't know and gave the same answer when asked what he was supposed to do. The stationery came to an end while I was in the office, but he had no idea how to change it or whom to contact. Nobody had been near him in the two weeks since the system had been implemented. Whereas previously he had written out despatch notes and felt part of the process, he now did virtually nothing because his new responsibilities had not been defined or described. The man was confused, frustrated and, understandably, insecure.'

Apart from demonstrating an inept approach to implementation, the systems analyst in charge of this project revealed a total lack of judgement about the human and social implications of introducing change. It is small wonder if projects encounter passive resistance and have a chequered introduction; it is surprising that staff subjected to these changes do not as a rule take more direct action. A lot will depend on whether or not they are unionized and, if they are, on the stance adopted by union officials. The unions generally seem to have a good understanding of the impact of technology on office work, and the more enlightened ones seek to obtain a fair share of the benefits of change rather than blindly to resist it. Thus, one encounters situations where:

• the union is briefed on the intentions of the long-term computer development plan, and may even contribute to it;

- procedures are in operation to give union representatives the opportunity to examine proposed new systems individually;
- changes to procedure and job content are subject to negotiation in terms of job grades, pay scales and other conditions of work;
- there are formal technology agreements and 'no redundancy' policies that shape the pattern of development and implementation.

The answer increasingly is for management to anticipate likely difficulties and to formulate a policy to deal with them, otherwise they may lose the initiative in controlling change.

Industrial relations among computer staff

For a long time it was confidently assumed that unionism would not have much impact on computer staff, both because pay and conditions were generally good and because it would be difficult to organize such a group of individualists, concerned more about their technology than broader issues. This complacent view received some sharp rebuttals during the early 1970s as economic recession began to affect even computer staff; for example, selective action by civil service unions at government computer centres has caused significant disruption, as witness the recent lengthy and costly strike of DHSS computer operators. Organized action by computer staff and the identification of the computer as a target will be depressingly regular features of future industrial disputes, and management must devote attention to developing a policy to cope with these problems.

Causal factors

It is difficult not to be highly cynical of the motives for the majority of disputes involving computer staff or computer installations. In very broad terms, one can identify three situations in which industrial action in any working environment is likely to arise.

Pay and conditions Organization of the workforce for collective bargaining on pay and conditions was quite rightly the initial and prime motivation for the development of trades unionism. However, by no stretch of the imagination could the pay and conditions generally available to computer staff from the outset be considered a source of industrial unrest. Normally, in relation to the rest of the employees of an organization, computer staff are very well paid and, in terms of average productivity, possibly rewarded excessively in some cases. There may be peripheral issues such as shift working which create feelings of hardship, but these are usually adequately catered for by allowances and other ameliorations, which may be subject to negotiation. There may also be situations in which the organization's pay structure for computer staff gets out of line with the market place, or individual jobs are insufficiently recognized, but I have yet to come across any cases that would justify militant action.

Exercise of power One is forced to conclude that in many disputes involving computer staff we are witnessing the exercise of circumstantial power rather than the manifestation of genuine grievance. Where companies or institutions are heavily dependent on the use of computers to carry out their business routines, they are clearly vulnerable to any actions that disrupt normal production processes. These actions are often taken in support of some other dispute that may have little or nothing to do with computer staff, who are merely being used as a valid weapon in confrontation. Whatever the justification may be, it is a practice that is likely to become popular and which has to be taken seriously by management.

Resistance to change There is more justification for industrial unrest among computer staff when their jobs or livelihood appear threatened. This can arise through the effects of recession, leading to direct redundancies or reductions in staff requirements because projects are cancelled or postponed. However there are subtler forces at work which computer staff are beginning to resist in an organized fashion. For example, the development of on-line systems and decentralization of facilities to users is having a marked effect on the need for certain centrally-located workers such as data preparation staff, data control clerks and computer operators. In addition, improved techniques and software for the automation of many tasks previously carried out by computer staff is having an impact on job content and job opportunities.

Similar changes are occurring in the systems development function, which has been subject to progressive de-skilling of jobs over the years. Now we have an increased emphasis on productivity, the assumption of systems tasks by users, and the emergence of software facilities that will erode the special position of the programmer by putting more development tools in the hands of the users.

These changes, which may not have their origins in a wish to undermine the unique position of computer staff, certainly have just that effect, and will clearly influence the number and types of job available and the levels of remuneration. In these circumstances it would be wise to expect resistance and the possibility of disruptive actions on the part of computer staff. Most computer managers make standby arrangements, to be invoked in the event of equipment failures, and it would make sense to draw up similar plans for contingencies arising from industrial action.

Problem areas

The risk of industrial action and the degree of impact on the organization as a whole will vary from case to case. For example you may operate in an environment that is well used to industrial disputes, in which case another variation will excite no great interest. However most computer managers are novices in industrial relations and, without guidance, may provoke or exacerbate a situation that could easily be avoided. It is important for both general and computer management to recognize the dangers and to formulate a policy for handling them.

1   In the first place, many computer users have reached a stage of systems development where the computer is fundamental to the routine operation of the business, and they are thus highly vulnerable to industrial action. The capital concentration involved in the creation of central installations supporting terminal networks increases the disruptive power of quite a small number of computer staff, as has been illustrated in a number of recent cases.

2   Furthermore, it is most unlikely that these advanced systems will have comparable fallback procedures that could be relied

on to support the organization for a substantial period of time. Quite apart from the difficulty of devising clerical systems that would mirror the data processing routines, the user might have problems in finding staff who understand the work well enough to carry them out.

3 Decentralization of computing facilities offers some safeguards against complete paralysis of the organization, and will no doubt figure prominently in the future plans of users who are most vulnerable. However it is not an absolute guarantee of peace, especially where the workforce is organized on a national scale and realizes that it can make its point by selective action rather than total disruption.

4 In some cases the source and progress of a dispute may be outside the control of your management, although it may be you that suffers the consequences. For example, if maintenance engineers belonging to your supplier go on strike, your installation will be affected unless you have alternative services available.

5 Some installations have been kept going during a dispute by the assumption of production responsibilities by managers and senior staff. Exercising this option depends on the quality and availability of suitable documentation and operating procedures; as we have commented previously, these conditions do not apply in every installation.

6 Some disputes are caused and prolonged by the inexperience of computer managers in handling a workforce. If they come up against professional union representatives, who have been trained in bargaining and negotiation, they will be ill-equipped to cope with even the simplest dispute. The situation may be worsened in the early stages if the manager is required to negotiate with a possibly junior member of his own staff. There is also the question of divided loyalties when an erstwhile technician, now manager, has to deal with his former associates on issues he may not fully comprehend in general organizational terms.

Courses of action

As with most facets of computing, a degree of foresight helps, and careful planning will go a long way to minimize the incidence of industrial relations problems and to mitigate the effects of any disruptive action.

Pre-emptive actions

1   The first requirement is to recognize both that the potential for disruption exists, whatever the level of your commitment to computers, and that there is no substitute for an intelligent and circumspect approach to industrial relations and personnel policies, whether or not your organization is unionized. Ingredients in this approach are:

- an adequate awareness of the pay and conditions appropriate to the jobs to be done;
- a clear understanding of the work required by all parties, and firm but fair management practices in controlling performance;
- a constructive policy for the recruitment, training, appraisal and progression of computer staff; and
- the avoidance of hard line, dictatorial and intractable management styles in favour of participative, human relations-oriented practices.

    It is surprising how much more productive and amenable staff can be if they have job satisfaction, are ably led and treated fairly, in addition to being well paid.

2   If your organization is unionized and there are established industrial relations procedures, including a pattern of formal/informal contacts with union officials, make sure that your computer manager is familiar with these arrangements and the way in which they operate. (It goes without saying that such familiarization should in any case be part of the development of management skills of senior computer staff.) Insist that established procedures are observed and, in the event of an issue developing, make sure that the computer manager has access to and uses the professional industrial relations experts in the organization.

3   In preparing development plans and in designing individual

systems, you should make adequate provision for the participation of all staff and give proper consideration to the efforts of the system on working methods. If it seems appropriate, involve the union in the formulation of these plans, even if it means trading some of the expected benefits for a smooth passage. If you operate a job evaluated structure, allow ample time for re-specification and grading of the new or modified jobs that will emerge from computer systems. If you delay involving the unions, you may have serious implementation problems. Attention can be directed to these critical areas by including an item on the union implications of proposals in a checklist of tasks to be completed in systems development.

4 Concentrate on maintaining a high level of communication between general management, computer management and computer staff on such issues as business policy and plans, the role of data processing, and personnel policies. Apart from being intrinsically right to do so, a relaxed attitude to communication will reduce feelings of alienation from the rest of the organization which commonly occur among computer staff.

Precautions
No matter how much attention you pay both to creating an environment in which change can be introduced without chaos and to encouraging a constructive approach in the industrial raleations policy towards computer staff, you may still run the risk of disruption of computer services. On the basis not only of trusting these arrangements but also 'keeping your powder dry', you should make positive plans both to remove the opportunities for disruption and to minimize its effect.

1 The starting point is an analysis of the risks involved for your organization in the present set-up. Your vulnerability will depend on such factors as:
  ● the location of equipment;
  ● the number and type of staff involved;
  ● the nature of the systems – on-line or batch;
  ● the operational importance of the systems to the continuance of business.
The quantification of risk will be an initial guide to the

importance of taking remedial actions. For example, disruption of billing routines will have cash flow implications that can be calculated and will determine not only how long the disruption can be borne but also the value of making alternative arrangements.

2 Based on this analysis of risk, you should prepare a comprehensive plan to accommodate a breakdown of production services. The plan should relate the actions required to the expected duration of the dispute and should take account of the following factors.

- Identification of the importance of systems in relation to the length of time they can be put out of service; for example, payroll has an undeniable priority (unless you wish to point up the lack of fellow feeling displayed by computer staff), whereas you may be less concerned about a stock control system.

- Initiation of clerical fallback procedures, where this is practicable, provided the dispute does not involve the rest of the staff.

- Arrangements for management to run the computer installation and provide a skeleton service on key applications. In this respect, you have to weigh carefully the short-term benefits of this action against the possible damage done to long-term industrial relations.

- Transfer of critical applications, such as payroll or billing, to other computer installations or computer service bureaux. The danger here is that if the industrial action is union-based there may be mandatory or sympathetic blacking of diverted jobs.

It is also particularly important to plan how full recovery is to be achieved once the dispute has been settled. Assuming that the rest of the organization is working normally and business continues, there will be a build-up of unprocessed transactions, including of course those which have been generated in place of computer actions. The potential for chaos is clear.

3 Whereas your plan for dealing with a disruption of production services should be concerned with remedies, any plan for future systems development should concentrate on avoidance of risk. Thus, in contemplating future systems strategies, you

may decide that a primary objective should be to design applications that can be protected against industrial action. This approach would consider such features as:

- duplication of equipment facilities in different locations, each capable of carrying the whole work load;
- decentralization of computing in order to preserve some operational routines;
- dedication of minicomputers to specific applications in order to minimize the risk of all applications being affected;
- integration of computing facilities with normal office procedures in order to lower the target profile;
- simpler system design in order to facilitate transfer to a bureau, or even conversion to a smaller machine;
- systems designed with the expectation that they may be halted for a prolonged period and have to cope with exceptional processing conditions during recoveries, e.g. record structures, where field sizes and processing sequences may have to be flexible;
- increased use of on-line systems and decentralized data entry;
- increased automation of computer operations.

4 An antidote to the potential threat posed by computer staff is the growth in user control of data processing. This is an additional reason for management to encourage such features as:
- the establishment of systems analysis teams in user departments;
- a limited decentralization of programming resources, where this makes sense;
- alternatively, selective use of subcontract staff to develop user applications;
- simpler systems design based on programming languages that can be exploited by users, e.g. RPG and 4GL;
- the use of software packages on a much wider basis.

5 Finally, ensure that your contingency plans are kept up to date with changes in technology and with the introduction of new applications.

It should be apparent that many of the effects of a disruption to computer services through industrial action are identical to the consequences of a breakdown caused by equipment or software failures. Thus an analysis of risks will fulfil two requirements, although the remedies may be quite different. In mobilizing emergency services because of a breakdown you are likely to have the full cooperation of your computer staff; in overcoming industrial action, you will have no support, and quite possibly active resistance, raising other issues concerning the security of the installation and, more significantly, the integrity of data and systems. However unpalatable it may be, your precautionary measures should take account of all eventualities. Nevertheless, in the interests of longer-term stability in industrial relations, your actions should be designed to minimize lasting resentment and to remove the causes of discontent.

14   Future developments

You cannot fight against the future. Time is on our side.

(W. E. Gladstone)

Introduction

I have always held the view that the limits of computer usage are set principally by our own ability to conceive uses and our confidence in pursuing them. If you can describe what you wish to achieve, you can rest assured that before long the hardware facilities and software techniques will emerge to enable you to attain your objective. Forecasting future developments in computer technology and applications has proved delightfully hazardous for most pundits; in prophesying the outcome of trends one can be wildly wrong or occasionally near the mark. Consequently, I have no reservations about contemplating the future: if I am wrong it does not matter, and I shall be in good company; and if I am right the accuracy will be ephemeral.

However, organizations that are considering their future data processing requirements, perhaps over a 5-10 year period, have to base their prognostications on premises that are not only readily understood by the purse bearers but that also seem credible in the light of their knowledge. In addition, the direction of future developments for an individual organization may be predetermined by its existing computing commitments, and will almost certainly reflect its assessment of its business prospects and the socioeconomic fabric of the organization. Consequently, it may not be possible to incorporate the latest or forecast technology in its long-term strategy because of inherent problems of absorbing and using it. For example, on examining the forward plans for a large financial institution I was struck by the prevalence of batch oriented systems, when pressures in similar organizations were in favour of on-line applications. In this case, however, management had made a careful assessment of the organization's ability to exploit computers, particularly at junior- and middle-management levels, and had concluded that a more cautious approach would be more suitable than an unstable period of radical change.

So, any speculation about the direction of future developments has to be interpreted in relation to the needs of the individual organization – what proves useful and beneficial to one company may be wholly inappropriate to the next. In this chapter I propose to indicate which of the foreseeable trends in computer and related technology I consider to be significant for the average user, and what the implications might be. You will have to decide if these trends are likely to have any impact on the activities of your own organization and how they should be exploited.

Developments in hardware

It does not require a great stretch of the imagination to appreciate that we are nowhere near the limits of developments in hardware technology.

1   We can expect the recent phenomenal progress in semiconductor technology to continue, whether or not it is based solely on silicon chips. The use of very large scale integrated (VLSI) circuits will facilitate the introduction of small processing systems of tremendous power, which may in turn be dedicated in particular functions in an overall computer system, i.e. microcomputers dedicated to specific tasks.

2   The same developments will also further stimulate communications technology, and the liaison between computers and communications will become a bond that will increasingly influence the pattern of both national and international data processing. Communications satellites and fibre optics will facilitate high-speed transmission of information between processors and across networks.

3   At a more mundane level, the features available with micro- and minicomputers will be extended in terms of power and capacity. As communications facilities improve, microcomputers will tend to supplant conventional terminals in computer networks.

4 As hardware becomes cheaper, functions previously carried out by software will be increasingly incorporated in the equipment, as they are to a limited extent already.

5 The cheapness and power of equipment, and improved communications facilities, will provide the user with the opportunity almost to tailor his own computer system from proprietory items in order to suit specific applications or local needs.

6 These same characteristics will foster the already apparent growth of interest in personal computing and provide the means by which individuals will be able to exploit not only the processing capacity of computers but also the mass of information available in their own organization's systems and in an increased number of national and international databases.

These advances in hardware, at progressively more economic costs, will stimulate developments in the manipulation of nonnumeric data in such forms as text, images and voice communication. These developments will have profound implications for the automation of office functions, and are treated separately later in this chapter.

From the standpoint of the average user, the developments in hardware technology will lead to:

- vastly improved cost/performance ratios;
- more storage capacity and peripheral flexibility at less cost;
- cheap, accessible and efficient communications systems;
- flexibility in constructing data processing configurations to suit individual needs;
- an impetus to personal computing services;

all of which will hasten a popularization of computer usage that should help promote the success of individual applications.

Developments in software

Our thesis, that the equipment will not work without software, may be dented by certain developments that 'hard-wire' some functions at present normally carried out by software. We already have computers solely devoted to the maintenance of databases, in which those functions normally vested in software are often carried out by circuitry. Clearly, as hardware costs decline and software costs increase, both relatively and absolutely, there will be an incentive to embed more functions in the hardware, provided flexibility in using or combining functions is not impaired.

Notwithstanding these changes, we can expect developments in software to be directed towards enhancing the non-professional user's ability to access and manipulate data in computer systems, in keeping with the hardware facilities at his disposal.

1   Thus there will be improvements in languages that will enable the user to write programs, to set up files, to manipulate and to extract data, without excessive technical training or over-rigid disciplines.

2   These facilities will probably extend into the less structured area of systems design, allowing interactive system building and prototyping by users utilizing fourth generation languages.

3   Access to existing systems and databases will be made easier by the development of more flexible query languages capable of coping with unstructured questions in a rapid response mode.

4   Database management systems will become commonly available at all levels of computer equipment, including microprocessors.

5   Software will be devised to complement hardware features, enabling voice and image communication with computers for purposes of interrogation, information recording, system development, command and control.

6   In terms of applications, the range and quality of the packages available to potential users will increase, particularly those which offer versatile database facilities.

7   Improved system building techniques and the increased use of application packages will reduce the large proportion of systems resources currently devoted to application maintenance. This trend will obviously affect the demand for conventional programming resources and emphasise the role of the user.

While some of these developments may take time to come into common use, there is little doubt that they are all feasible and likely to be available within the next few years. These and related features would go a long way towards establishing a true partnership between man and machine, without which the full potential of the computer cannot be realized. Up until now we have settled for a relationship in which each partner carries out the tasks for which he/it is best suited. As humans we have imagination, flexibility, discretion and a wealth of knowledge that would be difficult to pass on to a machine, but the signs are that computers, with our guidance, are becoming better at performing human tasks, as witness the developments in expert systems and AI. Computers can now store vast amounts of data, communicate in natural language, recognize speech and images, and display adaptive reasoning abilities. There is no reason to feel uncomfortable or uneasy about these developments so long as we remember that we are in control . . . aren't we?

Office automation

At the beginning of the 1980s it was fashionable to enthuse about the opportunities presented by rapid developments in information technology that would lead to the creation of the fully automated office. The arguments advanced by suppliers and theorists were broadly as follows.

1 Office work consists of a large number of activities that have not been amenable to conventional data processing techniques, e.g. exchange of information by voice, representation by image, the ambiguous and often unstructured nature of text; such information is difficult to represent in a form that could be communicated to and manipulated by the computer.

2 Advances in hardware facilities and communications now make it possible to store, process and transmit vast quantities of text, image and verbal information at a low enough cost to make it attractive so to do.

3 Furthermore, the new technology enables us to link together those media which had previously dealt with this information in isolated fashion, i.e. the telephone, the copier, the facsimile transmitter and the word processor.

4 The reason why we should combine this media and the

power of the computer is that we would vastly improve the productivity, not only of office staff, but also of managers, and markedly change the nature of office work.

It has even been suggested that in the long-term the office as we know it will cease to exist and people, armed with personal terminals, will be able to work from home or anywhere from which the system could be accessed. This prognostication is fascinating and, on balance, I think I agree with it, subject to a few reservations about the practicalities and some worries about future implications.

Current situation

A major reservation about the upsurge of interest in office automation is that, like data processing, it receives its impetus from the marketing activities of people who supply the equipment. If you examine their platform for promoting office automation it invariably matches closely the better features of their product line. Thus, one group of suppliers base their approach on the use of their mainframes while another considers that their word processing minnows are the correct starting point. Some suppliers now have the general communications facility and software flexibility to exploit these processing capabilities, although I suspect we are further off voice actuation than its proponents would imply.

What is somewhat more disturbing, is that suppliers have seemed a lot more interested in office automation than their prospective customers and will therefore have to do a great deal more 'selling' to generate a market for their total approach to office systems (as opposed to the activity in the subsidiary markets for word processors, facsimile machine and the like). Nevertheless, some companies have made good use of available technology and can boast modest achievements in the development of electronic office services.

Implications

For office automation in the fullest sense to succeed generally, and not merely to evolve in a few cases of 'paperwork factories' or in special departments, will require not only a major culture change but also a complete revision of commonly accepted bases for organizaing and managing work processes. To begin with, the abolition of the office would remove an institution which has considerable social and psychological significance for staff, apart from being a place of work. An employee spends the greater part of his waking life at work and necessarily develops group relationships that are as important to him as job content; some individuals may even be happier at work than in a domestic environment! Can the prospect of a man-machine interface, with no supportive relationships, be an adequate and acceptable substitute for the office?

Whether or not this version of the office of the future materializes, it is certain that the expected integration of information processing systems and computing would have a profound effect on the performance of work and on the nature of management. Conventional departmental boundaries would be overridden and opportunities would be provided to revise accepted concepts of organization structures and management practices; different work flows would be created and new control mechanisms would have to be developed. However, the most critical issues would be those arising from the human and industrial relations factors. How would you deal with an industrial dispute with a scattered workforce? Perhaps industrial conflict would not arise?

The future of service companies

Several years ago it was forecast that the computer service bureau, as a purveyor of machine time, would go into a decline as access to relatively cheap processing power became generally available. This decline has happened to a number of service companies which have not adjusted to the market; the survivors are those bureaux that have broadened the range of their services, offered new software products and absorbed new technology. There has been a reduction in the number of bureaux and the emergence of some large and extremely successful companies as a result of acquisitions, mergers and general expansion. Nevertheless, the continuing developments in cheap computing power strike at the existing and prospective customer base of many bureaux, and their cost structure and facilities are under constant pressure.

So what does the future augur for the computer service bureau and will it survive? We have already seen that, unlike most users of computers, the bureau is subject to great pressure to keep pace with advances in technology and expectations of their clientele. These pressures will increase, and it is the bureau which shows the greatest flexibility and adaptability to market conditions that will survive. This would suggest that those bureaux which are already large and with a variety of facilities and services will be in a stronger position than the medium-size company committed to one location, one type of equipment and perhaps a limited range of services. The very small bureau with a local clientele might also survive, but would be unlikely to grow. Generally I would expect the following types of development.

1   Establishment of a network of computers and on-line services designed to give maximum coverage in terms of size and variety of computing equipment and products.
2   These facilities would be designed to allow a variety of microcomputers to be linked to a powerful processor with large storage, thereby enhancing the power and capacity available to the small user.
3   I would expect a greater emphasis on the development of applications software and related services, to the extent that the larger bureaux would make inroads into markets currently largely the preserve of software houses and computer consultancies.
4   Some large bureaux with extensive coverage of the market might be in a position to offer private viewdata networks to organizations wishing to set up information storage and retrieval systems.

Software houses are likely to become involved in two types of application development.

•   Systems which enhance the user's capability to access and manipulate data in relatively large-scale computing environments.
•   Provision of cheap, flexible application packages to extend the use of small machines.

They will also have a continuing role as an alternative source of development staff, but must expect to adjust to an overall decline in user dependence on computer experts.

Effects on computer staff

There is no doubt that we will still need a large number of computer specialists, but as equipment and software become easier to apply by the average user, there will be a decreased demand for conventional data processing skills.

1 I would expect the assumption of systems analysis and design responsibilities by users to continue and be encouraged by the mechanization of some systems design tasks. While the transfer of systems responsibility might in the short-term increase the demand for systems analysts, the duties they carry out will increasingly be absorbed by users.

2 User skills will be extended into the programming field by the development of software aids, and the traditional tasks of program design and coding will be undertaken by user staff utilizing on-line program development facilities. The resultant applications may not be optimal but are likely to be quickly implemented, disposable and cheap to replace.

3 The main avenue for the development of the programming function will be in accumulating expertise in highly specialized areas, such as databases, information systems, systems software, telecommunications software, and in providing flexible programming tools for users to develop conventional processing applications.

Although we may not see the total demise of the systems development and programming functions, especially in the very large organizations with central installations and networks, the transfer of many activities to users and the increased use of packaged systems will reduce the need for basic skills, averagely performed.

Effects on users

The acceptance of training in computers in schools, tertiary education, the professions and management, which is still sometimes looked upon as a novelty, will become commonplace; before long most senior staff will be as familiar with data processing techniques as they are with the use of the telephone. This familiarity will encourage the demand for individual use of computer facilities, without the need to depend on specialist resources, and will provide a further inducement to the development of simple user-oriented software aids, a current example being the extensive availability of easy-to-use spreadsheet software.

The availability of cheap computers, capable of giving access to larger more powerful facilities, will enhance the personal computing capacity of the individual user. Not only will such facilities enable users to develop their own systems but, more importantly, they will allow them to explore data and information held in the whole computer system. This accessability will be extended to information stored in other computer systems, such that a manager involved in planning at a strategic or tactical level may be able to interrogate data banks held elsewhere for public use, e.g. trade statistics, economic forecasts, manpower data.

Within the individual organization, depending on its commitment to an existing computer strategy, the emergence of cheap hardware and flexible software tools will make it easier to develop or modify applications and certainly easier to exploit existing data for decision making purposes. The range of decisions that computer systems are allowed to undertake will increase, to the point where conventional approaches to the coordination of work at supervisory and junior management levels will have to be revised. I would hope to see the development of the concept of the systems manager, as opposed to function managers, and a consequent revision in the structure of many organizations. The introduction of integrated office and information processing systems would provide an added impetus to this style of operation.

Conclusion

The pace of development in computer technology has been awesome and breathtaking. In an incredibly short period of time, the computer has developed from a research aid to a vital tool for management and business. Nothing about current trends suggests that the pace will slacken, and all the signs are that it may quicken with new applications of technology following in rapid succession. In particular, we can see signs that the originally lauded 'general purpose' computing capability is being supplanted by dedicated, single purpose, function-oriented computers.

It is highly likely that mistakes will continue to be made, especially by the average user anxious to exploit the opportunities presented by cheap computing facilities, but the correctness of the trend towards the user is undeniable. If mistakes cannot be avoided, we should do what we can to minimize their consequences, and I would suggest that past experiences underline some commonsense rules.

1 Do not get carried away by the technology and do not pioneer new equipment or new software, or both. Allow someone else to find the 'bugs' and take full advantage of their experience.

2 Do not buy a Rolls-Royce when closer examination might reveal that you could make do with a bicycle. After all, a Rolls-Royce will need an expensive chauffeur, whereas you can ride the bicycle yourself.

3 Try not to be too ambitious; don't try to run if you can't walk. Pace your development according to the needs of your organization and its ability to absorb change. Never mind what others are doing.

4 Avoid investing in major applications development programmes if there are adequate software packages available. Sacrifice a few percentage points of your requirements in order to achieve benefits.

5 Do carry out a proper costs/benefits evaluation before you commit the organization, remembering to be generous on costs and tight on benefits.

6 Even so, do not expect miracles, and accept that payback periods for investment in computers may be longer and more uncertain than with other ventures. However, be suspicious of computer managers who want more money or more resources before they have delivered any system.

7 Do make sure that your computing function is correctly organized, properly resourced and sensibly managed. The normal management practices of the organization should apply.

8 Do make sure that computing is directed towards the user's needs and actively encourage user control over all aspects of developement.

Above all, take the trouble to identify what you are trying to achieve, to understand the means that will be used and to plan your exploitation of computers, and you may end up by controlling it satisfactorily.

Appendix 1
Short glossary of data processing terminology for management

access time The time taken following instruction before reading from, or writing to, a location in memory takes place. The access time can vary between nanoseconds for a register in a fast processor, seconds for a magnetic tape deck, or even longer for some forms of storage. The reading and writing access times are not necessarily equal for a particular device or class of devices.

address Name of a place where information is stored, *or* Make reference to a location in memory.

algol A high-level, machine independent language for scientific applications. The original language is known as Algol 60. Algol 68 is a different but similar type of language.

algorithm A series of instructions formulated to solve specific problems.

alphanumeric Relating to letters of the alphabet, punctuation signs and digits. A term commonly used to describe computer input and output.

analogue (also **analog**) Measured or defined by a smoothly changing physical entity such as the hands of a clock or mercury in a thermometer.

ANSI American National Standards Institute.

application Practical use to which a computer is put, such as process control, design, accounting, word processing.

assembler A program which translates a program written in assembler language into machine code. Sometimes called assembler program or assembler routine.

Basic Beginner's All-purpose Symbolic Instruction Code, the most popular simple computer language.

batch A quantity of data material such as source documents or punched cards processed by computers as a single unit. Hence

batch processing, which may be effected some time after actual delivery, as opposed to real-time working, in which items are processed as they arise. Also **remote batch processing** in which data is transmitted to a computer via a remote terminal for storage and subsequent processing.

baud Measure of band width of a digital communications channel expressed in code elements per second.

binary Using the base of 2 for computation or storage, rather than, say, the decimal system.

bit BInary digiT. Basic unit of information in the binary coded information system. Either 1 or 0.

block Sequential area of storage records, etc. Also a group of data items or instructions transferred as a single entity.

buffer A small memory which serves as a temporary storage space.

bug A thing that was wrong in a program or hardware. Hence **de-bugging** – removing the bugs.

burster A device for separating sheets of continuous printout stationery by pulling them apart at perforations.

byte A character, usually consisting of 8 bits of information.

card One of the standard storage media used in computers, particularly in the input/output system. Information is commonly stored in one of three ways: punched holes; pencil or other marks in standard locations; and magnetically on special cards coated with magnetic oxide.

cassette A small magnetic tape in a holder, originally developed from the cassettes used in small tape recorders.

central processor Part of a computing system, consisting of arithmetic unit and control unit. Main memory is sometimes considered to be part of the central processor.

channel Communication path or circuit.

character The smallest distinguishable, and often addressable, block of information which is processed as a unit; usually 6 or 8 bits. Four characters make a standard 32-bit word.

check digit Digit, over and above the minimum numeric code necessary to define information, which is used to detect error.

Cobol Common Business Oriented Language. A high level machine independent language for commercial data processing. The most commonly used language for commercial applications.

code The activity of coding, *or* A defined set of bit-patterns, digits, symbols, etc., *or* Defined relationship between two sets of bit-patterns, digits, symbols, etc.

COM Computer Output Microfilmer. A system of developing computer output directly on to microfilm. The advantage lies in the compactness of the medium (compared with paper) combined with the ability to read it directly with the aid of a viewer.

compatibility The ability of two or more systems to work together.

compiler A program, or set of programs, which operates on a program (source program) written in a high-level language (source language) such as Cobol, Fortran or PL/1 to produce a program (target program) in a target language which will generally be assembler code.

console The station, equipped with keyboard, operating switches, lights and displays, where the operator sits (or stands) when communicating with the computer.

conversational mode A method of interactive working in which the user is connected on-line to the computer, and can interrogate it to obtain an immediate response to input questions and requests. Remote terminals can function in conversational mode in time-sharing and real-time applications.

data Information in digital form. Also the facts on which a computer program operates, as opposed to the instructions in the program.

database An organized set of files providing a common pool of information for several or many users. The essential object of database systems is simple; it is to ensure that all parts of an organization are using information which matches, rather than independent files which may not correspond to each other at a given time.

database management systems (DBMS) Software systems for structuring, organizing and managing large filing systems, or database systems.

data entry The preparation of data in a suitable form for input to a computer, *or* The actual entry of data into a computer.

data preparation The preparation in suitable form, verification and correction of the basic data for introduction into a computing system. This may be done on to punched cards, punched tape or direct to disk storage.

data transmission The sending and receiving of data over the telecommunications system.

debugging The activity of removing the bugs (malfunctions) from equipment and programs.

disk (disc) A thin flat, circular plate coated with magnetic material on which data is recorded as magnetized spots. The spots are arranged in concentric circles on the surface of the disk. These circles are called tracks. When in use the disks rotate under read/write heads.

disk drive The unit which drives the magnetically coated disks of a replacable disk pack.

diskette A small magnetic disk used, for example, in data-entry systems.

disk file The most commonly used form of direct access storage device. It is a backing memory consisting of a number of rotating disks, read/write heads and an electronic control system. The controller handles addressing, reading and writing, error detection and correction, as well as providing buffer storage and other functions.

disk pack Interchangeable unit of magnetic disk used on a replaceable disk file.

display Visual computer output, usually shown on a cathode ray tube of a visual display unit (VDU).

downtime Time a machine or system is out of action due to malfunction (sometimes also for routine maintenance).

dump Transfer the contents of main memory, or a substantial part of the contents, on to backing memory, *also* To transfer the contents of a disk file(s) on to tape.

duplex Duplex working data transmission means that data can be transmitted in both directions simultaneously, as opposed to **simplex**, which is one direction at a time.

feasibility study An appraisal of a particular problem to be solved by computer techniques, or an assessment of whether certain aspects of a company's operation can be, or should be, profitably computerized.

field Area of data in a record, *or* Area with standard format in some storage unit, such as a punched card, to which information of a given type is assigned.

file An orderly collection of information and records maintained for reference, processing and updating.

fixed-disk file Disk file in which the spindle of disks cannot be removed or replaced in normal use.

floppy disk A small replaceable magnetic disk which will hold about 1 million bytes and is typically used for data preparation.

flow chart Graphic or diagrammatic representation of a process, project or problem, showing a sequence of operations.

Fortran FORmula TRANslator. The most commonly used high-level scientific and engineering computer language.

generations of computers A rough classification of the evolution of computers and computing systems.

graphics Generally signifies the visual display of graphical or diagrammatic computer output on a cathode-ray tube (VDU) or on paper by means of an X – Y coordinate plotter.

hard copy Readable printout on paper.

hardware The physical equipment forming a computer system. The term has come into use in contrast to software.

hexa decimal Using the number base of 16.

high-level language A computer language in which one instruction corresponds to several or many instructions in machine or assembler code. High-level languages are usually intended to be independent of a particular computer or range of computers.

housekeeping A term applied to program functions which are not concerned with problem solving but with tidying up and setting up internal computer routines so that programs can be handled more effectively.

hybrid A hybrid computer is one which combines analogue and digital techniques. Used mainly in industry, e.g. process control, rather than commerce.

information In computing, any bit pattern, or coded signal, with defined meaning.

input Data and programs must be fed into the computer memory before any useful work can be performed at all, and this is achieved by means of input devices (peripherals) using computer codes and languages written by programmers. Input can be achieved by punched cards or tape, magnetic cards or tape, terminals, disks, optical character readers, etc.

instruction Character, or group of characters, which defines an operation. Referring to a computer program, it is the part of the program which tells the computer what to do at any particular stage in the program.

integrated circuit An electronic circuit not much larger than a pinhead in which many components are deposited by chemical diffusion upon a silicon chip. Large scale integration (LSI) involves circuits with up to 1,000 components on a single chip.

intelligent terminal Instead of having as a terminal a simple typewriter or display screen without processing power, there are a number of terminals which include processors.

interactive The situation of working with a computer system in such a manner that the user secures immediacy of response.

interface Well-defined boundary between two logical or physical systems. A simple example of an interface is the household plug and socket. A far more complex interface is that between peripheral devices and input/output channels in a digital computer.

job Data processing activity imposed on a computer or computing system for a user.

job control language (JCL) Language used by the operator to give instructions to the computing system. It is a subset of the operating system.

k – kilo = 1,000 Hence K-byte = 1,000 bytes; kilocycle = 1,000 cycles per second, etc.

key Bit pattern used for identification purposes. Keys have many uses, for example in collating and in permitting access to data or programs restricted for security or other reasons.

keyboard-printer Usually an electric typewriter which is, or can be, connected, possibly through controllers appropriate to a particular system, on-line to a computer.

key-to-disk A data preparation office system in which information is keyed directly on to a small disk. A computing installation may have perhaps 8-24 or more key stations. Information is typed into the system and usually appears on an alphanumeric display. After verification it is transferred to the magnetic disk. The system includes a minicomputer which provides checking and editing facilities.

language In data processing, a method of communication between people and machines, in which step-by-step instructions are written in the form of a program for conversion into machine code for subsequent processing by the computer system.

library Set of volumes kept on shelves. Hence: **tape library**, a library consisting of information held on magnetic tapes;**program library**, a library of programs held on disk and/or in folders.

light pen Device for identifying a point on a display screen. It is called a 'pen' because it looks somewhat like one and draws a pattern in light on a screen. It does so when it is pointed at a cross or other marker, which it then pulls across the screen, leaving a trail behind.

line printer A computer printer which prints a whole line at a time at high speed, as opposed to a character printer, which prints one character at a time.

machine coding Writing short programs in machine code, which is usually the basic numerical code which the computer itself uses to identify store locations and to address locations for data storage. Also **machine language**, instructions written in machine code which can be processed by the computer without further translation.

machine independent Programming languages are machine independent if a program can be transferred without change from one computer to another, e.g. Cobol, Fortran. In practice machine independence is a matter of degree.

mainframe The centre of a computer comprising the arithmetic unit, control unit, main memory and console.

main memory also **main store** The memory which holds the instructions and data in current use in a computing system.

mark sensing A data entry system in which information is formed by presence or absence of pencil marks in predetermined positions on cards or pieces of paper.

matrix-printer Usually an impact printer in which letters are formed by selection of the appropriate set of wires from a matrix.

memory *also* **store/storage** System or device which is or can be used to hold information in such a form that it can be accessed, understood and used by a computer or data processing system.

message Group or sequence of words which must be transferred as a whole for its meaning to be understood. Typically a message consists of an identity label, which may include the address, the text of the message and an EOM (end of message) symbol.

message switching System used to route, store and retransmit messages between computers and remote terminals.

MICR Magnetic Ink Character Recognition. A data entry system in which characters of stylized form are printed with a magnetic ink, permitting them to be read by an appropriate automatic reader, e.g. cheques.

microcomputer A computer in which the central processor is made on a single chip of silicon or on a few chips.

microsecond A millionth of a second (10^{-6} seconds).

millisecond A thousandth of a second (10^{-3} seconds).

minicomputer A physically small, but possibly powerful, computer which does not merit the term mainframe.

modular programming Writing programs in such a way that they consist of a set of modules. Each module can then be separately developed and easily moved around.

module Self-contained part of a program which can be removed without affecting the operation of the remainder of the program, merely removing the functions performed by that module. The module can then be separately tested, debugged and modified.

multiprogramming An operating system in which a computer runs, or can run, several programs effectively simultaneously.

nanosecond A billionth (thousand-millionth) of a second (10^{-9} seconds).

networks Computer networks are groups of computers connected together on-line by a data transmission system.

numeric data A series of characters containing only numeric digits.

OCR Optical Character Recognition. An input system in which characters are scanned and identified optically by a machine which may be either on- or off-line.

octal Using a number base of 8.

off-line Applied to data processing functions which are not directly connected with nor under the immediate control of the computer, and therefore not under program control.

OMR Optical Mark Recognition. Same as a mark sense reader.

on-line Under the direct control of, or directly connected to, the computing system.

operating system The assembly of programs by which a computer carries out its internal housekeeping. It is usually bought with the computer and ideally most programmers wish to know nothing about its internal mode of operation, being satisfied if they can get on with applications programming or other work. Communication with the operating system is probably effected by a job control language.

output Information which is put out by a computer. It may take many different forms, either transitory, as on a visual display unit (VDU), or permanent, as in the case of a printout.

package A series of generally written programs for processing a particular application or function, e.g. payroll, data validation.

paging A system for automatic dynamic interchange of programs and data between main memory and backing memory. Also known as **virtual memory**.

paper tape Reels of paper tape with rows of holes punched across the paper, one row defining a character.

parity An extra bit (the parity bit) is commonly added to each character in a binary representation in such a manner that the sum of the 1s in the character and parity bit combined is always even (even parity) or always odd (odd parity).

peripherals The units attached to the main frame. Typical peripherals include printer, typewriter, display system, card reader, card punch, paper-tape punch, diskette, disk file, drum, magnetic tape deck, cassette, cash terminal and document sorter.

picosecond A million-millionth of a second (10^{-12} seconds).

plotter A peripheral device which makes drawings according to instructions received from a processor or store.

program A sequence of instructions to a computer to carry out a given task. One program may be part of a larger program.

random access Information so structured that one piece of information can be reached in approximately the same time as any other.

reading The action of extracting information from a memory.

real-time A system in which data input is processed immediately to provide output which can control or influence the event creating the input (as in industrial process control and airline seat reservations).

record Group of data items relating to a single (physical) entity. A file comprises of a number of records, each of which contains a number of data items.

reference files Files used for retrieval in information systems; files containing descriptions defining documents and reference records.

register A single storage location. Thus, for example, a register to hold a word, or character.

response time The time it takes for a computing system to respond to a request, interruption, or changing situation. For example, in a time sharing system a user sitting at a terminal will require a response by the system within a few seconds to simple requests.

ROM Read Only Memory. A memory in which information is physically fixed and cannot be altered by program. Also devices from which such memory is made.

RPG Report Program Generator. A high-level language, simpler than Cobol.

run Execution of a program.

serial access Information which is or must be reached in a simple predetermined sequence, as in the ancient scroll. Also devices which must be accessed serially and the process of assessing information serially. A magnetic tape is an example of a device which must be accessed serially.

software Programs; as opposed to hardware.

stand-alone Having the ability to function without connection to a central processor. Many small computers can be used either in a stand-alone mode or as systems peripheral to a more powerful processor.

string Sequence of records, words or characters.

subroutine Small program which is called up as a whole to execute some chosen operation.

systems analysis The task of a system analyst in data processing is to analyse the way in which an existing system functions, to recognize and define problems and malfunctions, to design and specify a new system, making the most efficient and economic use of available hardware and software facilities, and finally to implement the new system and ensure that it is maintained and updated as necessary.

tape Ribbon of material which is, or can be, used to store information; for example, punched paper tape or magnetic tape.

tape library Library holding the magnetic tapes on which is stored the bulk of large files in most data-processing systems.

telecommunication Communication between two or more locations, probably remote from each other, by electromagnetic means.

teleprocessing Computing which makes use of the communications system for on-line processing. It utilizes machine-to-machine communication, usually through the telephone system.

terminal An input/output device, often remote from the computer, using data transmission facilities to access the central processor. Although a terminal is usually considered to be a keyboard machine (with or without visual display facilities), it may in fact be any kind of input/output peripheral, including tape or card readers and punches.

time-sharing A system in which many users have instantaneous access to a central computer. The computer divides its time into many small slices which are distributed among the users, so that it appears to each user that he has a computer entirely at his disposal.

transaction processing Individual commercial transactions are processed interactively as they take place and the power of the computer is used to facilitate the transactions. Access may be made to a database holding information such as credit rating, stockholding, delivery schedules and so forth. The development of transaction processing depends on the use of time-sharing. The extension of transaction processing to remote terminals requires the development of teleprocessing.

translate Change information from one representation to another without altering its meaning.

transmit Send information from one storage area to another. Similar to transfer but more commonly used to denote transfer between locations or devices physically remote from each other.

turnkey operation The supply and installation of a computing system in so complete a form that the user (figuratively) need only turn a key to start the system in working order.

unpack Take a record stored, for example, on magnetic tape and unpack the information into separate units (characters or words) for placement in storage locations.

update Alter information on a file to bring it up to date.

up-time The period when a computer is serviceable and capable of being used, as opposed to downtime.

utility program A service routine designed to carry out certain prescribed operations on data files, irrespective of their content, such as transferring them from one type of store to another, rearranging sequence, copying, etc.

validation A check routine to ensure that data is tested against known limits, such as numerals appearing in alphabetic fields and vice versa, or that a person's age is not recorded as 275, or that a date such as July 45th cannot be accepted by the computer.

VDU Visual Display Unit. A terminal device incorporating a cathode-ray tube which will display alphanumeric characters or graphs and diagrams on the screen, sometimes with facilities for amendment of data and updating by means of a light pen.

verification Process of checking data which has been keyed on to some medium or memory, usually by keying the information a second time and comparing results.

VRC Visible Record Computer. A special type of small computer designed to meet basic accounting needs. The information is stored on a typed ledger card and simultaneously on a magnetic strip attached to the top of the ledger card. The user reads the typescript and the computer reads the magnetic tape.

word The basic entities of a language with defined meaning and possible relationships, *or* The unit of information treated by the arithmetic unit as a whole.

word length Number of bits in a standard computer word.

writing The action of putting information into a memory.

Appendix 2
Data processing job descriptions

I POSITION IN ORGANIZATION		
	Job Title :	SYSTEMS DEVELOPMENT MANAGER
Division : MANAGEMENT SERVICES	*Immediate Superior* :	MANAGEMENT SERVICES MANAGER
Department : SYSTEMS DEVELOPMENT	*Subordinates* :	Project leaders, systems analysts and programmers

II OBJECTIVES

1 To identify areas throughout the group that would benefit from the application of data processing techniques.

2 To act as the source of advice to management on the use of computer facilities.

3 To provide an efficient and effective systems and programming service to users.

III PRINCIPAL DUTIES

	AUTHORITIES		
1 System guidance	*Expenditure* :		*Capital* :
2 Project identification			
3 Planning	*Staff* :		*Annual Wage* :
4 Resources			
5 Quality of work	*Equipment* :		
6 Technical			
7 Recruitment and development of staff	Signature of job holder		Date
8 Administration			

Key tasks	Performance standard required	Means of measurement
1 To provide guidance to management on the development of computer and related systems.	1 Provision of advice and guidance on the use of computer techniques in the development of the association's systems.	The SDM is able to respond constructively to enquiries or problems raised by general management, the management services manager, or users.
	2 Maintenance of an up-to-date technical and systems knowledge.	Personal training.
2 To assist management with the identification of problem/opportunity areas for further development.	1 The SDM is constantly in touch with management on future requirements.	Periodic user meetings.
	2 Initial appraisal of problem/opportunity areas.	Preliminary investigations. New project authorizations.
	3 Preliminary analysis of project scope, likely costs/benefits and resources.	User discussions. Classification of projects. Project authorizations.
3 To prepare and maintain a long-term systems development plan.	1 Preparation of an annual systems development plan (plus a 2-year look ahead) recording all current and proposed projects, including estimates of time and resources required.	The existence of an annual department plan that has been agreed with: ● the management services manager; ● users and prospective users.
	2 Quarterly review of plan to take account of revised priorities, availability of resources, etc.	A revised annual plan. Supporting justifications.
	3 Recommendations on new projects as a result of: ● directives from general management;	New project authorizations.

Key tasks	Performance standard required	Means of measurement
	• requests from user managements; • observation of needs; • liaison with other management services departments; • scope for improvement to DP systems.	
	4 All projects have defined terms of reference, time and cost estimates.	Project authorizations.
4 To plan and allocate the use of systems and programming resources.	1 Adequate resources are available to meet the agreed systems development plan.	Manpower plan. No project postponed through lack of resources.
	2 Resources are allocated to project teams as required.	No project delayed through lack of resources.
	3 Changes in the quantity, quality and skills of staff resources are constantly monitored.	Monthly SDM meetings.
	4 Guidance to project leaders on the estimating and planning of projects.	Project estimates. Project plans.
	5 Liaison with computer operations and O&M to ensure feedback on existing systems and cooperation on new developments.	Monthly SDM meetings. Daily/weekly incident meetings.
	6 New systems are tested using systems test data and live data before going live.	Results of trials.

Key tasks	Performance standard required	Means of measurement
	The new systems are implemented gradually.	Implementation reviewed against original plan.
	7 Users are adequately trained in the new clerical procedures.	Results of trials. Errors experienced on live running.
	8 New files are established and found to have less than 5% errors during live running.	Analysis of errors attributable to file creation.
	9 Systems are implemented within 10% of agreed time and cost estimates.	Comparison of actual with plan.
	10 Action is taken to ensure expected benefits are achieved.	Subsequent systems audits.
	11 Immediate help is provided to users to find solutions to identified and agreed problems.	Record of man-days spent assisting users.
	12 A continuous program of training is established to familiarize users with computer systems.	Actual man-days spent on orientation training. Actual days spent by users on courses.
5 To ensure that the work of the systems development department is produced to agreed quality standards, on time and to agreed costs budgets.	1 Agreed systems and programming standards are observed.	Periodic review of documentation. Detailed review of systems specifications.
	2 Project progress is reviewed on a regular basis, deviations from plan are investigated and remedial action is taken.	Weekly project progress reports. Monthly SDM meeting. Revised project plans.

Key tasks	Performance standard required	Means of measurement
	3 The most appropriate systems and programming methods are exploited by project teams.	Review of systems and programming specifications. Walkthroughs.
	4 Utilization of resources and associated costs is in line with agreed time/costs budgets.	Monthly SDM meeting. Monthly report to management services manager.
6 To maintain the technical knowledge and expertise of the systems development department.	1 Knowledge of equipment and software is regularly updated and is available to new projects.	Personal training programme. Availability of internal/external courses for staff.
	2 Regular liaison with appointed manufacturer and other suppliers.	Monthly meetings.
7 To be responsible for the recruitment and development of systems and programming staff.	1 Availability of resources and skills inventory is constantly monitored.	Manpower plan. Recruitment plan.
	2 Action is taken to upgrade technical competence.	Training plan.
	3 Staff are appraised on a regular basis and counselled on performance and future progress.	Performance appraisals in personal file.
8 To be responsible for the administration of the systems development department.	1 Completion of all duties required of department managers by the association's rules.	Personnel records. Attendance records. Leave roster. Salary/increment reviews. Performance appraisals.
	2 Contribution to the management of the management services division.	Monthly MSM meetings.

I POSITION IN ORGANIZATION

Job Title	:	SYSTEMS ANALYST
Immediate Superior	:	PROJECT LEADER/SYSTEMS DEVELOPMENT MANAGER
Subordinates	:	Analysts; programmers as allocated within project context

Division	:	MANAGEMENT SERVICES
Department	:	SYSTEMS DEVELOPMENT

II OBJECTIVES

As directed, to analyse existing procedures in order to determine user requirements and, in conjunction with users, to develop, design and implement computer systems within the framework of the systems specification to agreed time and cost budgets.

III PRINCIPAL DUTIES

1 Work organization
2 Fact gathering
3 Analysis of findings
4 Proposals
5 Systems design
6 Programming
7 Liaison with users
8 Implementation
9 Team responsibilities
10 Department responsibilities

AUTHORITIES

Expenditure	:	*Capital*	:
Staff	:	*Annual Wage*	:
Equipment	:		

Signature of job holder	Date

Key tasks	Performance standard required	Means of measurement
1 To plan the use of his time and to complete the work allocated to him either as an individual or as a team member.	1 Analysis of activities and tasks to be performed in the allocated assignment.	Activity/task list.
	2 Agreed estimate of work content and target dates.	Activity estimate sheets. Activity bar chart.
	3 Documented completion of allocated assignment.	Written stage reports. Achievement of target dates.
2 To carry out detailed investigation and data collection in the area allocated.	1 Determine the principal purpose(s) of the area under review.	Assignment documentation according to management services division standards.
	2 Document: • organization structure; • staffing; • workflow; • work load – volume data and frequencies; • existing costs; • problem areas.	
	3 Establish management information requirements.	
	4 Liaison and discussion with user staff and management.	
3 To analyse results of investigation.	1 Identification of areas where new or revised systems would assist the department/the association as a whole.	Written stage report(s) according to management services division standards.

Key tasks	Performance standard required	Means of measurement
	2 Consultation with project leader, O&M or other specialists and user for interpretation and analysis of findings, as necessary.	Written evaluation/justification report to management services division standards.
4 On the basis of investigation and subsequent analysis, to review alternative solutions.	1 Identify alternative approaches.	
	2 Evaluate alternatives.	
	3 Consultation within management services division and with user.	
	4 Identify the preferred solution.	
	5 Document the solution with supporting cost/benefit analyses; implementation plan.	Written stage report.
	6 Present positive recommendations agreed with user.	Supporting documentation. Verbal presentation. Project authorization for next stage.
5 To prepare a full systems specification for the proposed system(s) in accordance with prescribed management services division documentation standards.	1 Detailed work schedule available.	Activity/task lists. Activity bar charts.
	2 After authorization, development of full specification of requirements for proposed system(s) incorporating: • system/procedure charts • input/output/file details • information requirements • computer/clerical interface.	Completion of a systems specification and supporting documents.

Key tasks	Performance standard required	Means of measurement
	3 Consultation with project leader and senior programmer on systems design.	Sound and effective systems design to meet user requirements and to make optimum use of hardware/software facilities.
	4 Consultation and agreement with user as project proceeds.	User agreement. Minutes of meetings.
	5 Adherence to project plan.	Achievement of milestones on time. Project progress meetings. Project progress reports.
	6 Written/verbal presentation of specification to: ● users ● project team ● management for subsequent authorization	Written stage reports. Presentations. Project authorization. Walkthroughs.
6 During the programming stage to liaise with: ● senior programmer ● programmers ● user	1 Provision of additional data as required.	
	2 Liaison with user.	
	3 Monitoring program progress.	Regular meetings. Weekly progress meetings. Project schedule.
	4 Remedial action if progress falls behind schedule.	Revised schedules. Investigation into cause of slippage.
	5 Provision of test data.	
	6 Supervision of testing phase.	Test results. Delivery of system that works on time. User agreement.

Key tasks	Performance standard required	Means of measurement
7 To maintain constant contact with users through all stages of project.	**1** Full understanding and anticipation of requirements.	No user changes once system enters 'frozen zone'.
	2 Good working relationships.	No user complaints.
	3 Prompt handling of queries.	No delays to project.
8 To plan and control implementation of new/revised system(s).	**1** Prepare and agree implementation plan covering: ● timing ● management services resources ● user resources ● parallel running ● handover procedure	Existence of agreed plan.
	2 Availability of full documentation including: ● computer operations requirements ● procedure manuals ● job breakdowns ● stationery requisites, etc.	Existence of documents. User agreement.
	3 Adequate training of users.	Training schedule. Training sessions.
	4 Handover of operational system on time.	'Signed off' by user. No operational faults.

Key tasks	Performance standard required	Means of measurement
9 Team responsibilities: ● technical guidance ● project leadership ● counselling	**1** Maintenance of up-to-date systems and technical knowledge.	Contribution to systems design. Walkthroughs.
	2 Assistance to project leader in planning, controlling and executing the work of the project team, including, if necessary, fulfilling the responsibilities of the project leader in his absence.	Effective control of project.
	3 Assistance with the guidance and development of project team staff.	Improved performance of staff.
10 Department responsibilities.	**1** Contribution to the upgrading of systems development department and the maintenance and improvement of management services division standards.	New techniques. Department meetings.
	2 Fulfilment of any specialist duties that may be assigned by the SDM from time to time.	SDM review.

I   POSITION IN ORGANIZATION

Division   :   MANAGEMENT SERVICES

Department :   SYSTEMS DEVELOPMENT

Job Title   :   PROGRAMMER

Immediate Superior :   SENIOR PROGRAMMER

Subordinates   :   None

II   OBJECTIVES

To write and test programs, as specified, to an agreed time and cost budget and to established installation standards for quality, presentation and documentation.

III   PRINCIPAL DUTIES

1 Undertaking the problem
2 Planning the work
3 Writing the program
4 Testing
5 Documenting
6 Team responsibilities

AUTHORITIES

Expenditure :   *Capital*   :

Staff   :   *Annual Wage* :

Equipment :

Signature of job holder   Date

Key tasks	Performance standard required	Means of measurement
1 To read (and in some cases prepare) the program specification and to understand the requirement before commencing work.	1 The program specification is read and discussed and all queries answered.	No subsequent problems arise that indicate inadequate briefing.
	2 The relationship of the program/ module to other programs/modules is understood.	Team walkthroughs. No subsequent problems with linkage.
2 To plan the structure of the program and the tasks involved.	1 Preparation of structured flowchart.	Flowchart.
	2 Analysis of tasks to be completed.	Task list/milestone chart.
	3 Estimate of time required to complete.	Agreement with senior programmer estimate.
	4 Program design is simple and logical and conforms to installation standards.	Design is approved/amended by senior programmer.
	5 Flowcharting standards and techniques are observed and all processing is represented.	
3 To write the program/module as specified.	1 Coding is simple and easy to follow, making full use of: ● meaningful data names ● paragraph names ● comments ● established techniques/practices ● technical support unit	Desk checking. Supervision. Walkthroughs.
	2 Conservative use of core.	Modules to be ±50 statements. Program size ±??K.
	3 A pre-set coding rate is achieved.	Installation standard to average 40 statements/day over elapsed time for job.

Key tasks	Performance standard required	Means of measurement
	4 Intelligent use of installation software.	Supervision.
	5 All possible exception conditions are catered for.	No major additional coding after completion.
	6 All coding errors are corrected after first compilation.	No major additional coding after initial compilation.
	7 Programs are thoroughly desk checked.	No more than three compilations for average program/module.
	8 Completion of program/module on time.	Achievement of target dates.
4 To carry out testing to prescribed installation standards.	1 Creation of comprehensive test data.	No part of program/module untested.
	2 Adherence to established procedure for: • program testing • systems testing	Liaison with senior programmer and operations. Testing instructions.
	3 Satisfactory completion of program tests and subsequent systems test, within time requirement.	Test results. No more than five test shots for average program/module. Achievement of target dates. Programs that work.
5 To document the program/module fully in accordance with installation standards.	1 Provision of all documents before release of programs, including any subsequent changes.	Completeness of program file. Release procedure.
	2 Programs can be easily understood (unaided) by another programmer.	Ease of maintenance.

Key tasks	Performance standard required	Means of measurement
6 Team responsibilities: • personal development • walkthroughs • training	1 Maintenance and improvement of technical knowledge. 2 Active participation in walkthroughs. 3 Technical and practical guidance to trainee programmers (as required).	Rate of improvement in personal contribution. Rate of improvement in trainees.

Appendix 3
Computer selection – specification of requirements

Introduction

This Appendix is intended as a guide for preparing a specification of requirements to be sent to computer manufacturers with an invitation to submit proposals. It lists items which are usually relevant, but it is not meant to be exhaustive.

The reason for attempting to achieve some measure of standardization is to facilitate the subsequent evaluation of manufacturers' proposals. By asking the right questions in the first place, the number of supplementary questions arising during evaluation, which waste a lot of time, can be reduced to a minimum. The evaluation process is also simplified by laying down the sequence in which manufacturers must present the information in their proposals.

The specification of requirements should be issued to those manufacturers who are being asked to quote, with a covering letter stating the deadline for receipt of proposals, the number of copies required, and naming the contacts from whom further information can be obtained.

In those cases where it is thought appropriate to give manufacturers an indication of the sort of configuration which is envisaged, this should be done verbally. It must be emphasized that manufacturers should not be given any opportunity to evade their responsibilities in connection with the ability of the equipment proposed to carry out the work specified.

Example of specification of requirements

Title page
Company name
Specification of requirements
Date

List of contents and appendices

Body of the report

I   *Introduction* The XYZ Company, after an examination of its procedures, has decided to install a computer (or replace its existing computer) during the . . . quarter of 19 . . Selected manufacturers are being asked to submit proposals for the supply of a computer to carry out the work described in this specification.

II   *The XYZ Company* Background information on company.

III   *Plans for the development of computer systems* Brief description of the existing data processing situation, e.g. existing service bureau work and/or computer, punched card and accounting machine equipment.

Brief description of the major areas of the business where existing and proposed computer systems are to be implemented. Give an indication of the time scale envisaged and, if systems are to be implemented in stages, explain how they will be phased.

IV   *Proposed computer applications* List the applications and refer to appendices where input/output volumes, file sizes and processing are given in detail. Relate to the phased implementation programme where applicable.

Explain the time constraints, e.g. number of shifts worked, defining hours worked per day and per week. For phased implementation, explain how you expect the increased work load to be handled, e.g. enhance machine for later phases and/or work more shifts.

V   *Information required from manufacturers* This section specifies the information to be given by manufacturers in their proposals, for example as follows.

In submitting your proposal you should include the following information, in the sequence listed.

  1   A full technical specification of each item of data preparation and computer equipment proposed. Also provide, on loan, one set of those user manuals relating to

this equipment which will enable us to assess its speed, capability and method of operation.

2 Purchase, annual rental and annual leasing costs and terms, and annual maintenance costs and terms, for the data preparation and computer equipment proposed, in total and by individual items of equipment, for one shift (x hours/day, y days/week) and two shift, etc. (define as appropriate) operation. If costs are dependent on contract period, give prices for 1, 3 and 5 year periods. Provide copies of your standard purchase, rental leasing and maintenance contracts.

3 Details of delivery and installation charges, and any insurance costs to be borne by the XYZ company.

4 Trade-in value after 2, 3, 4 and 5 years.

5 Quantity and cost of magnetic file storage media estimated to be required during the first year after installation.

6 Proposed delivery and hand-over dates (plus any special information about later enhancements).

7 The latest date the proposed configuration may be altered without affecting the hand-over date.

8 Physical planning requirements:
   - Temperature range
   - Humidity range
   - Filtration
   - Floor area
   - Floor loading

9 Whether a voltage stabilizer is required, and who supplies and maintains it. Its purchase and maintenance cost.

10 Where the maintenance engineer will be based, and how long on average it will take him to arrive on site when called. When the machine will have to be made available to your engineer for routine maintenance.

11 Details of how the proposed computer systems will carry out each procedure. Outline system flowcharts should be provided, as well as recommended file designs for all input, output, working and main files. Give estimated run times for each program, with information on how the times have been calculated. Give an estimate of core

storage requirements for each run, showing requirements for software, input/output buffers and user program separately. In the case of real-time systems, give
detailed estimates based on caculation or simulation of
response times and queues for the system of terminals/
line network/central facilities.

12   Run times should be summarized by procedure, by
daily, weekly, monthly (etc. as appropriate), commitments.

13   A recommended data preparation and computer daily
and weekly work schedule. (Here specify any time constraints and deadlines not covered elsewhere in specification.)

14   (Any particular questions on proposed system, e.g.
error handling and correction, audit trail, accounting
controls restarts.)

15   Recommendations on the software to be used, i.e.
executives, operating systems, high level languages,
assembly languages, database and data communications
handlers, and application packages. For each item of
software recommended give the following information.
● General description.
● Storage requirements in core and on disk.
● Number and type of peripherals needed and capable
of being used.
● Operating performance, e.g. average statements
compiled per minute, as appropriate.
● Date operational in UK.
● Current release number.
● Whether written and maintained in UK.
● Number of users in UK.
● Purchase and/or annual rental costs and terms. Pro-
vide copies of standard contracts.
Provide one set of manuals on loan giving detailed tech-
nical and operational information on each item of
software proposed.

16   The amount of systems and programming assistance
that could be provided, and the cost of this assistance.
Provide copies of standard contracts.

17   Details of the training facilities available for manage-

ment, systems, programming and operational staff, and the cost of this training.

18   Details of the free program testing time provided, and the cost of additional time, with details of the machines available for program testing.

19   If work is initially to be carried out, before delivery, on a bureau or other user machine, request details of these machines and of the costs involved.

20   Information on machines which might be available as standby in the event of a serious failure of the machine proposed. Give company names and locations and show in what way these machines are compatible with the machine proposed. Indicate present and expected future loading of these machines.

21   Any special requirements, e.g.:
- benchmark test;
- programming situations;
- terms for reprogramming existing punched card or computer work.

Appendices

1   One for each major application.
2   Specify file sizes and data content (show whether numeric or alphabetic).
3   Specify input volumes and data content.
4   Describe processing to be carried out, and frequency.
5   Specify output volume, lines or sample format.
6   Specify in detail the message traffic characteristics, the acceptable service time, and the security and restart requirements for real-time systems.

Appendix 4
Checklist for software package evaluation

Will it solve my problem?

1   Does it do what I want? If not, how easily can the extra procedures be attached?
2   Does it do more than I want? If so, can the unwanted procedures be unhitched?
3   Will it meet my deadlines?
4   Are there convenient input routines and documents?
5   Does the I/O link easily with my own systems and other software, if required to do so?

Will I be able to get it to work?

1   Will it fit the hardware environment – memory size, peripherals, etc.?
2   Will it fit the software environment, operating systems, file handlers, etc.
3   How much consultancy is included in the basic cost of the software?

Will it be reliable?

1   Where did the package originate? Who owns it?
2   How many people are using it?
3   Of these, how many have paid for it?
4   May I talk to them?
5   Will I have both source and object programs?
6   How good is the documentation?
7   In case of program failure, who will correct it? What is his name? How long after failure will it be before he starts work?
8   Is the vendor's business stable, or is he likely to disappear and leave me without support?

What conditions will apply to its use?

1 Who else will be allowed to use the package?
2 Is there a periodic payment or a single payment?
3 If I make a single payment and the package is made obsolete by a new one, do I get a trade-in discount?
4 If I make periodic payments, do they temporarily cease when program errors occur?
5 Is the software licensed for one computer, one company or a group of companies?
6 In the case of one-computer licenses, what happens when the licensed computer breaks down?
7 Do I get a free trial?

Legal points

The enforcement of any legal rights in software is fraught with difficulty. Nevertheless, it is prudent to seek whatever limited protection is afforded by the law. In particular, the company's legal advisers should consider these points.

1 Who owns the title to the software?
2 Are we relinquishing our common law rights?
3 Does the Sale of Goods Act or the Trade Descriptions Act apply?
4 If we are buying hardware as well as software, are there any patents involved?
5 Should the vendor idemnify us against any possible legal action by third parties?

Costs

Some or all of the following costs will be incurred when using a software package.

1 Cost of the package – single payment or periodic payments.
2 Cost of extra hardware.
3 Cost of own staff's time in getting the package operational.
4 Cost of specially written routines to be attached to the package.
5 Cost of extra computer capcity if the package is less efficient than a tailor-made program would be.

6 Cost of extra clerical labour if the package's I/O facilities are less good than those of a tailor-made program.

These costs must be set against the cost of producing tailor-made programs to do the same job.

Index

Reference, language and information

☐	**The Story of Language**	C. L. Barber	£2.50p
☐	**North-South**	Brandt Commission	£2.50p
☐	**Test Your IQ**	Butler and Pirie	£1.50p
☐	**Writing English**	D. J. Collinson	£1.50p
☐	**Illustrating Computers**	Colin Day and	
		Donald Alcock	£1.95p
☐	**Dictionary of Famous**		
	Quotations	Robin Hyman	£2.95p
☐	**Militant Islam**	Godfrey Jansen	£1.50p
☐	**The War Atlas**	Michael Kidron and	
		Dan Smith	£5.95p
☐	**Practical Statistics**	R. Langley	£1.95p
☐	**How to Study**	H. Maddox	£1.95p
☐	**The Limits to Growth**	D. H. Meadows et al.	£2.50p
☐	**Your Guide to the Law**	ed. Michael Molyneux	£3.95p
☐	**Ogilvy on Advertising**	David Ogilvy	£6.95p
☐	**Common Security**	Palme Commission	£1.95p
☐	**The Modern Crossword**		
	Dictionary	Norman Pulsford	£3.50p
☐	**A Guide to Saving**		
	and Investment	James Rowlatt	£2.95p
☐	**Career Choice**	Audrey Segal	£3.95p
☐	**Logic and its Limits**	Patrick Shaw	£2.95p
☐	**Names for Boys and Girls**	L. Sleigh and C. Johnson	£1.95p
☐	**Straight and Crooked**		
	Thinking	R. H. Thouless	£1.95p
☐	**Money Matters**	Harriet Wilson	£1.75p
☐	**Dictionary of Earth Sciences**		£2.95p
☐	**Dictionary of Physical Sciences**		£2.95p

☐ **Pan Dictionary of Synonyms and Antonyms**		£2.50p
☐ **Travellers' Multilingual Phrasebook**		£2.50p
☐ **Universal Encyclopaedia of Mathematics**		£2.95p

Literature guides

☐ **An Introduction to Shakespeare and his Contemporaries**	Marguerite Alexander	£2.95p
☐ **An Introduction to Fifty Modern British Plays**	Benedict Nightingale	£2.95p
☐ **An Introduction to Fifty Modern European Poets**	John Pilling	£2.95p
☐ **An Introduction to Fifty Modern British Poets**	Michael Schmidt	£1.95p
☐ **An Introduction to Fifty European Novels**	Martin Seymour-Smith	£1.95p

All these books are available at your local bookshop or newsagent, or can be ordered direct from the publisher. Indicate the number of copies required and fill in the form below   12

Name_____
(Block letters please)

Address_____

_____

Send to CS Department, Pan Books Ltd, PO Box 40, Basingstoke, Hants
Please enclose remittance to the value of the cover price plus:
35p for the first book plus 15p per copy for each additional book ordered
to a maximum charge of £1.25 to cover postage and packing
Applicable only in the UK

While every effort is made to keep prices low, it is sometimes
necessary to increase prices at short notice. Pan Books reserve
the right to show on covers and charge new retail prices which
may differ from those advertised in the text or elsewhere